A Manual of Copyright Practice

A Manual of COPYRIGHT PRACTICE

for writers, publishers, and agents

by Margaret Nicholson

SECOND EDITION

New York · OXFORD UNIVERSITY PRESS · 1956

Preface

THIS IS A BOOK FOR THE AUTHOR, editor, agent, permissions department, publisher and his secretary—for anyone in the literary world who wants to know what to do in a specific situation involving copyright. It is not for copyright lawyers or even for law students who plan to specialize in copyright law. As one editor lamented, there are scores of books on the market to save you thousands of dollars and many lawyers to get you out of copyright difficulties and to redress your wrongs. The real difficulty is to find out what to do in day-to-day routine.

This *Manual of Copyright Practice* leans on the Copyright Act, bulletins of the Copyright Office, decisions of the court in cases involving authors and publishers, and ordinary publishing practice. In an effort to avoid legalistic complexities I have undoubtedly over-simplified from the specialist's point of view, and in attempting to resolve small difficulties I have included what to many not in the publishing field will seem to be obvious. Certainly the book is repetitious—deliberately so. Any person who read this book from cover to cover in one sitting would find many passages to use in what one contemporary magazine calls the 'infatuation with sound of own words department.' But this is not a book to be read from cover to cover at one sitting. It is a book for reference, for quick reference, and although the 'q.v.'s' are interspersed generously, there are many cases in which it seemed that a line of repetition would save minutes that would otherwise be spent in page turning. For the same reason, bibliographical and legal citations have been omitted. If the novice in copyright will read Part I (the background of copyright; its subject matter and procedure; and the outline of the law) and follow this with perhaps the articles in Part II on Assignment, on Books, on Classification, on Applications, on Affidavits and the Manufacturing Clause, he may put the book on his desk and pick it up next only for a specific answer—unless he wishes to get an overall view of the practical problems of authors and publishers by browsing in the section of Questions (Part III). For a general survey of any topic, the reader is urged to refer to the Index. Although not given in the text, most of the cases cited for illustration are listed alphabetically in the Appendix.

v

The articles on copyrighting works not directly related to the literary world—music, motion pictures, television, radio, prints and labels, art, and architecture—are 'for the record,' and considered only in their possible connection with book publishing. The whole question of legal procedure and penalties for infringement is completely omitted; these are matters not of copyright practice, but of copyright law, and require the service of a copyright lawyer. One bit of advice that cannot be repeated too often: in case of infringement, in case of any copyright trouble, consult a lawyer—and the best copyright lawyer available.

But if the minutiae of copyright routine, which is the subject matter of this book, have been observed, there is little cause for worry. Anyone who scans the record of copyright cases from 1909 to the present will be convinced of the court's sympathy for the author, the true copyright proprietor; invariably the literary pirate and the opportunist seem to come to grief. Another point brought home by the record is the fact that many of 'the best people' of the publishing world are involved at one time or another: Henry Holt, *The New York Times,* Theodore Dreiser, Charles Scribner, Eugene O'Neill, the Macmillan Company, Harper & Brothers, Ernest Hemingway, the Oxford University Press, 'Frank Merriwell,' the *Atlantic Monthly,* Yale University Press—the list is endless; not to mention the moving picture, music, and radio companies. Furthermore, a distressing conclusion is that many of the legal difficulties could have been avoided by attention to some minor routine detail.

The Copyright Office is more than generous in answering questions and guiding the copyright claimant toward adequate protection, as anyone who has appealed to it knows. But the Copyright Office is bound by the Copyright Act.

The publication of this revision was repeatedly postponed during the past four years in the ever-recurring hope that it could incorporate changes in the law to be enacted on our joining in some sort of world copyright union. It is of the greatest satisfaction to both author and publisher that this edition can now appear with the text of the Universal Copyright Convention as part of the Appendix—that when it is published the United States and fifteen other countries of the world will be actively participating in UCC.

Inevitably some of the interpretations of UCC clauses in this book will have to be revised as the regulations of UCC become better understood through practice. At the time of writing none of the English-speaking nations except the United States has yet adhered. But the new changes in our own law are in effect and it is hoped that familiarity with these and with the basic principles of UCC will make it easier for those dealing with copyright routines when the number of participating countries increases.

My indebtedness to books and people is comprehensive. Amdur's *Copyright Law and Practice*, Bowker's *Copyright, Its History and Its Law*, Howell's *The Copyright Law*, Ladas' *The International Protection of Literary and Artistic Property*, and Weil's *The American Copyright Law* have been my chief sources of consultation, and I cannot recommend any of them too highly for the person who wants an authoritative discussion of copyright law. They do not always agree, but in each you will find abundant citation of law and precedent for the point of view expressed. The material in the present volume on the European background of the copyright law owes much to the Howell and Ladas books, as well as to the Encyclopaedia Britannica. The *Copyright Decisions* from 1909–1952 have been the greatest help, for here are the records of court decisions on the actual problems that face us.

My indebtedness to people is equally great. In the preparation of the first edition, the staff of the Copyright Office were extraordinarily cooperative and encouraging, and I want to express my gratitude especially to Mr. DeWolf and Mr. Howell and to Mrs. Iradell Rafter. Mr. Howell's article on the Copyright Office was a welcome contribution to the text. The advice of Mr. Frederic Melcher and the late Mr. Benjamin Stern in regard to some of the more controversial questions was also of great value. Mr. Stern's and Mr. DeWolf's further kindness in looking over the galleys was one that only those who have performed a similar labor can fully appreciate. Miss Caroline Sauer was also most generous in giving her time and many helpful suggestions. In view of the professional status of these people, let me hasten to add that any oversights, omissions, misinterpretations, or errors in the text are my own.

Then there were the many publishers, agents, and staff members of publishing houses whose letters and personal consultations helped to create what I believe is one of the most useful parts of the book—the section of questions.

I also want to thank the many people who have helped in the preparation of the revised edition. Members of the staff of the Copyright Office have given freely of their time and guidance, but I must emphasize at once that all matters of interpretation are my own and that I speak in no way for the Office. In the early days of the preparation, when UCC was only a hope, the late Mr. Arthur Farmer of Stern and Reubens kept me advised on many developments and helped greatly in clarifying problems that seemed to me then insurmountable. Mr. Lawrence Reed has also been of great help, not only by discussing with me many controversial questions but also in suggesting topics for inclusion. Mr. John Cushman and Miss Barbara Russell both contributed much in the mechanical preparation of the manuscript and in their provocative and helpful questions. Lastly I want to thank my many friends at Oxford University Press for their patience and encouragement.

M.N.

Hillsdale, New York
December 1955

Contents

PREFACE   v

I

Background of Copyright Law   3

The Copyright Office   9

The Subject Matter of Copyright   13

How to Copyright Literary
   Property   16

Outline of the Copyright Law   19

Outline of the Universal
   Copyright Convention   25

Check List for Copyrighting
   a Literary Work   28

II

Abridgments and Adaptations   35

Ad Interim Copyright   37

Advertisements   40

Affidavits of American Manufacture   43

Alien Authors   45

Applications   47

Architecture   52

Art and Design for Works of Art   54

Assignments   57

Author   61

Books   69

Choreography   73

Classification   74

Common-Law Rights   79

Compilations (Anthologies)   82

Deposit   84

Dramas and Music Dramas   87

Duration   89

Fair Use   91

Fees   94

Illustrations   95

Infringement   97

International Copyright
   Relations   101

The International Copyright
   Union   110

Lectures   114

Letters   115

License   117

Magazine Articles
   Short Stories, Poems (Con-
   tributions to Periodicals and
   Newspapers)   119

CONTENTS

Manufacturing Clause	121	Search	164
Maps	123	Titles	165
Moral Rights	124	Unfair Competition	169
Motion Pictures	126	Universal Copyright Convention	171
Music	129	Unpublished Works	174

New Editions, Revisions, Reprints, and Reissues ... 132

III

Newspapers and Periodicals	134	Questions on Copyright Practice	179
Notice	137	Forms	207

APPENDIX

Photographs	141	Copyright Law of the United States	227
Posthumous Works	144		
Proprietor	145	Universal Copyright Convention	242
Public Domain	147	The Berne Convention	248
Publication	150		
Quotations (Permissions)	154	Selected Bibliography	255
Radio and Television	158	Cases Cited	257
Renewals	160	INDEX	261

Part 1

Background of Copyright Law

'The Congress shall have Power . . .
   To promote the Progress of Science and the useful
Arts, by securing for limited
   Times to Authors and Inventors the exclusive Right
to their respective Writings and Discoveries . . .
   To make all Laws which shall be necessary and
proper for carrying into Execution the Foregoing
Powers . . .'

THE CONSTITUTION OF THE UNITED STATES

IN THESE WORDS the framers of the Constitution laid the foundation for the protection of literary property in the United States. Not that the idea of copyright was new in 1789. Even when the only books available were laboriously hand-copied manuscripts, it was generally acknowledged that ownership was vested in the creator of a work, though glory might be his sole reward. When books began to bring material profit, however, after the invention of the printing press, the problems of proprietorship became more complex; for with the mechanical means of multiple reproduction came literary piracy. Once a book was placed in circulation, publishers the world over felt free to print it in quantity, 'for the good of the people' and of their own pocketbooks.

The first statute concerning modern copyright was the English 'Act of 8 Anne.' From 1476, when William Caxton began to print books in England, until the Statute of Anne in 1709–10, authors, or more often their 'publishers,' who were then really booksellers, were considered to have a perpetual common-law right in their works. The actual licensing of printers and publishers was controlled by the Crown, and was a matter of special privilege. In the Act of Queen Anne, the author for the first time had legal protection of his rights. The necessity for such an act was made clear in its opening words:

Whereas printers, booksellers, and other persons have of late frequently taken the liberty of printing, reprinting, and publishing books without the consent of the authors or proprietors . . . to their very great detriment, and too often to the ruin of them and their families: for preventing therefore such practices for the future, and for the encouragement of learned men to compose and write useful books, be it enacted . . .

3

To protect the author from this abuse, the law conferred upon him the exclusive right to print his book for a period of fourteen years, with a second fourteen-year renewal period, if he registered the title at Stationers' Hall and furnished nine copies for deposit at various university and official libraries. Furthermore, the law had 'teeth':

And that if any bookseller, printer, or other person whatsoever, shall print, reprint, or import any such book or books, without the consent of the proprietor . . . then such offender shall forfeit such book or books to the proprietor of the copy thereof, who shall forthwith damask and make wastepaper of them; and farther, that every such offender shall forfeit one penny for every sheet which shall be found in his custody.

Other European countries were slow to follow England's example. Denmark's first copyright law was enacted in 1741. It declared that books could be reprinted only with the consent of the author or the first publisher, with several notable exceptions: hymnals, Luther's catechism, and 'abc books.'

It was not until 1793 that France enacted her copyright law, which was passed on to Italy, Belgium, Switzerland, and Holland as each came under the influence of Napoleon. The law assured to all authors, artists, and composers, regardless of citizenship, the exclusive right during their lifetime to sell, distribute, or assign their works throughout the Republic. Spain's copyright law was passed in 1847. One of the few progressive steps in the turbulent reign of Isabella II, it protected the works of Spanish authors, whether published in Spain or in any of the many Hispanic colonies; but if the works of colonial writers were in the Spanish language, they could be imported into Spain only with the consent of the Government.

In Germany, a federal law was much more difficult to enact because of the absence of a strong central government. From the time of Napoleon's defeat until after the Franco-Prussian War, Germany was comprised of many autonomous States, loosely bound in a Confederation. The primary functions of the German Diet, especially during its earlier years, were to maintain peace between the States and provide for self-defense if German territory was attacked by a foreign power. However, the Diet did pass a copyright law in 1838 (seven years after Heine had gone to France) to protect the subjects of the confederated kingdoms. The protection, unfortunately, proved to be only theoretical. The States failed to enforce the law, and pirating continued. Germany's first national copyright law was enacted in 1870, when she at last attained the unity that resulted the following year in the establishment of the Empire.

The most important step forward in international copyright was taken in 1887 by the Berne Convention, resulting in the International Copyright

4

Union, to which all the important European countries, then or later, became signatories. The Union abolished all formalities in securing copyright, and each member State granted to foreign authors whose works were first published in any unionist country the same rights that it granted to its own nationals.

The American colonists' ideas of copyright were naturally based on the practices prevailing in England. In the first few months of 1783, Connecticut, Massachusetts, and Maryland adopted copyright laws; in May of that year Congress recommended to the states that they establish copyright protection for 'United States citizens.' New Jersey, New Hampshire, and Rhode Island immediately did so, and by 1786 all the states except Delaware had some sort of copyright provisions. But individual state legislation was unsatisfactory, as was inevitable. Happily, the Constitutional Convention perceived this, and Section 8 of Article 1 of the Constitution, quoted above, gave Congress the authority to enact a national copyright law.

In 1790 the first federal Copyright Act was passed. It applied to 'books, maps, and charts,' but although it protected the rights of United States citizens and residents (for fourteen years with a fourteen-year renewal period, as in the Act of Anne), it virtually gave its blessing to what would now be considered the pirating of foreign books; without bothering about authorization, printers and publishers imported any foreign books they thought would be popular and reprinted to their hearts' content. This actually was a service to the book-hungry Americans, as the cost of importing enough copies to supply the demand would have been prohibitive. Moreover, at that time the practice was not confined to the United States. It prevailed even in England, whose copyright laws were then the most advanced in the world.

Other provisions of the Statute of 1790 stipulated that a copy of the title page of a forthcoming book should be deposited before publication, and that during the first two months after publication the copyright owner should run a newspaper advertisement of the facts of publication for four weeks. Within six months of publication a copy of the book itself had to be deposited with the United States Secretary of State. Should a printer deliberately infringe any work the copyright of which had been so established, by issuing a piratical edition, not only would he have to forfeit all the copies he had on hand, but he also became liable to a fine of fifty cents for every sheet found. Half of this went to the author, the other half to the United States Government.

Amendments to this act followed at fairly regular intervals during the next century. In 1802 it was required that the book should carry a notice of copyright, and the law was extended to include designs, engravings, and etchings. In 1819 United States circuit courts were declared to be the courts of original jurisdiction in all copyright cases. A statute in 1831 consolidated the earlier acts and provided for the protection of music. It also extended the first term of protection to twenty-eight years, though the renewal term remained fourteen. Public advertisement, except in the case of renewals, was no longer necessary, but, probably because the postal system was improving, the six months' grace before deposit was cut to three months. Except for an amendment providing for the recording of assignments (1834), this act remained unchanged for the next fifteen years.

As early as 1837, American authors and publishers, inspired by Henry Clay and George Putnam, began to agitate against the unrestricted pirating of foreign books. It was not only English authors who were suffering from our indifference to piracy, but also those of other foreign countries whose nationals were immigrating to the United States in large numbers. A piratical American edition sometimes followed foreign publication within two weeks — an amazing fact, considering the time necessary to publish a book today.

In 1846 the Copyright Act was again amended. It was now necessary to send one deposit copy to the Library of Congress, instead of to the Secretary of State, and a second to the newly founded Smithsonian Institution. The importance of this amendment is considerable, because by using the Library of Congress as a depository, a permanent index of United States copyright material was begun. Since then anyone wanting to determine the copyright status of a book has been able to have a search made for a nominal fee.

Another series of amendments began in 1855. In that year, deposit copies were granted free postage. Performance rights were granted to dramatists in 1856. In 1859 copyright matters were transferred from the State Department to the Department of the Interior. In 1861 it was provided that all copyright cases could be appealed to the Supreme Court, regardless of the amount involved. (Other cases were barred from appeal unless $5000 or more was at stake.) In 1865 protection was extended to photographs, and the period for post-publication deposit was cut to one month; two years later a $25 fine was set for failure to deposit.

In 1870 another general act was passed, this time permanently placing copyright matters under the Librarian of Congress. This act extended protection to paintings, drawings, statues, chromos, models, and designs. It was still necessary to register the title of the book before publication and to deposit in the mail two copies of the book within ten days after publication. A fine of $100 was fixed for the fraudulent use of a copyright notice.

6

Four years later the form of official copyright notice was established: the word Copyright, the year of publication, and the name of the copyright owner. Engravings, cuts, and prints were then defined as applying only to pictorial illustrations or works connected with the fine arts; 'prints and labels' for articles of manufacture were transferred to the Patent Office.

In 1891 the Chace Act was passed. By it copyright protection was at last extended to foreigners, but only if their books were manufactured in this country and bore a notice of United States copyright. The foreign author was required to register his book in the Copyright Office and deposit two copies there. Deposit copies had to be placed in the mails on the day of publication. The manufacturing clause and the requirement of the formalities of notice, registration, and deposit remained the chief obstacles to the United States' joining the International Copyright Union.

In 1897 provision was made for a Register of Copyrights and his staff (and *Register,* not *Registrar,* is his official title).

In 1905, in a further attempt to protect the rights of foreigners, an ad interim copyright clause was introduced, allowing foreign copyright proprietors of foreign-language books one year to decide whether it was worth while to reprint in the United States.

The Copyright Act of 1909, our present basic law, contained several noteworthy improvements over the earlier provisions. Books of foreign origin in a foreign language were not required to be reprinted here to secure copyright; the copyright term now started from the date of publication instead of the date of registration and deposit; the renewal term was extended to twenty-eight years.

In 1940 the registration of prints and labels was transferred from the Patent to the Copyright Office.

By an act of 30 July 1947 the copyright law, Title 17 of the United States Code, was codified and enacted into positive law. In April 1948 the section dealing with fees and the selling price of the Catalogue was amended; in June of that year sections dealing with procedure were repealed.

An important amendment to the basic act was Public Law 84 passed in 1949, extending ad interim copyright protection. According to it, books of foreign origin written in English, which formerly had to be manufactured in the United States to secure copyright, could be imported up to 1500 copies within 5 years of their first publication abroad, provided ad interim copyright was secured within six months of their first publication and that all imported copies carried a copyright notice. This ad interim copyright, which still is in effect for all except Universal Copyright Convention countries, protects the work for 5 years and can be extended to the full legal term — 28 years plus 28 years renewal term — if an American edition is produced within the ad interim period.

Another great deficiency in the law was corrected in 1952. Previously, writings that were classified as 'books,' including short stories and poems as well as full-length nonfiction books and novels, had had no protection against unauthorized public performance. By the amendment of Article 1c of 17 July 1952, not only were all 'nondramatic literary works' protected against being delivered, read, or presented in public for profit without the express consent of the copyright owner, but works of all classes were protected against unauthorized oral delivery for profit and unauthorized use by recordings, radio, television, and exhibition, representation, and reproduction for profit 'by any method whatsoever.'

The greatest step forward came in 1954 when after a century of copyright isolationism as a result of the manufacturing clause, the implementation bill (HR 6616) was passed permitting the amendment of the act to allow citizens and nationals of countries who become members of the Universal Copyright Convention to obtain United States copyright protection by publishing their works with the brief copyright notice, ©, the name of the copyright owner, and the date, without compliance with our formalities of registration, deposit, and fee, or our manufacturing clause. (It also permitted American citizens and nationals to take advantage of ad interim importation if their works in English were first published abroad.) Thus in 1955 the United States joined with 11 other nations of the world in a universal copyright system to 'facilitate a wider dissemination of works of the human mind and increase international understanding.'

The Copyright Office *

THE COPYRIGHT OFFICE is a quasi-autonomous bureau in the Library of Congress. Its office and catalogue rooms are in the Library Annex, a white Georgia-marble building completed in 1939, directly behind the old Library. The most important function of the Copyright Office is the administration of the provisions of the Copyright Act relating to (a) the registration and certification of all original and renewal claims to copyright; (b) the recordation and certification of assignments of copyright; (c) the preparation of catalogues for each class of copyright entries; and (d) the preservation of all copyright records and other things required by law to be preserved. The Copyright Office also acts in an advisory capacity in interpreting the Copyright Act in so far as it is necessary to do so for administrative purposes, and maintains a Public Information Office to assist the public in filing applications and to answer inquiries in regard to copyright procedure. The final decisions in disputed matters of law are made by the federal courts in copyright cases brought before them for settlement.

Before 1870 there was no central clearing house for copyrights. Every entry of title for the purpose of securing copyright had to be made in the clerk's office of the United States District Court in the district in which the author or proprietor resided. Hence there were as many title catalogue systems as there were District Courts throughout the country. This situation was remedied by the Consolidated Act of 1870, by which the whole copyright business, including the custodianship of previous record books and copies, was centralized in the office of the Librarian of Congress, who was required to 'perform all acts and duties prescribed by the law touching copyrights.'

During the next quarter of a century the growth of the copyright business was so great that Congress provided for a special department of the Library to deal exclusively with it, including the handling of copyright fees and the reception and examination of deposit copies. In making appropriations for the ensuing fiscal year, an Act of 1897 provided for a new officer,

* Material furnished through the courtesy of Herbert A. Howell, former Assistant Register of Copyright, and from the records of the Copyright Office.

the Register of Copyrights, who as head of the Copyright Department was charged with the performance of all duties relating to copyrights, under the direction and supervision of the Librarian of Congress. In 1900 the official designation was definitively changed to 'Copyright Office,' and in the general revision of the copyright law that took place in 1909 the Office acquired an even more distinct individuality, and the duties and powers of the Register were more specifically defined and considerably increased.

The Register of Copyrights serves as the legal, technical, and administrative head of the Copyright Office. He is responsible for the development of rules and regulations for the registration of copyrights and the interpretation and application of the provisions of the Copyright Act. With the assistance of his administrative and legal staff he is also concerned with proposed amendments to the copyright law and with revisions of international conventions and treaties.

The more routine work of the Copyright Office is carried out by four 'divisions':

The Service Division, which receives and routes incoming material, accounts for money received, and files the various records of deposits, applications, et cetera.

The Examining Division examines the applications for registration and deposits to see if they are in accord with the law.

The Copyright Cataloguing Division indexes the registrations and compiles the *Catalog of Copyright Entries*.

The Reference Division handles inquiries about material on file and requests for information about procedures, policy, and rules.

The Copyright Office is primarily an office of record. In addition to the material recorded on the applications for registration, the Office will record, for the statutory fee, assignments of copyright, licenses, contracts, mortgages; changes of corporation titles; wills, and decrees of distribution; and documents of power of attorney.

A section of the Regulations of the Copyright Office reads as follows:

Information relative to the operations of the Copyright Office is supplied without charge. A search of the records, indexes and deposits will be made for such information as they may contain relative to copyright claims upon application and payment of the statutory fee. The Copyright Office, however, does not undertake the making of comparisons of copyright deposits to determine similarity between works, nor does it give legal opinions concerning rights of persons in cases of alleged infringement, contracts between publisher and author, the copyright status of any particular work other than the facts shown in the records of the Office, or other matters of a similar nature.

10

Under the law, the Copyright Office *cannot* furnish opinions on the merits of any particular work, recommend publishers, or advise applicants about their contract arrangements. Nor can it furnish applicants with legal advice about their problems. This is particularly true of questions involving possible infringement, which would ordinarily have to be decided by a court. In such cases, it is best to consult a lawyer.

An excellent account of the organization and functions of the Copyright Office may be found in a booklet issued by the Library of Congress in 1952 (reprinted 1954) entitled *The Copyright Office of the United States of America*. The following paragraphs are taken from its closing pages:

COMMON MISCONCEPTIONS REGARDING THE COPYRIGHT OFFICE

That the Copyright Office issues copyrights. The Copyright Office does not issue copyrights in the sense that the Patent Office issues letters patent. Although the certificate issued by the Copyright Office shall be admitted in any court as prima facie evidence of the facts stated therein, the Copyright Office does not investigate or adjudicate the validity of any copyright. There is no provision in the copyright law, as there is in the patent law, for scrutiny of applications or copies to determine questions of originality or authorship. In such matters the claim of the applicant is its own evidence.

Thus the certificate of registration issued by the Register of Copyrights is limited to a certification only that the statements set forth in the application have been made a part of the records of the Copyright Office. If the provisions of the law for securing copyright have been complied with by a person entitled to claim copyright the copyright is secured.

That the Copyright Office retains at least one copy of all copyrighted works in its files. This is untrue. The copyright law provides in section 213 that 'Of the articles deposited in the Copyright Office under the provisions of the Copyright Law of the United States, the Librarian of Congress shall determine what books and other articles shall be transferred to the permanent collections of the Library of Congress . . . and what other books or articles shall be placed in the reserve collections of the Library of Congress for sale or exchange, or be transferred to other governmental libraries in the District of Columbia for use therein.' Furthermore, of such articles as remain undisposed of, the Librarian and the Register decide those it is desirable to preserve in the permanent files of the Copyright Office and may, under certain conditions, cause the remaining articles to be destroyed, or returned to the copyright claimant.

Blanket transfers made from the Copyright Office to the Library have included all periodicals, published maps, published music and magazine contributions received for registration. A large selection is made by the Library of books, pamphlets, prints, motion-pictures and other deposits.

As a general rule, the Copyright Office retains in its files unpublished music, lectures, unpublished dramas, commercial prints and labels and other works of

11

the graphic arts. Selected titles from these classes may also be transferred to the permanent collections of the Library.

That the public can obtain legal advice from the Copyright Office concerning the copyright status of particular works. The Copyright Office is an office of record and lacks the authority to give legal opinions. Requests for legal opinions, therefore, should not be addressed to the Copyright Office, but should be referred to an attorney.

The Subject Matter of Copyright

THE PRESENT UNITED STATES COPYRIGHT LAW offers protection to all original 'writings' of an author. No mention is made of literary quality, artistic merit, or the purpose of the author; advertisements, photographs, symphonic compositions, Limericks, telephone books, cartoons, statues, architectural designs — these are but a few of the varieties of writings embraced by the law. Even the definition of 'originality' is stretched to its utmost limits. In reply to an infringer who attempted to justify his theft of copyright material, one presiding judge blandly declared that there could be little force to the argument that copyright material must have originality; 'Very few literary, musical, or artistic ideas,' he said, 'are really novel.'

The Act itself enumerates various reworkings of material that are entitled to independent copyright: compilations, abridgments, dramatizations, translations — or, broadly, 'other versions.' What is subject to copyright in the contribution of the second 'author' — the editor, adaptor, translator, or dramatist — is the product of the exercise of his judgment and selection, his creation of a new form and expression of the ideas of the original author, though the essential ingredients remain the same.

For copyright resides essentially in 'expression,' in the relation of words, sentences, paragraphs, or any other units of the expression of ideas, to each other — in the choice of language and sequence. The idea itself, once it is expressed, is for the most part free to the public (but see *Radio and Television* page 158). An author who related to his friend a short story he was about to write would have no redress if his friend published the tale himself. But if our first author had written his story, and given the manuscript to his friend to read, he would have grounds for a suit if his friend's story plagiarized his in expression or sequence of events. The author's property right in his expression of an idea can be defended at common law the moment the expression is put into writing.

To return to the variety of writings included in the subject matter of copyright, the law itself enumerates thirteen different 'classes' of works, each with several subdivisions, in one of which each work should be placed when application for registration is being made (see *Classification*). The most important of these from the point of view of book and magazine publishers and authors are the first two — 'books' and 'periodicals, including

13

newspapers.' In the first, all sorts of things not commonly regarded as books are included: advertising catalogues, magazine articles, short stories, poems, dictionaries, descriptive atlases, anthologies, directories, contributions to newspapers and journals if they are not just factual 'news,' essays and collected essays, any written description or text accompanying noncopyrightable material (such as games, mechanical devices, or other things for use), picture books, art catalogues, maps that have extended accompanying text, single cards that have pictures and text, novels or nonfiction published serially or in installments, encyclopedias — practically any written published expression of an idea. The physical form of the 'book' is unimportant; it may be bound, stapled together, or just folded; it may be printed, photographed, plated, mimeographed, typewritten, or, conceivably, handwritten or lettered, if copies are actually sold or publicly distributed in that form. This expansive definition of 'book' must be thoroughly understood if the proper application form for registration is to be selected. A poem published in a newspaper, with a separate copyright, is a 'contribution,' but if the same poem has several stanzas and some illustrations added to it, and it is printed in a folder as a Christmas card, it is a reissued book. Any collection or compilation is registered as a book, whether it is of pictures, published plays, lyrics from musical comedies, or whatnot; tables and charts are books; the published description of a motion picture is a book; interest, tax, and wage tables are books.

'Periodicals' include magazines, daily and weekly newspapers, quarterlies, proceedings of conventions and meetings if they are published more than once a year, bulletins, serial publications, literary journals, reviews — anything that would be second-class matter in the mails. The contributions to periodicals if they bear a separate copyright may be registered independently. If they have no separate notice, but are covered only by the general copyright on the periodical, the author may have the copyright on his contribution reassigned to him after publication, if the publisher is willing to do so.

In addition to books and periodicals, there are many other classes of material subject to copyright: Lectures, radio and television scripts if worked out, sermons, drama, including television and radio plays, music, and motion pictures — works that depend chiefly on presentation or performance, which can be copyrighted before publication or after; products of the various graphic arts — design, architectural drawings, maps, photographs, many of which can also be copyrighted before publication. The scope of copyright is indicated by the list of subjects given on pages 77–8 in the article on *Classification,* most of which are dealt with specifically in the text of this book.

14

To complete the picture of what the copyright act classifies as 'books,' its obverse should be examined. A play or musical play, though published in book form, is not a 'book' but a 'drama.' The libretto of an opera is a 'drama,' even if published as a book without music. (But selections from it are a book.) An advertising circular with pictures and/or text, if it has only four folds, is not a 'book' but a 'print.' More than four folds — two or more sheets — are a 'book.' An advertisement in a periodical is not a 'contribution,' but a 'print.'

In addition there is a whole body of material not subject to copyright under any classification. Things intended primarily for practical use are usually protected by patent, not copyright. Other material that has specifically been denied copyright protection by the courts includes:

titles of books, magazines, series, radio programs, or any other titles (though they are sometimes protected at common law)

names, pen names, trade names, business names (sometimes protected at common law or by patent)

calendars having no text or pictures

conventional and stock figures

games, dolls, toys, primarily for use, not 'perusal' *(but explanatory material accompanying them may be copyrighted as a 'book')

dances unless they are dramatic in character (as a ballet or dance pantomime; published descriptions of dances may be copyrighted as a 'book')

laws and opinions of courts

legal forms, without original matter

slogans, mottoes, 'wisecracks,' and gags (but a slogan or title may be a trade mark, protected at common law or by patent)

blank books, record books, checks, journal books, index cards, or other material designed for physical use rather than perusal

ideas, plots, themes, theories, opinions, apart from their literary expression (sometimes protected at common law)

price lists, railway tickets, and time tables

standardized expressions, clauses, phrases

mere 'aggregation' of old material, as opposed to a 'compilation'

systems, schemes, methods, plans

immoral, seditious, or piratical works

news, facts

works in the public domain

government publications

works on which copyright has expired

works still in copyright in other countries but that have been published and sold in the United States without notice

works with fatally improper copyright notices

* Some recent decisions do not bear this out — see page 54.

How To Copyright Literary Property

FOR A WORK TO BE ELIGIBLE for copyright in the United States, its author must be (a) a United States citizen; (b) an alien making his residence * in this country at the time of the book's first publication; (c) a citizen of a country with whom the United States has reciprocal copyright relations (see *International Copyright Relations*); or (d) a citizen or national of a country belonging to the Universal Copyright Convention (UCC) or the author of a work first published in a UCC country.

The claimant of copyright must be (1) the author himself; (2) a proprietor who has derived his title directly from the author; or (3) an executor, administrator, or assignee of the author or proprietor. If the author himself could not claim copyright protection as a United States citizen or domiciled resident, or as the citizen of a country having a copyright agreement with the United States by treaty, proclamation, or copyright convention, neither can his proprietor or assignee.

Books † and periodicals (magazines, journals, newspapers, etc.) of foreign origin in the English language not claiming protection under UCC may be copyrighted in the United States only for the ad interim period (5 years, and not over 1500 copies to be imported) unless they are completely manufactured in this country. Books of foreign origin in a foreign language may be copyrighted here without having been manufactured in this country, providing they comply with our laws in other respects.

To secure copyright for any work that may be classified as a 'book' or 'periodical' (qq.v.), the first step is to publish it with the proper notice — Copyright, Copr., or ©, year, name of claimant (see *Notice*). In the case of a book, the notice must be on the title page or the verso of the title page — i.e. the page immediately following; under UCC it may be in any reasonably conspicuous place, but this does not apply to books first pub-

---

* The Copyright Act reads 'domiciled.' This is usually interpreted as 'residing with intent to remain,' but there are dissenting opinions. It is safe to assume, however, that the casual tourist is not intended to come within the meaning.

† Throughout this volume, 'book' means any material registered under Class A, regardless of its physical form: i.e. story, novel, poem, nonfiction, pamphlet, etc., published with its own copyright notice.

lished here. In periodicals and newspapers, the notice must appear on the first page of text or on the title page (see page 134), it must appear once in each separate issue. If a contribution to a periodical bears a separate notice, it should be on the first page (i.e. the 'title page') of the contribution itself. For imported books seeking ad interim copyright, no notice is required on the deposit copy, but the notice must appear in the copies imported for sale or distribution (see *Ad Interim Copyright*). Books protected by UCC must carry the notice on first publication and in all copies.

As soon as the work is published (see *Publication*) with proper notice, if it is by a United States citizen or national or is first published in this country, application for copyright registration should be made to the Copyright Office. (For proper application form, affidavit of manufacture, and fee, see *Applications*.) Two copies should be sent for deposit promptly after publication (see *Deposit*).

The Register of Copyrights issues to the copyright holder a certificate of registration, stating the name and address of the claimant; the name of the author, if it is available (an author can remain anonymous if he insists), his citizenship, his address, and whether or not he is domiciled in the United States; the title of the work; the dates of deposit and of publication; and the class designation and entry number. He also acknowledges the receipt of the affidavit of manufacture, if one was required. This certificate bears the seal of the Copyright Office and is admitted in any court as prima-facie evidence.

Although books of UCC countries or in foreign languages by non-resident authors need not be manufactured in this country to secure copyright, they must bear the proper notice in order to be protected. If their first publication takes place here, they must comply with our formalities, two copies must be deposited, with the application for registration and the fee; if non-UCC books are published abroad and seek registration here, one copy and the $4 fee should accompany the application, or two copies and a catalogue card (see page 213).

Unpublished manuscripts of books, stories, poems, articles, or anything that may reasonably be included in Classification A, 'books,' cannot be copyrighted before publication. The worried or the wary author will find comfort in knowing that his work is protected by his common-law rights (q.v.). Lectures and sermons and dramatic, radio, television, and musical works not 'reproduced in copies for sale' can be copyrighted without publication. In this case, the copyright claimant must file one complete copy of his work, with the proper application form and fee ($4). If these works are later published, then two copies of the best edition must be deposited, with the usual application and fee of $4. The copyright date remains that of the first registration.

The period of the copyright is 28 years from the date of publication, ending then unless the copyright is renewed for a second 28 years. For most books, the application of renewal must be made in the name of the author, or if he is dead, his widow, his children, executors, or his next of kin depending on circumstances (see *Renewals*). In the case of posthumous works, periodicals, cyclopedic or composite works, or works copyrighted by an employer or corporation hiring someone to do the work, if they were copyrighted by the proprietor originally, the proprietor of the copyright is entitled to the renewal. Application for renewal must be made within the last twelve months of the original term.

To repeat: For a non-dramatic literary work sold or distributed in the United States — a 'book' or periodical — copyright originates with publication with notice, on all copies sold or distributed in this country. After publication, if the work is not protected under UCC, the proprietor must comply with certain formalities in order to be assured of full term protection. But without publication with notice as stated above, no statutory copyright in the United States can exist for published works.

Outline of the Copyright Law
UNITED STATES CODE, TITLE 17

*A résumé of the sections most pertinent to the author, publisher, and agent of 'literary works.' ***

I. REGISTRATION OF COPYRIGHTS

§ 1: The rights granted:

(a) To print, reprint, publish, copy, and vend.

(b) *If a literary work,* to translate or make any other version, to dramatize. *If a drama,* to convert it into a novel. *If music,* to arrange or adapt it. *If art,* to complete, execute, and finish it.

(c) *If a lecture* or similar, *or any other non-dramatic literary work,* to deliver, read, or present it in public for profit; to make any transcription or record by which it can be delivered, presented, produced, or reproduced; to play or perform it in public for profit, and to exhibit, represent, produce, or reproduce it in any way or by any method.

(d) *If a drama,* to perform it in public; to sell any manuscript or record (if unpublished); to make any record or transcription by which it can be exhibited or performed; to exhibit, perform, produce, or reproduce it in any way or by any method.

(e) *If music,* to perform it in public for profit; to record it (but not granted to foreign authors unless the State of which he is a citizen grants similar protection to United States citizens). But if once recorded, others may record and pay royalty of 2 cents for all use except public performance for profit (as of this writing, use on a coin-operated machine is not 'performance for profit' unless admission is charged) . . .

§ 2. The author retains unlimited right at common law or in equity to prevent the copying, publication, or use of his unpublished work without his consent.

§ 3. The copyright on a work protects:

(a) All new copyrightable parts of the work.

(b) All material in the work that has already been copyrighted, but without lengthening its term of copyright.

(c) In composite works and periodicals, each copyrightable part, as if it were individually copyrighted.

§ 4. All the writings of an author are subject to copyright.

§ 5. In applying for copyright registration the material should be classified in one of the following groups:

(a) Books, including composite and cyclopedic works, directories, gazetteers, and other compilations.

(b) Periodicals, including newspapers.

(c) Lectures, sermons, addresses, or similar material prepared for oral delivery (radio and television scripts, if non-dramatic).

(d) Dramatic or dramatico-musical compositions (including radio and television plays).

(e) Musical compositions.

(f) Maps.

(g) Works of art; models or designs for works of art.

(h) Reproductions of works of art.

(i) Drawings or plastic works of a scientific or technical nature.

(j) Photographs.

(k) Prints and pictorial illustrations, including prints and labels used for articles of merchandise.

(l) Motion-picture plays.

(m) Motion pictures other than photoplays.

---

* Many clauses not relevant to the literary author or publisher are omitted, as are also the details for infringement. The Act is given in full on pages 227–41.

These classes do not limit the subject matter of copyright and an error in classification will not invalidate or impair the copyright.

§ 6. Since 1 July 1940 copyright of prints and labels connected with the sale and advertisement of merchandise (but not trade marks) is handled by the Register of Copyright. Fee for registration, $6.

§ 7. The following kinds of writings become new works, subject to independent copyright, when they are created either from material in the public domain or from copyrighted material with the consent of the copyright owner:

compilations	translations
abridgments	new editions with
adaptations	new copyright
arrangements	matter
dramatizations	new versions

However, the copyrighted publication of these works does not affect the validity of any copyright in the source material, or extend its duration; nor does it prevent others from making similar use of the same material.

§ 8. There is no copyright on the following material:

Works in the public domain.

Works published before 1 July 1909 and not at that time copyright in the United States.

Any publication of the United States Government or any reprint from government publications (except certain copyrights allowed to the Postmaster General).

The use of copyrighted material in a government publication does not, however, annul the copyright, nor does it authorize further use of such material without the consent of the copyright owner.

§ 9. The author or proprietor, or his executor, administrator, or assigns, is entitled to copyright under the terms of this law when

(a) he is a United States citizen, or he is domiciled in the United States at the time of first publication of his work, or

(b) he is a citizen of a foreign State that grants by treaty, convention, agreement, or law to United States citizens the same copyright benefits it grants to its nationals; or substantially the same copyright protection given foreigners in the United States; or is party to an international agreement that provides for reciprocity in copyright, which the United States may join if it wishes. These states are designated by the President by proclamation. . .

(c) When the Universal Copyright Convention is in force between the United States and a foreign State of which the author is a citizen or subject, or in which the work is first published. In such instances the following requirements are waived:

(1) reciprocity in granting mechanical reproduction rights for music (see § 1e);

(2) obligatory deposit (see § 13);

(3) United States manufacture and filing of affidavit (§§ 14, 16, 17, and 18);

(4) the prohibition against importation of foreign manufactured books in English during term of United States copyright (§ 107);

(5) the requirement that the notice be in the specific places stated in §§ 19 and 20, provided from first publication all copies shall bear the notice ©, the name of the proprietor, and the year of publication, placed in such a way as to give reasonable notice of claim of copyright.

Ad interim copyrights in effect when a foreign State becomes a member of UCC are automatically extended to full term (28 years from first publication) without further formality (see § 23).

The provisions of this subsection (9c) are not applicable to works of an author who is a citizen of or domiciled in the United States or to works first published in the United States,

§ 10. Copyright is secured, by a person entitled to it, by publishing the work with a copyright notice (see § 19) affixed to every copy published or offered for sale in the United States, except in the deposit copies of books seeking ad interim protection.

§ 11. Copyright registration may be made by complying with the provisions of the Copyright Act, including the deposit of copies. Upon compliance, the Copyright Office will issue a certificate of copyright.

§ 12. Works not reproduced for sale may obtain copyright by registration and deposit as follows:

(a) lectures, dramas, music (Classes C, D, and E), 1 complete copy;

(b) motion picture plays (Class L), title

and description, with 1 print from each scene or act;

(c) photographs [Class J], a photographic print;

(d) motion pictures, non-dramatic [Class M], title and description, with not less than 2 prints taken from different sections;

(e) work of art or plastic work or drawing [Classes G and I], a photograph or other identifying reproduction.

If the work is later published, 2 copies must then be deposited.

§ 13. Registration of published works [optional for UCC works of foreign origin]:

After publication with notice, the proprietor must deposit in the Copyright Office 2 complete copies of the best edition; *or*

If the work is by a foreigner and is published in a foreign country, 1 complete copy; *or*

If the work is a contribution to a periodical, for which special registration is requested, 1 copy of the issue or issues containing it; *or*

If not reproduced in copies for sale, deposit of special classes as stipulated in § 12. No action for infringement can be maintained before deposit and registration.

§ 14. Penalty for failure to deposit: If the copyright proprietor fails to make deposit, as outlined in § 13, the Register of Copyrights may any time after publication demand deposit within 3 months from any part of the United States, or 6 months from an outlying possession or a foreign country. If the deposit is not made then, the copyright proprietor is liable to a fine of $100 and twice the retail price of the book, and the copyright becomes void.

§ 15. Deposit copies may be mailed free by being given to the postmaster, who will give a receipt if requested.

§ 16. Manufacturing provision: Printed books and periodicals in the English language as specified in § 5 (a) and (b) must be printed from type set within the limits of the United States . . . or from plates made within the limits of the United States from type set therein, or if the text is produced by a lithographic or photo-engraving process, the process must be wholly performed within the limits of the United States, as must also be the

printing and binding. This extends also to illustrations produced by lithography or photo-engraving, except where the subjects illustrate a scientific work or work of art that is located in a foreign country. This does not apply to works in raised characters for the blind, or to books or periodicals of foreign origin in a foreign language, or to works printed or produced in the United States by any other process, or to up to 1500 copies of books or periodicals in English imported into the United States within 5 years after first foreign publication, if the copies contain proper notice of copyright and have been registered for ad interim copyright. [UCC works of foreign origin exempt.]

§ 17. Affidavits setting forth that the books have been manufactured in accordance with the provisions of § 16 must accompany the deposit copies. The affidavit must be under an official seal, made by the copyright claimant, his agent, or the printer, and must state where the work was done, and the date of the completion of the printing, or the date of publication.

§ 18. Anyone deliberately making a false affidavit is liable to a fine of not more than $1000 and forfeiture of the copyright.

§ 19. The copyright notice in a printed literary, musical, or dramatic work consists of Copyright, or Copr., or ©, the year of publication, and the name of the copyright proprietor. In copies of works in classification F to K, it may be © and the initials or symbol of the proprietor if his name appears elsewhere.

§ 20. One notice of copyright must appear in each volume of a set of books or each number of a newspaper or periodical:

In a book or other printed publication, on the title page or the page immediately following it.

In a periodical, on the title page or the first page of text, or under the title heading.

In a musical work, on the title page or first page of music. One notice in each volume or issue of a newspaper or periodical is enough.

§ 21. Omission of notice through error:

If the copyright proprietor has sought to comply, the omission of the notice by mistake or accident in one copy or a few copies will not invalidate the copyright or prevent recovery from a deliberate infringer. However, the copyright owner must reimburse the outlay of an innocent infringer before a permanent injunction will be made.

§ 22. Ad interim copyright:
A book or periodical in English first published abroad may secure ad interim copyright protection by the deposit of 1 copy in the Copyright Office, not more than 6 months after its foreign publication, with the request for reservation of copyright. This must state:
The name and nationality of the author.
The name and nationality of the copyright proprietor.
The date of publication.
The copyright thus secured is good for five years after first publication abroad. [Not applicable to UCC works of foreign origin.]

§ 23. American edition of books or periodicals having ad interim copyright:
When the American edition is published, within the ad interim period, and in compliance with the terms of the Copyright Act in regard to manufacture, notice, affidavits, registration, and deposit, the copyright is extended for the full term. [No registration required for American editions of foreign UCC works.]

§ 24. Copyright endures for 28 years from the date of first publication, plus a renewal term of 28 years.
In the following cases the proprietor makes the renewal:
(a) Posthumous works, periodicals, cyclopedic or composite works in which the copyright was originally secured by the proprietor.
(b) Works copyrighted by a corporate body, otherwise than as an assignee or licensee of the individual author.
(c) Works copyrighted by an employer for whom the work was done for hire.
In all other cases, including contributions of individual authors to periodicals or to cyclopedic or other composite works, the renewal is made by the author, if he is still living; if not by
(a) the widow (or widower) or children of the author;
(b) if no widow(er) or children, by the authors executors, or, in the absence of a will, his next of kin.
The application for renewal must be made and registered during the last twelve months before the original copyright expires.

§ 25. Copyrights registered in the Patent Office before 1 July 1940 may be renewed during the last year of their 28 year term.

§ 26. The 'date of publication' is the earliest date when copies of the first authorized edition are placed on sale, sold, or publicly distributed by the copyright proprietor or under his authority. 'Author' includes an employer in the case of works done for hire.

§ 27. The work copyrighted is distinct from the copyright itself, and the owner may sell or give away the material object [manuscript] without transferring his rights. In the same way, the assignment of the copyright does not imply that the material object must be transferred too.

§ 28. A copyright may be assigned, granted, or mortgaged by a written statement signed by the proprietor, or it may be bequeathed by will.

§ 29. An assignment of copyright executed in a foreign country must be acknowledged before a consular officer or secretary of legation of the United States authorized to administer oaths.

§ 30. Every copyright assignment must be recorded in the Copyright Office within 3 calendar months if it is executed in the United States, 6 calendar months otherwise, or it will be void against any subsequent purchaser, without notice, whose assignment has been recorded.

§ 31. The Register of Copyright will record the assignment, upon payment of the required fee, and return it to the sender with a certificate of record. A certified copy of it will be furnished to any one who wishes it, on payment of a fee.

§ 32. When a copyright has been assigned and recorded, the assignee may substitute his name for that of the assignor in the copyright notice . . .

II. INFRINGEMENT PROCEEDINGS

§ 101. [Treats of penalties for infringement; §§ 102–3 were repealed.]

§ 104. Deliberate infringement for profit is a misdemeanor and punishable by imprisonment, fine, or both. However, the use of religious or secular works, such as cantatas, oratorios, masses, etc., for charitable or educational purposes is not prohibited.

§ 105. Anyone who uses a copyright notice fraudulently on material that is not copyrighted, or removes or alters a valid copyright notice, is punishable by a fine from $100 to $1000. Anyone who knowingly sells a work with a false copyright notice, or imports one into the country, is liable to a fine of $100.

§ 106. The importation of any article bearing a false copyright notice or of piratical copies of books that are copyrighted in the United States is prohibited.

§ 107. During the existence of the American copyright on a book it is forbidden to import either piratical copies or authorized copies not manufactured in accordance with § 16 of the Copyright Act. In regard to the latter, however, there are the following exceptions:

(a) Works in raised characters for the use of the blind.

(b) Foreign newspapers or magazines, even though they contain material in English copyrighted in the United States if it is authorized, unless they also contain unauthorized material holding a United States copyright.

(c) The authorized edition of a book in a foreign language of which only the English translation is in copyright here.

(d) Any authorized foreign publication under the following conditions:

(1) If only one copy is imported at a time, for individual use and not for sale. This does not apply to a foreign reprint of a book by an American author copyrighted in the United States.

(2) If it is imported by the authority of or for the use of the United States.

(3) If only one copy is imported at a time, for use and not for sale, by or for a religious, educational, literary, scientific, or philosophical society or school or library.

(4) If books of this type are part of a library or collection purchased *en bloc* for the use of institutions or libraries listed in (3), or are part of a library or personal baggage of people arriving here, and are not for sale.

[(5) UCC books of foreign origin.]

However, if books imported in this way are used to violate the rights of the United States copyright owner, or limit his copyright protection, they will be considered infringement.

§ 108. Books imported illegally are seized and destroyed. However, authorized editions of copyrighted books may be returned to the country of export if it is proved in a written application to the Secretary of the Treasury that their importation does not involve wilful negligence or fraud . . .

[§§ 109–16 have to do with regulations and injunctions.]

III. Copyright Office

[§§ 201–8 have to do with regulations of the Copyright Office.]

§ 209. The Copyright Office furnishes the copyright claimant a certificate of registration containing the name and address of the claimant, the nationality of the author, and, if he is an alien domiciled in the United States, his address; the author's name if it is given in the application, the title of the work, the date of the deposit of copies, the date of publication, class designation, and entry number. In the case of a book, it also states the receipt of the affidavit and the date of the completion of printing or publication. This certificate is admitted in any court as prima facie evidence of the facts stated in it. A receipt for the deposit copies will also be furnished on request.

§ 210. All copyright registrations and assignments are indexed and catalogued. The Copyright Office indices and catalogues are admitted in court as prima facie evidence of the facts stated in them regarding any copyright registration . . .

§ 211. The catalogues of copyright entries are not only available to officials, but also for sale to the general public (priced at not over $25 for the complete yearly catalogue).

§ 212. All indices, record books, and deposits in the Copyright Office are open to the public and copies may be made upon request.

§ 213. The Librarian of Congress determines what deposit copies shall be transferred to the permanent collection of the Library of Congress and what shall be placed in the reserve collections for sale or exchange, or be transferred to other governmental libraries.

23

§ 214. The Librarian of Congress and the Register of Copyrights jointly decide what records and deposits should be kept permanently and what may be destroyed after a given time. A catalogue is published listing the years of receipt of the material to be destroyed so that any copyright claimant may claim material he wishes to preserve. No manuscript of an unpublished work is ever destroyed during the term of copyright without the copyright proprietor's first being notified.

§ 215. Fees:

Registration: $4 for any work not a print or label; $6 for a print or label; only one registration fee is required when several volumes of the same book are published and deposited at the same time; with regard to foreign works, in lieu of the payment of the fee of $4 together with one copy of the work, the foreign author or proprietor may within six months of publication deposit two copies accompanied by a catalogue card.

Renewal of copyright: $2

Additional certificates of registration: $1

Certifying an application for registration, and for all other certifications: $2

Recording assignments, agreements, powers of attorney, or other papers not exceeding 6 pages: $3; for each additional page: 50 cents; for each title over one in the papers recorded: 50 cents

Recording notice of use for not more than 5 titles: $2; each additional title: 50 cents

Searching Copyright Office records or works deposited: $3 an hour

Outline of the Universal Copyright Convention

I. Each Contracting State provides for the protection of the rights of authors of literary, scientific, and artistic work, including writings, music, drama, motion pictures, painting, engravings, and sculpture.

II. *Who is protected.* § 1. Published works of a national of each Contracting State and works first published in each Contracting State enjoy in other Contracting States the same protection that those States grant to nationals for works first published in their own territories.

§ 2. Unpublished works enjoy the same protection that other Contracting States grant unpublished works of their own nationals.

§ 3. Any Contracting State may assimulate to its own nationals anyone domiciled in it.

III. *How protected.* § 1. Any Contracting State that requires formalities (deposit, registration, manufacture, etc.) as a condition of copyright shall regard these formalities as satisfied if from first publication all copies bear the notice ©, the name of the proprietor, and the year of publication *except* if the author is one of its nationals or the work is first published in that state.

§ 2. Any Contracting State may require formalities, etc., of its own nationals wherever published, and for work first published in its territory.

§ 3. Any state may require that a person seeking judicial relief must comply with its requirements (such as appearing through domestic counsel or making necessary deposit of copies), but failure to comply will not affect the validity of the copyright.

§ 4. Each Contracting State must have legal means of protecting the unpublished works of nationals of other States, without formalities.

§ 5. If a State has two or more terms of copyright and the first term is longer than the minimum required in Article IV, it need not extend its protection without formalities to the second or later periods.

IV. *Duration.* § 1. The duration of protection is governed by the law of the State in which the protection is claimed.

§ 2. The minimum term of protection is the life of the author plus 25 years, *or* 25 years after registration of unpublished works and publication of published works, depending on the system of the individual State.

If any State limits certain classes of work to a period after publication, it may keep the exceptions, and extend them to other classes.

If two terms are granted, the first must be no less than the minimum stated above.

§ 3. Photographic works and works of applied art are excepted, but if they are protected (as artistic works) in any state, the term must be at least 10 years.

§ 4. No Contracting State need grant protection to a work for a period longer than that fixed for the class of works to which it belongs, if unpublished, by the law of the State of which the author is a national; if published, by the law of the State in which it is first published. In this context, if a State grants two or more terms, the period of protection of that State will be the aggregate of the terms (but if the work in question fails to comply with the requisites for the subsequent terms, other States need not protect it after its copyright has expired).

§ 5. In regard to § 4, the work of a national of a Contracting State first published in a Non-Contracting State shall be treated as though first published in the Contracting State of which the author is a national.

§ 6. Also in regard to § 4, in the case of simultaneous publication in two or more Contracting States, a work will be treated as though first published in the one that has the shortest term; publication within 30 days will be regarded as simultaneous.

V. *Translations*. § 1. Copyright includes the exclusive right of making or authorizing translations.

§ 2. However, any Contracting State may, by domestic legislation, restrict the right of translation as follows: If an authorized translation has not been published within 7 years of first publication of a work into the national language or languages of any Contracting State, any national of that State may obtain a non-exclusive license to translate and publish it, if he can establish that he has requested and been denied the permission of the proprietor, or that he was unable to find the owner of the right. (A license may be granted on the same conditions if all previous translations are out of print.) If the owner of the copyright cannot be found, the license may be obtained from the diplomatic counselor or representative of the author's country or the organization designated by the government of the author's state. 'Just compensation' is to be made to the copyright owner and the original title and name of the original author must appear on all copies of the translation. The license is not transferable and the translation can be exported only to those countries of which the language is also the national language and where domestic law permits it. If all copies of the original work have been withdrawn from circulation, such a license will not be granted.

VI. *Publication.* 'The reproduction in tangible form and the general distribution to the public of copies . . . from which it can be read or otherwise visually perceived.'

VII. *Retroactivity.* The Convention does not apply to works already in the public domain in the state in which protection is claimed.

VIII. Any State may ratify or accede to the Convention by deposit of its papers of ratification or accession.

IX. The Convention comes into force 3 months after the deposit of 12 instruments of ratification, of which 4 are of non-Berne States. Subsequently it comes into force for any Contracting State 3 months after the deposit of its ratification.

[X–XVI. Regulations and organization; see Appendix, pages 244–5.]

XVII. The Convention does not affect provisions of the Berne Convention.

XVIII. It does not abrogate copyright agreements between American Republics.

XIX. It does not abrogate copyright agreements between Contracting States.

XX. Reservations to the Convention are not permitted.

XXI. The Director-General of UNESCO shall notify all interested states of acceptances and denunciations. [For Appendix, Resolutions, and Protocols, see pages 246–7.]

Check List for Copyrighting a Literary Work

I. *Is the author entitled to copyright protection?*

(a) Is he an American citizen? *or*

(b) Is he a resident of this country? Do you have his address? *or*

(c) Is he a citizen of a UCC country or of one with which the United States has reciprocal copyright relations? *and*

(d) Has he preserved common-law copyright in his work by never having sold, assigned, or licensed it to anyone else; by never having publicly sold or distributed copies; and by never having dedicated it to the public?

If (a), (b), and (c) or (d) are answered in the negative, his work *cannot* be copyrighted in the United States.

II. *Is the material subject to copyright?*

(a) Is it an 'original' writing? *or*

(b) Is it a new version of material already published?

(1) Does it have new copyright material such as substantial revision, additional chapters, notes, commentary, introduction, index?

(2) Is it an adaptation, abridgment, translation, compilation, collection, anthology, dramatization?

(3) If the material on which it is based is not in the public domain, does the author have permission of the copyright owner(s) to use the material?

(4) Does he have permission from the present copyright proprietor for all quotations from copyrighted material?

(5) Is the work free of infringing, plagiarizing, blasphemous, obscene, seditious, and libelous material?

(c) Has it ever been published, publicly distributed, sold or placed on sale in the United States before? If it has,

(1) If it was first published in the United States, did it carry a United States copyright notice? (If so, it cannot be copyrighted again unless it has substantial new material added or is a new version.)

(2) If it is of foreign origin and in the English language and did not carry a UCC notice, did it secure ad interim copyright, or is it now seeking it?

III. *If it is in English and is a book or periodical by a United States citi-*

zen or national or was first published here, has it been manufactured in accordance with the copyright requirements?

(a) Has it been completely printed, plated, or photographed in this country?

(b) If there are illustrations, have they been photo-engraved or lithographed in this country? *or* Are they reproductions of scientific or artistic subjects located abroad?

(c) Has it been bound in this country?

If the answer is 'no' to (a), (b), or (c) the book cannot be copyrighted.

IV. *If it is in English and of foreign origin,*

(a) Is it a United States manufactured edition having first publication here or simultaneous publication with the foreign edition?

(b) If it was first published abroad and not protected by UCC, was ad interim copyright registration made within 6 months of its publication?

(c) If it is an American edition of a book previously protected by ad interim copyright, has it fulfilled the manufacturing requirements, were less than 1500 copies of the foreign edition imported for sale here, and is it within 5 years of first foreign publication?

V. *Is the copyright notice in proper form?*

(a) Is it on the title page or the back of the title page, if it is a book, or on the first page of text or under the title heading, if a periodical?

(b) Is it worded properly (Copyright or Copr. or ©, the year, the name of the copyright holder)?

(c) Is the name of the proprietor in the notice the same as that specified in the contract with the author? (A copyright proprietor *must* be able to trace his title to the author.)

(d) Does the year correspond with the year of *first* publication?

(e) If this is a reissue with new copyright material, does the year of the old as well as the new publication appear? (This is advisable though not explicitly required legally.)

VI. *Have you sent deposit copies?*

(a) Were two copies of the best edition sent, if it is an American book, magazine, or newspaper?

(b) If it was an ad interim book or book or other work first published abroad, was a fee enclosed if only one copy was sent, or a catalogue card if two copies were sent in lieu of a fee?

(c) Was one complete copy of the periodical sent if it was a contribution to a magazine or newspaper, bearing a separate copyright notice?

(d) Were the deposit copies properly wrapped, addressed to the Register of Copyrights, Washington, D. C., with your return address?

VII. *Is the application for registration in order?*

(a) Is it classified properly? (Do not select an application form until you have considered *all* alternatives.)

(b) Is the form filled out properly?

(1) Does the name of the copyright owner correspond with that in the notice of the book?

(2) Is the author's name spelled correctly, and does it correspond with that on the title page?

(3) Is the author's citizenship stated? His address given, and whether or not he is domiciled in the United States?

(4) Does the title of the book correspond with that on the title page? (*Not* that on the spine or on the jacket.)

(5) Is the correct publication date given? Does it correspond with that given in the affidavit?

(6) If this is a translation of a published work, is the name of the translator given? (The translator is the 'author' of a translation — the original author is not.)

(7) If this is the American edition of an ad interim book, or of a book that was first published abroad, is the year of the foreign publication given as well as the American publication date?

(8) If it is a book that has been previously published serially or a revised edition, is the nature of the new material indicated?

(9) If it is a contribution to a periodical on which separate copyright is requested, are the title, date, page, and volume of the periodical in which it appeared given? (Form BB.)

(10) If it is a periodical, is the date of actual publication (public release) given, not just the date given on the cover? Is the name of the deposit account given?

(c) Is the affidavit properly filled out?

(1) Is the status of the person making it properly indicated?

(2) Are the state and county in which it is made given?

(3) Is it dated on or after the date of publication?

(4) Does the date of publication agree with that given in the application?

(5) Is it signed?

(6) Is it notarized and sealed?

VIII. *Is the proper fee enclosed* ($4, *but see* IX *below;* $6 *for commercial print or label*)?

(a) Is it a check, money order, or a certified check?

(b) If not, do you have a deposit account, and is the name under which it is held indicated on the application form?

IX. *If a catalogue card is being sent in lieu of a fee,*

(a) Is the work of foreign origin?

(b) Is the author a citizen or national of a country with which we have reciprocal copyright relations?

(c) Is all the information requested given under Option B (see p. 213)?

X. *If it is a renewal, is it being made in accordance with the law?*

(a) Is it being renewed in the name of the proper person?

(1) the author, if he is living

(2) the widow(er), children, executor, or next of kin, if the author is dead (see *Renewal*)

(3) the proprietor, if it is a posthumous book, or a compilation, periodical, cyclopedic work, or one made for hire, and originally copyrighted by the proprietor.

(b) Is it being made within the last 12 months of the first copyright term?

Part II

Abridgments and Adaptations

AN ABRIDGED VERSION of a published work must carry the word 'abridged' in clear and conspicuous type on the front cover, title page, jacket, and any advertising copy (ruling of Federal Trade Commission). The words 'special edition' or any other variation will not do. It must be labeled 'abridged.' If a new title is used, the original title must also be given wherever the new title is used — the cover, title page, beginning of the story, jacket, et cetera.

Abridgments of works in the public domain and abridgments of copyrighted works authorized by the copyright owner are regarded in the copyright statute as 'new works,' and on first publication can be registered under classification A. To be entitled to copyright, the abridgment must be the result of intellectual labor, of the 'exercise of reason, judgment, and taste.' If it is of material in public domain, its copyright will protect only the new form and any editorial notes or changes; another person is free to make a second abridgment of his own, using the original source, and to copyright his abridged version.

So far as the abridgment of material still in copyright is concerned, the Copyright Act grants to the original author the right to make 'any other version' of his work. Hence an abridgment made without permission of the copyright owner constitutes infringement. If the author makes the abridgment himself, it is not necessary to secure new copyright. If there are substantial alterations, a new copyright may be justified, but as the law states that there can be only one copyright on a work, the author must guard against copyrighting the same material twice. This would throw the whole book into the public domain. If an abridged version is published before full-length book publication, a new copyright notice must be carried by the book to protect the new material. However, the date of the abridged version, if an earlier year, should also appear in the notice.

An abridgment in a 'digest' magazine is entitled to a new copyright, either by the original copyright owner or by the digest magazine, according to the terms of the contract. It should also carry the notice of its original publication.

Unauthorized abridgment or adaptation is not always infringement. A plot résumé in a book of stories of the opera has been declared 'fair use.'

35

On the other hand, a digest of a textbook, given in installments to pupils on separate mimeographed sheets at successive class meetings, has been declared an infringement. In this case (Macmillan Co. *v.* King), some of the sheets gave quotations from the text, some a digest, and some abridgments. The author and source were given in each instance, and only parts of the book were included. However, the author's permission was not asked, and he successfully demonstrated that the sale of his book would eventually be affected by the continued use of the abstract. In infringement by abridgment and adaptation, the question is whether so much has been reproduced that the author's right to make 'other versions' has been violated; also, whether the use of the material competes with the original work.

Included in the right to make 'other versions' of a work is the right to adapt it to various other purposes. When an adaptation is made by anyone other than the original author, but with his permission, if it is original and creative it in turn is subject to its own copyright (application form A). To meet this requirement it must not be a mere copy of the original, verbatim but with deletions. It must retain the essence of the work, but be something different in form and structure. A complicated historical novel retold for children is a type of adaptation justifying a new copyright.

The right to make adaptations of his work is also granted to the musician and artist. Musical adaptations, such as orchestrations of compositions for piano or violin or popular dance arrangements of classical melodies, are 'new works' and entitled to a new copyright. So also a painting or photograph of a piece of sculpture. If the original material is not in the public domain, the permission of the original artist or musician must be obtained. If it is in the public domain, although the adaptation is entitled to copyright, this does not give the author any exclusive right to the original source material, which may be used by anyone else.

When a license is granted for an adaptation or abridgment of copyright material, it is often assumed to be exclusive when the fact is not expressly stated. Legally this is only determined by the specific contract.

In most European countries the original author has a 'moral right' in regard to the new version, even though he grants a license for the adaptation. He can object, for example, if his tragedy is given a comic ending. A case on record concerned a German artist's objection to having the nude figures in his painting clothed when the painting was adapted for use as a mural. Most American courts do not recognize this 'moral right' if there is an assignment or license, unless the contract states that the final version must have the author's approval, or the subsidiary work defames character or results in a libel suit.

36

Ad Interim Copyright

Form A-B Ad Interim; deposit 1 copy and $4 fee, or 2 copies and a catalogue card (see pages 210 and 213).

EXCEPT FOR WORKS PROTECTED under UCC, a book or periodical in the English language first published outside the United States can secure copyright here only through ad interim registration. The application, deposit, and fee (or catalogue card) must be filed within six months after first publication, but will not be accepted if filed before publication.

(a) The application: The application calls for name, address, and citizenship of copyright claimants; title of the work; the volume, number, and date of a periodical; author(s)' name, address, and citizenship, and whether domiciled in the United States; the place and date of publication; and if it contains previously published material a statement of the new matter. It must be signed by the copyright claimant or his authorized agent, but does not need to be notarized.

(b) The deposit copy: The Copyright Act does not specify that the 'best edition' need be deposited for ad interim registration, but it does require a 'complete' copy; any copy of the foreign edition will probably be accepted. The deposit copy need not carry a notice, but any copies imported for sale or distribution must. Deposit and registration cannot be made until *after* publication (i.e. when the work is first published abroad), but must be in the Copyright Office within the first six months allowed by law.

(c) The fee for ad interim registration is $4, but the proprietor may if he chooses elect to send two deposit copies and a catalogue card properly filled out, in lieu of the fee. (This alternative does not apply to works by U.S. citizens, nationals, or proprietors.) A form and sample card are supplied on a separate sheet issued by the Copyright Office. If the fee is sent, it should be a certified check or money order, and sent with the application by first-class mail, not enclosed with the book.

Unless there has been a written assignment of copyright (and most foreign contracts for publication are licenses, not assignments), the name of the copyright claimant in the registration and in the notice should be that of the author, not the foreign or American publisher. When the American

37

edition is published, it should carry the same name unless there has been a later assignment recorded in the Copyright Office before publication here (see *Assignments*).

The purpose of ad interim ('in the meantime') copyright is to give temporary protection to books in English that have had first publication outside the limits of the United States and are not protected under UCC. According to the U.S. Copyright Act, no book in the English language sold in this country, unless it is protected by UCC, is entitled to a full term of copyright if it has not been completely manufactured in this country (see page 121). Without some protection, the prospective American publisher of books in English of foreign origin would run the risk of piratical editions' being imported or manufactured here (thus putting the book in the public domain) before he could bring out his authorized American edition in accordance with the law. The law therefore provides that the author (or proprietor) may secure a temporary copyright for 5 years and import as many as 1500 copies during this period, while the American edition is being manufactured. Since September 1955 American citizens and nationals whose works in English are first published abroad may also take advantage of this provision.

After ad interim copyright has been secured, an authorized American edition may be published in accordance with copyright law requirements within 5 years. The proprietor then must register the American edition and deposit two copies of it in the Copyright Office (Form A), with an affidavit of manufacture (see *Affidavit*) and a $4 registration fee. The copyright then extends 28 years — from 'first publication,' not from the date of the application or of the publication of the American edition. The copyright notice in the American edition therefore carries the date of the first foreign publication.

If the American edition has a new title, a statement to that effect should be on the copyright page. This is not required by the copyright law, but it will protect the publisher against 'innocent infringers.' Also it is required under laws relating to fair trade.

If a whole book is submitted for ad interim copyright, and only a part of it (a few chapters) is subsequently published, it is not entitled to copyright, according to an opinion of the Attorney General. The reason for this ruling is that the publication of a fragment of the book with a United States copyright would deter any other publisher from bringing out an edition containing the remaining parts, and therefore the American public would effectively be denied any edition of the complete work.

After ad interim registration, only the holder of the import statement may legally import copies. If after having registered a book for ad interim copyright the publisher decides he needs more than 1500 copies and does not want to bring out an American edition, the copyright may be abandoned, with the consent of the copyright claimant. The Copyright Office should receive authorized notification of abandonment of the copyright (from the copyright claimant, not the holder of the import license, if they are in different names) and there should of course be no copyright notice in copies imported after abandonment or any still on hand of the original 1500. The work is then in the public domain.

When UCC comes into force in any foreign country, every book or periodical of a citizen or subject of that country registered for ad interim copyright on the effective date is automatically granted full protection for 28 years from its first publication without the necessity of compliance with further formalities of U.S. manufacture, registration, or fee.

Advertisements (Prints and Labels)

Form KK, *deposit* 2 *copies, fee* $6.

COMMERCIAL CATALOGUES AND OTHER ADVERTISEMENTS, written or pictorial, that are original or 'creative' are subject to copyright. Catalogues may be registered as a 'book,' after publication with notice (Form A). Advertising circulars and individual pictures or cuts are registered as 'prints' under classification KK, as are also prints or labels for articles of merchandise. Each print must bear a separate notice. Certain companies that put stress on material used in newspaper and magazine advertising prefer to hold the copyright themselves rather than rely on the copyright of the periodical. These are registered as prints (KK) if they advertise an article of merchandise; otherwise as a contribution (BB).

Since 1940 the registration of prints and labels has been handled by the Copyright Office. Prints have been defined by the Office as 'single page works containing copyrightable pictorial matter, text, or both,' first published in a periodical or separately, advertising articles of merchandise. (It is safer to register multipage circulars as 'books.') A label is 'an artistic and/or literary work' that is either stamped or impressed directly on the article, or attached to it or its container. Both print and label must bear words to serve as an identifying title. Before they can be registered they must be published with notice. 'Copr.' or © and the initials, mark, or monogram of the claimant is sufficient if the full name appears elsewhere, but the type must be large enough to be legible. The year date and full name in the notice are not required, except for UCC protection. After publication they are registered on Form KK (see page 224), fee $6. Two copies must be sent for deposit.

Every time advertising material is used it must carry the original notice in clearly legible form. Failure in this invalidates the copyright. If the original material was copyrighted as a 'book' (Class A), the notice must be Copyright or © or Copr., the year, and the name of the claimant; © with the initials of the claimant is valid only if the copyright was obtained under the classification KK, and is valid then only for U.S. protection, not UCC. Advertising catalogues that are issued yearly may obtain new copyright (as a

40

compilation) if substantial new material is added, but the new copyright does not, of course, prolong the copyright of the old material.

If a book or map is enclosed in a container with descriptive matter on it, the container may be copyrighted only as a label, and must carry a separate copyright notice.

A copyright is not a patent. A merchant or manufacturer cannot monopolize an unpatented article by copyrighting a catalogue in which it is illustrated. Other manufacturers can copyright illustrations of it too, if they work from the original and not from a copyrighted pictorial reproduction. His copyright protects only the actual expression or illustration in his catalogue.

Neither is a copyrighted print or label a trade mark. A trade mark is a 'symbol' (picture, sign, word, or phrase) applied to goods to distinguish them from other goods of the same kind. Trade marks are protected under the Lanham Trade-Mark Act (under Interstate Commerce), passed in 1946 (for information, write the Commissioner of Patents, Washington 25, D.C.). Trade names are the distinguishing 'labels' of business, identified with their products, reputation, and good will. To be protected, trade marks and trade names must have a secondary meaning (that is, be more than merely descriptive), must be more than geographical (the *Oxford* in 'Oxford University Press' cannot prevent the use of 'Oxford' by the Oxford Book Company, Oxford Paper Company, and a host of others), cannot use the name of a living person without that person's consent, or of a deceased President of the United States if the President's widow is living, without her consent. The established trade mark and trade name are usually protected against unfair competition, whether by statutory law or at common law. In a frequently quoted decision the court said, 'Unquestionably in our ever-increasing complex business life, the trend of modern judicial decisions in trade mark matters is to show little patience with the newcomer who in adopting a mark gets into the borderline zone between an open field and one legally appropriated to another. As between the newcomer and one who by honest dealing has won favor with the public, doubts are always resolved against the former.'

A price list has been held uncopyrightable because it lacks any element of originality. But although 'a mere advertisement of articles,' such as a price list, is not copyrightable, any advertisement with 'artistic quality' and 'originality' is, and, as Weil points out in his excellent book, it requires very little originality indeed to render it so. A pamphlet in which a list of motor vehicles was given, with the numbers and dimensions of the piston rings of each, was held to be the result of 'labor and research' and therefore subject to copyright protection, as were also cuts of women's clothing illustrating the season's fashions. It should be noted, however, that only truthful advertisements are copyrightable, since the law will not protect a 'fraud' (misrepresentation).

The question of the legality of copyrighting pictures used for advertising, such as posters, calendars, and postcards, has come before the courts many times. Although in some of the earlier cases the copyright claimants were defeated, in all the more recent cases the courts have upheld them. Justice Holmes declared in a case challenging the copyright of a circus poster, 'Certainly works are not the less connected with the fine arts because their pictorial quality attracts the crowd and therefore gives them a real use — if use means to increase trade and help make money.' Some of the leading cases in which the copyright of advertising material has been upheld have concerned colored photographs of Colorado scenery, catalogues of cuts and pictures of statuary, a print of a young man clothed only in underwear, and a *Manual for Successful Drug Store Advertising and Merchandising*.

The protection of commercial art is not peculiar to United States copyright law. The Berne Convention protects as 'writings' (*écrits en tout genres*) guide books, catalogues, commercial prospectuses, and advertisements. In England the copyright has been upheld on *An Illustrated Book of Shopfittings, The Art and Virtue of Dressing Well, The Bath Drug Company's Price Current,* and other trade catalogues. Advocates of our becoming members of the International Copyright Union (by abolishing our copyright formalities and the requirement of domestic manufacture) have stressed the value to be gained by protecting in other lands 'our superior advertising creations.'

Publishers should guard strictly against the use in advertising of any material, whether protected by statutory copyright or at common law, without the author's consent. In most states, laws relating to unfair competition or the right of privacy forbid the unauthorized use for commercial purposes of a name, picture, or even a few quoted words, and publication may be stopped by injunction and result in damages. Laudatory letters should not be used in circulars without the writer's consent. Reviews may of course be quoted, but the practice of deletion in such a way as to obscure the reviewer's true verdict is not condoned and may result in damages.

Since the jackets of books are not protected by the book's copyright, any material used on them is thrown into the public domain unless it carries a special copyright notice. The art work on a jacket can, however, be protected as a print (K); if it is the text that is important, registration under Class A might be preferable.

42

Affidavits of American Manufacture

The verso of Form **A.**

APPLICATIONS FOR COPYRIGHT REGISTRATION of books in the English language published in the United States must be accompanied by an affidavit certifying that the typesetting, printing, and binding were done in the United States (see *Manufacturing Clause*).

The Copyright Office furnishes application forms (A) on the back of which are affidavits to be filled out by the copyright claimant or his authorized agent. According to the Copyright Law (§ 9) the printer is also entitled to make the affidavit, but in recent publishing practice he seldom does. The affidavit form is given on page 209.

The affidavit form should be filled out with care and rigorously scrutinized before it is submitted. The Copyright Office is constantly being forced to reject affidavits that have been incompletely or erroneously made. Some of the most common errors are:

1. Failure to fill in the state and county in which the affidavit is being made, and to have these data agree with the notary's statement.

2. Giving the name of a corporation or partnership instead of the individual affiant (a corporation cannot take an oath; only a person can). If the copyright claimant is a corporation, partnership, or firm, the affiant is the 'authorized agent' — a representative of the firm authorized to sign contracts and legal documents. He usually is an officer of the corporation, but this is not obligatory.

3. Failure to indicate the capacity in which the affiant acts. This is done by checking the proper box on the printed form: the duly authorized agent (i.e. the publisher, if the copyright claimant is the author), the printer, or the person claiming copyright.

4. Not giving the exact date of publication (or of the completing of the printing; the latter is assumed to be the off-press date, not the date of completing the binding or of delivery). Month and year are not enough. The date of publication must correspond with the date given in the application, and must be earlier than, or the same as, the date of the affidavit (see 8 below).

43

5. Failure to sign as an individual; a corporation or partnership cannot sign. (See 2 above.)

6. Failure to have the affidavit notarized, or to sign before a notary whose power is valid in the county in which the oath is taken.

7. Failure to see that the notary's seal is affixed. The seal is required by the Copyright Act, even though it may not be required on legal documents in the state in which the affidavit is made.

8. Dating the affidavit before the date given for publication. The form reads 'the book was published or printing completed on . . .' and the Copyright Act specifically states that the application should be filed after publication. Hence an affidavit dated before the day of publication or the completed printing is manifestly false and invalid.

9. Finally, inconsistency between titles, names, and dates in the affidavit and those given on the application or the book itself.

The Copyright Office will often call attention to errors in affidavits, but occasionally an irregular one will slip through unnoticed. This is not to the advantage of the claimant, as a certificate of registration is worthless to him if the facts on which it was issued do not conform with the law. Also, many cases in which an attempt has been made to justify copyright infringement, because of error in the affidavit, have come before the courts. When the errors are obviously matters of oversight, the court usually rules in favor of the claimant: for example, in one case in which the affiant failed to strike out an alternative statement in the printed form, the court declared that the copyright was not therefore invalidated. In another case an affiant was challenged because the date of publication entered in the affidavit was incorrect. Here the court declared,

. . . a mistake made as to the date of publication in the affidavit attached to the application . . . [does] not in my opinion invalidate the copyright. No prejudice resulted to the defendants or the public, and the misstatement of date is not of a character to justify a finding of purposeful falsehood.

But even though the courts usually protect the innocent though careless claimant, they cannot spare him the loss of time and effort required for his defense. Meticulous care in making out the affidavit will often protect him against the deliberate infringer who uses a technical flaw for his justification.

The penalty for wilfully making a false affidavit is a fine of not more than $1000 and forfeiture of the copyright. (Copyright Act § 18.)

Alien Authors

IN RESPECT TO COPYRIGHT, alien authors may be classified in four groups: (1) those domiciled in the United States or its possessions; (2) citizens of countries with which the United States has reciprocal copyright agreements; (3) citizens or nationals of countries adhering to the Universal Copyright Convention; (4) those belonging to none of groups 1, 2, or 3.

1. 'Domiciled' in this sense is usually interpreted as residing (here) and intending to remain (here). An alien domiciled in the United States at the time of first publication of his work is entitled to the same protection under the Copyright Law as if he were a citizen. He also enjoys full protection, as do United States citizens, at common law. In filing copyright applications for the works of alien authors domiciled in this country, it is important to give the place of residence, not merely a business or professional address, and, if he is stateless, to give his former citizenship.

2. Non-resident aliens who are citizens of countries not adherent to UCC but with which we have copyright agreements by proclamation, convention, or treaty (see *International Copyright*) are entitled to common-law rights in their unpublished works and may secure statutory copyright protection for published and unpublished works under the following conditions:

(a) With the exception of books in the English language, if the work is published with a copyright notice, and is registered (Form A-B Foreign for books and periodicals) in the United States Copyright Office, with deposit and fee (or alternatively two copies and catalogue card; see *Deposit*).

(b) If books in English are filed for ad interim copyright (see *Ad Interim*) and not more than 1500 copies of the foreign edition, bearing a copyright notice, are imported for sale or distribution in the United States. The copyright so secured is valid for five years after first publication and if an American edition is produced within that period, the copyright is extended to full term (28 years plus 28 years if renewed).

3. The works of citizens and nationals of UCC countries first published with a UCC notice (©, claimant, year) are entitled to the same protection as is given works of United States citizens, but without compliance with

the formalities of registration, deposit, and fee. The period of protection is that granted to United States citizens, but in order to take advantage of the renewal term, the formalities required by our law may be demanded (see also *Duration and Universal Copyright Convention*). Works of foreign origin entitled to protection under UCC may be registered on form A-B Foreign if the proprietor wishes to do so, but registration is not obligatory.

4. A non-resident alien who is a citizen of a country with which the United States has no reciprocal copyright agreement, including that of the UCC, cannot secure a United States copyright for his work unless his work is first published in a UCC state. Even if he assigns his work to an American or a citizen of another country who is entitled to protection under our laws, the work cannot claim copyright, since it is the citizenship of the author that is the determining factor, not that of the proprietor. It should be remembered, however, that translations and 'other versions' are 'new works' under our law. Thus although an Albanian as of this writing cannot secure United States copyright, a translation of an Albanian work by a Spaniard could secure copyright, as could also a dramatization of the work by a Frenchman. The original work, however, could be translated or dramatized by an American even without the Albanian's permission, since technically the original work would be in the public domain.

Although *all* copies of works by 'reciprocal' aliens (not UCC) not published or sold in the United States need not carry a copyright notice, some copies must, and all sold or distributed in this country must, or the copyright is invalidated. If the formalities of registration and deposit are not complied with promptly, the Copyright Office may demand compliance; the alien proprietor has six months after demand for compliance, rather than the three months allowed for works published here.

It is expected that many authors entitled to UCC protection will continue to register their works in the United States even though it will not be obligatory. Registration and deposit can legally be demanded in order to take advantage of our renewal term or defense against infringement, and it would seem wiser to go on record before the necessity arose.

See also *Universal Copyright Convention, International Copyright Relations,* and *International Copyright Union.*

46

Applications

ONE ESSENTIAL STEP in securing copyright registration is the filing of an application with the Copyright Office. On request, the Office will furnish various application forms; when asking for them, the applicant should state the number and kinds he needs. In general, the forms are divided into the 13 classifications indicated by the Copyright Act (see *Classification*), with one or two extra types and subdivisions. The book publisher will usually require only the A and R (Renewal) forms; the magazine and newspaper publisher, the A, B, and R forms, and so forth.

The available forms to be used are:

A: * Any 'book' printed and published for the first time in the United States. This form has the affidavit form relating to manufacturing requirements. It is used for the registration of 'fiction and nonfiction, poems, compilations, composite works, directories, catalogues, annual publications, information in tabular form, and similar text matter, with or without illustrations, published as a book, pamphlet, leaflet, card, single page, or the like' (Regulations of the Copyright Office). In addition to 'new books' first published in the United States, revised editions, translations, serials republished with new material, and United States editions of works protected by ad interim registration also use this application. Do *not* use it for advertisements (q.v.), published plays, periodicals or individual registration of contributions to periodicals, or American editions of books claiming protection under UCC.

A-B Ad Interim: * Ad interim copyright on a book or periodical in English first published outside the United States, by a citizen or national of a country with whom we have reciprocal copyright relations or by a United States citizen or national. The import statement is contingent on this application form. Do not use it for books claiming protection under UCC.

A-B Foreign: * A book *or periodical* or *a contribution to a periodical* of foreign origin first published outside the United States. No import state-

* Indicates that a sample of this form is given in the section on forms, pages 207–26.

ment necessary. No later United States edition necessary. Copyright is secured for full term (28 years plus 28 years renewal if renewal is properly registered) if all copies sold or distributed in this country have proper copyright notice. Do not use it for books in English seeking ad interim protection.

B: * A periodical, printed or produced in the United States. On this form should be registered newspapers, magazines, reviews, bulletins, and other publications that are issued more than once yearly (*not* annuals and *not* contributions to periodicals) — in general, periodical publications that would normally be accepted as second-class mail. Although periodicals in English must be printed in the United States in order to qualify for full-term copyright (unless protected under UCC), no affidavit is required.

BB: * A contribution to a periodical printed or produced in the United States — poem, story, article, series of narrative cartoons (comic strips, etc.). Advertisements of merchandise first published in periodicals, however, are registered on Form KK.

C: * A lecture, address, or similar work intended for oral delivery. Use this also for unpublished sermons, monologues, recording scripts, and scripts for radio and television (but not if they are dramatic with worked-out dialogue, etc.). If later published, a work in this class should then be registered as Class A.

D: * A drama or dramatico-musical work, published or unpublished. Plays, dramatic scripts for radio or television, pantomimes, ballets (if they contain a 'story'), musical comedies, operettas and operas, and new versions of such works are registered on this form. It may be used by both United States citizens and aliens. A published work does not have to be printed in the United States to be eligible for copyright. 'Publication' of dramatic works means 'reproduced in copies for sale or general distribution'; public performance is *not* publication, nor is the distribution of copies to actors.

E: Music, published or unpublished, by United States citizens or nationals, or first published in the United States. All musical compositions except 'dramatico-music,' included in Class D, are registered on this form — new versions, adaptations, arrangements, with or without words. The words, if any, are protected as well as the music. (But a song-poem — i.e. words *without* music — is a book and must be registered *after* publication

48

on Form A.) Even if it is first published abroad, the musical work of an American citizen or national is registered on this form. Public rendition of music is not publication but according to a recent decision a recording seemingly is.

E. Foreign: * Music of foreign origin, published or unpublished. If published it must bear a copyright notice.

F: * A published map. (Unpublished maps cannot secure statutory copyright but are protected at common law.) Register on this form atlases, marine charts, celestial maps, globes, relief models, as well as individual area-maps. This form is used for works of both domestic and foreign origin.

N.B. As of this writing, new application forms, such as those released in September 1955, have not been issued for classes G, I, H, and K, pending possible modifications of the law with respect to the deposit required for published works in these fields. Until new forms are issued, those described here should be used.

G: * A work of art (painting, drawing, or sculpture) or the model or design for a work of art, published or unpublished. As well as works of fine art, works of artistic craftsmanship are registered on this application — models and designs for jewelry, enamels, glassware, and tapestry — but not a published 3-dimensional work of art itself (see GG). Used for works of both domestic and foreign origin.

GG: A published 3-dimensional work of art, domestic and foreign.

H: * A reproduction of a work of art, reproduced in copies for sale — i.e. published lithographs, photo-engravings, etchings, etc., of a painting, sculpture, or other work of art (domestic or foreign).

I: A published or unpublished drawing or plastic work of scientific or technical nature. Unpublished relief maps are sometimes registered on this form; as also architectural and engineering plans and designs, technical drawings, and anatomical models (domestic and foreign).

J: * A published or unpublished photograph. Film strips, slides, and slide films, domestic and foreign. (But see K.)

K: A print or printed illustration. Included are pictorial illustrations, picture postcards, greeting cards, etc., domestic and foreign.

KK: * A published commercial print or label of an article of merchandise (but *not* a trade mark). 'Print' includes pictorial and/or textual matter, published in a periodical or separately; 'label,' pictorial and/or literary work impressed or stamped upon the article itself.

L-M: * A published or unpublished motion picture, intended for projection upon a screen or transmission by television. Use for both photoplays and 'nonfiction' motion pictures, including travelogues, newsreels, educational films, etc.

R: * The renewal of copyright of any classification.

[Form RR, formerly used for the renewal of commercial prints and labels, has been abandoned.]

U: Notice of Use of Music on Mechanical instruments.

Copyright registration is often delayed because the application form has been filled out hastily or carelessly. This wastes the time not only of the Copyright Office, in the extra correspondence, filing, and other clerical work, but also, in the end, of the publisher or claimant. The most frequent error is that of wrong classification.

A second frequent type of error is the omission of information — that is, some queries in the application are left unanswered, either through oversight or because the information requested is not easily available. The following omissions are the most usual:

The full name and address of the copyright claimant
The citizenship of the author
Title of material to be registered for copyright, especially of photographs and
    works of art
Place of publication
Nature of material on which copyright is claimed, if a new edition, compilation,
    or reissued book
Volume, number, and date of issue of periodical
Name of printer
Exact date of publication
Name of account, if fee is to be charged against a deposit fund

Still a third type of faulty application is that in which there is a discrepancy between the data supplied in it and the material sent for deposit. For example, the name of a magazine may be given as the copyright claimant on the application, whereas the copyright notice in the book reads 'by the Blank Publishing Company.' Or the publisher's name is given as the copyright claimant when the author really holds the copyright and is so entered in the notice. Memory (or even an office file) should not be trusted. Check against the book.

The following data must correspond exactly with the actual copy of the work to be registered:

Name appearing in copyright notice
Title of material to be registered
Name of author or composer on title page
Volume and number of periodical or series
Date of issue

It cannot be stressed too often that the date of publication given in the application must be exact and complete. Copyright runs for exactly 28 years from the date of first publication (or from the date of deposit of an unpublished work). Carelessness in regard to this may allow the book to go into the public domain before the copyright is renewed. It must also be remembered that applications for the registration of published works will not be accepted if they are received before the date of actual publication.

Once an application has been registered and a certificate has been issued, there is no way to withdraw it or correct it. In some cases the Register may, at his discretion, annotate it for clarification or explanation, or reference to other relevant facts that are on file in the Copyright Office. The Copyright Office is not responsible for checking errors, although if one is apparent it will notify the claimant. But the ultimate responsibility rests with the claimant.

Architecture

Form I *or* G; *published: deposit two copies, fee* $4; *unpublished: deposit photo or other reproduction, fee* $4.

THERE WILL PROBABLY BE NO OCCASION for the reader of this manual to copyright architectural models or plans. For the record, however, this is how it is done:

The artistic rendering of an architectural work is registered under Class G (see page 221). The architect's plans and models, however, are registered as a 'drawing or plastic work of scientific or technical character' (I). The plans are a drawing, not a plastic work; the model probably is plastic (which means a physical modelling, not the commercial material 'plastic' now on the market). It is often hard to decide what should be registered on G, what on I. The Copyright Office will probably accept either classification in doubtful cases.

In the United States the architect's protection is meager, both at common law and under the copyright statute. Even though his plan or projection is registered for copyright, only the actual drawing or projection cannot be copied. In a court decision it was once ruled that the filing of an architect's plans at the city hall constituted publication of the plans, and that the construction of the building was publication of the model, design, or rendering. Many copyright authorities do not agree with this interpretation, but in view of the fact that it has never been superseded, and that once a work is 'published without notice' it is in the public domain, it is well for architects to copyright their designs and plans before any possible 'publication' in order to secure their rights. If major changes are made in them from time to time, new copyrights may be obtained, but minor changes do not justify a new copyright.

Architects have reason to be gratified, however, by a recent court decision in their favor. A well-known architect copyrighted his plans and drawings for small California-type ranch houses, which were later copied by a competitor. As a result of the infringement suit the competitor was enjoined from copying the drawings and plans, using them in the construction of houses, and constructing houses that imitated those of the original architect in appearance, style, and character.

A photograph of a building, once that building is constructed, is neither publication nor infringement. Any building actually erected is in the public domain in so far as it may be photographed, sketched, or painted by anyone who wishes to do so. The resulting photograph or 'work of art' may then be copyrighted by its owner, but the copyright does not prevent anyone else from making other photographs or drawings of the building.

Architectural plans published in a magazine or newspaper are automatically protected under the general copyright of the periodical. After publication the copyright may be assigned back to the architect, or if the plans carried a separate copyright notice they may be copyrighted in his name originally and registered on BB as a 'contribution.'

Art and Design for Works of Art

Application forms G, GG, and H; deposit 2 copies if published, photograph(s) or other identifying reproduction if unpublished; fee $4.

THE WORKS OF THE ARTIST, architect, sculptor, and designer are included in the Copyright Act under Classes G, GG, and H; those of a technical or scientific character are registered under I; photographs under J; prints and pictorial illustrations under K. Products of the industrial arts, even if artistically made, are usually protected by patent. Inevitably there is much overlapping, and the artist sometimes has the choice of applying either for patent or for copyright. In 1954, a decision of the United States Supreme Court reversed much of our previous thinking on works of this kind. A statuette of a Balinese dancer wired for use as a lamp base was registered for copyright but was later denied protection because it was of a 'utilitarian purpose'; a similar one, but with no wiring, was protected. In upholding the validity of the copyright the Court said, ' "Works of art" and "reproductions of works of art" are terms that were intended by Congress to include the authority to copyright these statuettes. Individual perception of the beautiful is too varied a power to permit a narrow or rigid concept of art.'

A work of art or a model or design for a work of art (classes G and GG) includes not only painting, drawing, and sculpture, but also designs for murals, stage sets,* architectural buildings, and memorial monuments. Dress patterns, designs for fabrics, toys, or games, and other designs primarily for 'use' require patents.

Reproductions of works of art (Class H) — etchings, engravings, and so on of a painting, sculpture, or other product of fine art — are subject to copyright if the *reproduction* is a new work and has an element of originality. The fact that the subject or model is in public domain is immaterial. As Justice Holmes said, 'Others are free to copy the original. They are not free to copy the copy. . . The copy is the personal reaction of an individ-

---

* But it is the *picture* or *design* of the stage setting that is protected, not the setting itself. The setting can be used on the stage by others, but may not be published in a magazine or a book on theatre art.

ual upon nature. Personality always contains something unique. . . . A very modest grade of art has in it something irreducible, which is one man's alone. That something he may copyright.' It is not safe to assume that because a masterpiece is hundreds of years old that you may reproduce the copy of it found in another book. Mezzotint engravings of old masters, published in a catalogue and copyrighted, were protected against infringement because of the individual contribution of the engravers.

Copyright on published material in Classes G, GG, and H is obtained by publication (issuance of copies for sale or general distribution, or exhibition in public places with no restriction against copying) with a notice of copyright. Under the United States Copyright Act, the notice may be only c in a circle, ©, with the initials of the proprietor, providing that some place on it — the margin, back, permanent pedestal, or base — the full name of the proprietor appears. Under UCC, however, the full notice must be given: ©, proprietor's name, and year of publication. The notice must be large enough to be legible, and must be as stipulated — that is, artistic variations of the c in a circle are not acceptable. If the proprietor is a United States citizen or 'domiciliary,' deposit must be made of two copies of the best edition or, if it is a 3-dimensional work of art, as many photographs (preferably 8 x 10 inches, black and white or colored) as are necessary to identify it. (See *Deposit.*) Application for registration is then made on Form G, GG, or H (see *Classification*) with the fee, $4. The application * calls for the name and address of the copyright proprietor, the name and address and citizenship of the 'author' (artist, etc.), the title of the work (and it must have a title, no matter how abstract), the publisher, and the date of publication; if it was produced outside the United States by lithography or photoengraving, the country in which it was produced must also be given. Works of art by nationals of UCC countries, other than United States citizens and residents, are protected without the formalities of deposit and registration.

Unpublished works of art are of course protected at common law, but since statutory copyright is available to them, it is particularly advisable to take advantage of it for a class of works that may be 'published' — that is, dedicated to the public — inadvertently. The Copyright Act does not say that public exhibition necessarily means publication, but the courts have usually so ruled it when there is no restriction against copying, as in many museums. A mural in a hotel lobby was declared 'published,' and

---

* As of this writing, new application forms have not been issued for Classes G, H, I, and K, pending the outcome of a bill before Congress that would allow the deposit of photographs in certain classes. The forms described here are those available in 1955.

the artist had no recourse at common law against infringement. To copyright an unpublished work of art, a photograph (or photographs) or some identifying reproduction is sent for deposit with the application for registration and the fee ($4). The copyright term starts from the day of registration. If the work is later reproduced in copies for sale, two copies must be sent for deposit (with proper copyright notice bearing the date of first registration) but no new registration need be filed.

Art books are usually registered as Class A, as are also collections of cartoons, line drawings, et cetera. Any illustrations included that are already under copyright must carry the notice on the same page or on the copyright page of the book itself. Illustrations of any sort first published in a magazine or newspaper may be registered separately as a contribution (see page 119). (See also *Architecture, Advertisements, Illustrations, Maps, Photographs*.)

Assignments

Send original documents; fee $3 for 6 pages or less, 50¢ extra for each additional page, or less, 50¢ additional for every title over 1 in the paper recorded.

UNDER THE UNITED STATES COPYRIGHT ACT, any copyright may be 'assigned, granted, or mortgaged by an instrument in writing signed by the proprietor of the copyright, or may be bequeathed by will.'

Before the assignee's name can be used in the copyright notice, the assignment must be recorded in the Copyright Office. If it is not recorded in 3 calendar months after its execution (6 calendar months if executed outside the United States) it is void against any later innocent purchaser whose assignment is recorded.

The essential elements of an assignment are:

1. The full legal name of the assignor (copyright proprietor, if it has been copyrighted).
2. The title of the work to be assigned; its registration number and date of copyright, if available.
3. The full legal name of the assignee.
4. The signature of the assignor (an individual — if the assignor is a corporation, an officer of the company).
5. The place and date of the execution of the assignment.
6. If necessary under the laws of the state, a witness or notary public's seal.

To have an assignment recorded:

(a) Send the original signed document to the Copyright Office within the specified time (three months in the United States, six months abroad). The Copyright Office will record late assignments, but certain legal rights may be lost. It should be sent by registered or certified mail. There need be no fear that it will be lost or destroyed once it is received by the Copyright Office; a microfilm is made of it and the original is returned to the assignee with a certificate of record under seal, giving the volume and page numbers of the record book. It will be returned by registered mail only if registry fee is included for that purpose with the fee.

(b) Include a check or money order for the fee; $3 covers the recording of most assignments of one title. A document of over 6 pages will require 50¢ more for every fraction of an additional page. For many reasons it is preferable to have a separate assignment for each title; however, more than one title can be included in a single assignment, the fee being 50¢ for each title in addition to the first one. Thus if three different poems are being assigned in one document of not over 6 pages, the fee for recording would be $3 plus $1 for the two extra titles, plus the necessary fee for return registered mail.

There are many reasons for assigning a copyright. It may be assigned by the author to a publisher, when a uniform edition of his work is being brought out. It may be assigned back to the author by a magazine publisher because the author wishes to use the material in another medium. It may be assigned by a magazine publisher to a book publisher when a serial is being published in book form. It may be assigned by the author or publisher to someone to whom he is in debt. It may be assigned by one publisher to another who is buying out his whole business. Or it may be bequeathed by will as a separate part of an estate. Whatever the motive, in order for the assignment to be effective against the claims of any later purchaser or assignee without notice whose assignment has been recorded, it must be made in writing and it must be recorded in the Copyright Office.

The Copyright Office issues no special forms for assignments, nor can it act as an agent. The written document may be complicated or simple, drawn up by a lawyer or written out by the assignor himself. It should be borne in mind, however, that any statement that does not transfer 'entire and unqualified monopoly' is not an assignment, but a license (q.v.).

Common-law rights may be assigned verbally, and there is no statement in the Copyright Act that a verbal assignment is not binding. However, most countries do require written assignments, and it is certainly safer to have any legal transfer of ownership in writing.

The signature to the assignment must be the authorized signature of the copyright proprietor. For example, in the case of an article published in *Publishers' Weekly,* the signature would be by an officer of R. R. Bowker Co., not the magazine itself. The usual practice is to have the name of the corporation typed over the signature of the president, secretary, or other officer authorized to perform legal acts.

An assignment executed in a foreign country must be acknowledged before a United States consular officer or secretary of legation authorized to administer oaths or perform notarial acts. The certificate of acknowledgment must be attached to the original document. If it is impossible to have it acknowledged, it may still be recorded, but it should be accompanied by a letter specifically authorizing the Copyright Office to do so. In any case of a notarized assignment, the assignee should be sure that the notary has legal authority in the actual place at which the instrument is dated.

58

The instrument should also state whether it is an assignment, a transfer, or a mortgage. If it is a will or part of a will, the whole portion concerning the copyright should be placed on record.

Blanket assignments ('all the works by author John Doe published and copyrighted by the Book Publishing Company') are not recommended, although the Copyright Office will record them if requested to do so. There is too much danger of later dispute or innocent infringement.

In contrast to English law, United States copyright is indivisible and may be assigned only *in toto*. Specific rights, such as those of dramatization, serialization, translation, et cetera, are granted by license, not assignment. An assignee acquires all the existing rights of the original copyright owner, but he is bound by any licenses or grants made before the assignment. Thus, if A assigns his copyright to B without reservation, he may not later extend a specific license to C. That license can be granted only by B, the new owner. A magazine publisher, having once assigned the copyright on a short story back to the author, can no longer grant movie rights except by specific agreement with the author. Any reservation of rights in making an assignment destroys its validity, making it a mere license. To avoid possible complications, the whole copyright should be assigned, and any specific rights then licensed back to the assignor.

Whereas an assignee has all the rights of the original proprietor, and can sue infringers, a licensee cannot sue for damages in his own name, even though his license has been recorded; he can sue only by joining with the owner (see *License*).

An assignee cannot claim copyright ownership if the original assignor was not entitled to it. For example, if the assignor was not domiciled in the United States at the time of first publication, and was not a citizen of the United States or of a country with whom we have a copyright agreement, or if he was not the author and could not trace his ownership to the author, the assignment would be void. If a publisher takes out a copyright in trust for the author, even though the publisher is the legal and titular owner of the copyright, he can make no assignment, except when so stated in his contract or agreement with the author, without the author's consent. The author retains his original rights until they are expressly released.

In case of a bankruptcy, the publisher-proprietor's copyrights taken over by a trustee may be sold or assigned; the assignment should of course be recorded in the Copyright Office. The author, however, retains whatever rights he had according to the original contract of publication. If the new publisher to whom his copyright is assigned does not work the copyright, or fails to fulfil the terms of the original contract, the author can have the title reassigned to himself.

There has been much controversy about the assignment of copyright on magazine stories, articles, and other contributions to periodicals that are included in a single copyright for the issue in which they appear. The prevailing view now seems to be, however, that although the publisher-assignor assigns the copyright on only one part of the whole — i.e. the specific story or article — the assignee (i.e. the author) is properly and legally an assignee, not a licensee (see also *Newspapers and Periodicals*).

The fact that an assignment has not been recorded does not make it less binding between the two parties concerned, nor does it mean that the assignee cannot protect himself against wilful infringers. He would, however, have difficulty in collecting damages from an innocent infringer who had taken a second assignment in good faith. The recording is valuable in case of a subsequent sale, mortgage, or transfer. Then the proprietor has proof of the validity of his title, and the second party in the transaction can satisfy himself that there are no other assignments or liens against the copyright ownership. The recording of the assignment also makes it possible, as stated in the Copyright Act, for the assignee to use his own name in the notice.

It is important to the author to have the copyright of material that was first published serially or as a contribution to a magazine or newspaper assigned back to him, if no separate copyright was originally secured. Most book publishers (and virtually all motion-picture companies) will not consider publication of previously published magazine material until this is done. Even if book publication is not imminent, the author should have the assignment made in his own interest. In one case, an author wrote on his contract, 'The author reserves the right of book publication and dramatic rights,' but allowed the publisher to copyright the serial version of his novel. No assignment was later made. The publisher later sold motion-picture rights without consulting the author, who in the meantime had made other moving-picture contracts himself. When he tried to stop the production of the first motion picture by injunction, he failed, because the company had acted in good faith in securing their rights from the publisher.

With a few exceptions, an assignee cannot renew a copyright (see *Renewal*), but an assignor can agree by contract to renew his work. If he dies before the renewal year, however, only those entitled to renew under the law can do so.

In collaborations, both authors must be party to an assignment (though either one can grant a license, to be worked for their joint benefit).

Author

A FACT THAT the publishing, printing, book-producing world tends to lose sight of is that the protection of the author was originally the chief concern of copyright. The purpose of copyright legislation is not to provide employment for publishers, printers, bookbinders, salesmen, paper manufacturers, theatrical and moving-picture producers, labor unions, copyright lawyers, radio sponsors, or even book reviewers. It is to secure to the author a reasonable profit from his work, and thus to promote 'the progress of science and the useful arts.'

The author is the person who gives written or graphic expression to an idea. His right is in the expression. In a recent case the court remarked, in contrasting 'authors' and 'inventors' (who are protected by patent): ' "Original" in reference to a copyrighted work means that the particular work "owes its origin" to the "author." '

The Copyright Act states explicitly the few cases in which the writer of the work is not to be considered the true author: Work done 'for hire' — as newspaper or magazine staff-writing, employee-created house organs, murals painted 'as a job,' photographs taken by paid photographers — these belong not to the person doing the work, but to the employer, whether the employer is an individual or a corporation.

Borderline cases are the works of ghost writers and hired translators of an unpublished manuscript. There have been no test cases to determine the court's attitude, but a member of the Copyright Office once suggested that if the 'ghost' or translator is sought out by the author to do the job 'for hire,' he stands in the shoes of an employee. If, however, the 'ghost' conceives the idea, for example, of an 'autobiographical' account by a person who has had first-hand experience, and creates the structure and expression more or less independently, and with the subject's consent, he would be entitled to the copyright. For complete safety, however, the wise procedure in the latter case is to have the title read *'James McGilli- cuddy's Account of the Battle of Cyprus* as told to John Doe.' Mr. Doe will then encounter no obstacle in copyrighting the book in his own name. A translator, if he wishes to claim any rights in a book, should also have his name on the title page. In either case a written contract should clearly define the status of the 'ghost' or translator.

1. The first responsibility of an author is to determine whether he is entitled to a copyright for his work. If he is not an 'employee for hire,' as defined above, the answer is to be found in the work itself.

Is the material heretofore unpublished? This is easy to answer if it is a newly created short story or novel, but in many cases authors, wittingly or unwittingly, re-use their own published material. Perhaps a chapter or two of this book appeared in a magazine long ago. Perhaps one or two of the poems were published in a copyrighted college literary journal. Perhaps that account of a Diesel engine made its first appearance in a textbook the author wrote two years ago, which was so well done that he incorporated it as part of his new manuscript on *Internal Combustion Engines of Today*. The point is that if an author 'cribs' even from himself, he must give credit to the earlier copyright. Not to do so is manifestly unfair to the copyright proprietor of the magazine or book in which the earlier material appeared, and also weakens the copyright status of the new book, since the new copyright date would appear to prolong the life of an earlier copyright — which is, of course, illegal.

Is the work original? There is a discussion elsewhere in this book on that super-intangible, originality (see page 13). An honest author knows when he is deliberately copying the words, expressions, or thoughts of someone else. His danger is in unconscious plagiarism. Perhaps this plot that he thought up last night when he couldn't sleep is an almost verbatim duplication of a yarn he read on the train coming up from the South several years ago, and hasn't thought of since. It might even be something that he has stored in his subconscious mind since childhood. The intention to infringe is not essential to infringement. It is the author's responsibility to be sure that his work is his own.

Is the work a proper subject for copyright? The over-all range of copyright material is suggested by the classes of subject matter in the Copyright Act (see *Classification*). Generally, 'all the writings of an author' are subject to copyright. However, there are certain works that might be considered 'writings' that are not subject to copyright: titles, most games, toys, objects designed especially for use rather than perusal (blank books, check books, journal books — works conceivably protected by patent), clauses, slogans, or mere 'colorable' adaptations of work in the public domain or that has already been copyrighted (see page 15).

Are all the permissions cleared? The clearing of quotations from copyrighted works is essentially the author's responsibility. The citing of source is not enough (see *Quotations; Fair Use*). For a work of which the primary market is the United States only, the usual procedure is to clear permissions for the United States, the Philippine Republic, and, if possible, Canada. If there is any probability of a foreign market, the author usually asks for British or world rights or whatever seems necessary. Sometimes when foreign rights are not held by United States publishers, this involves a long and laborious search and correspondence; if the rights for publication in the United States are all cleared, the author may feel that the mere possibility of foreign publication is not worth the effort to clear foreign rights. However, he should so word his letters asking permission to quote that the replies will be an authentic record of the copyright status of all quoted material. When he quotes from material of foreign origin, even though it bears no copyright notice, he should make an effort to determine its copyright status and secure written permission from its legal owner. If it was published before 1955 it may have had ad interim copyright which was extended under UCC, or it may have been registered here but not sold in this country (see page 155).

Is the work free from libelous passages? Does it violate the right of privacy? Does it contain fraudulent, obscene, or seditious passages? These questions are not essentially of copyright, but the author must keep them all in mind. (a) Any statement injuring the reputation of a living person is potentially libelous. Even if not libelous, any statement invading the 'privacy' of a living person is potentially subject to suppression under the laws of many states. A book in which an author discusses living persons, or deplores their morals or ethics, should be read by a lawyer before publication. Fiction writers have got into trouble by unintentionally injuring someone's reputation. They may think *Jacquelaine Heimpoupqui* is a very amusing name, but if there is a real Jacquelaine Heimpoupqui she may rightfully take offense at ridicule. The license number of the story villain's car may bring shame to the real owner of the license plate, as will the street address of a fictional murderer to the real resident or property owner. Firm names should be used with caution. Even modelling an exemplary character on a living person may 'invade' privacy if the subject of the model is excessively modest. If a writer wishes to use real people for his subjects, he should obtain written authorization from all who are used.

(b) 'Fraud' is the deliberate deception of the public. It would seem that an author could not be innocently guilty of this crime, but sometimes the public is surprisingly easily deceived. When Arthur Train wrote the *Autobiography of Mr. Tutt* his intentions were surely honorable. The *Tutt and Mr. Tutt* stories had been published in leading magazines for years. Yet one person actually threatened legal action when he discovered that the 'autobiography' was a 'hoax.' There was no Ephraim Tutt. More seriously, an

American author wrote a novel that was published as a translation of a European writer's work. The copyright on it was denied because the public was being deceived and because the application for registration gave false information. Many laws concerning unfair trade practices are also designed to protect the public against deception.

(c-d) Obscene and seditious material, even though granted a certificate of copyright registration (it is not the duty of the Copyright Office to examine it), may be denied protection by the courts. The difficulty is in guessing what the courts will term obscene or seditious at any given time. It is like trying to guess what the Postal Authorities will deem immoral and bar from the mails — or what the censor will pass for the motion pictures. Byron was denied copyright on *Cain* in the early nineteenth century. Even his counsel, it is said, admitted the work contained 'much bad taste and many bad jokes.' Southey was denied copyright on *Wat Tyler.* Understandably, most publishers tend to be reactionary rather than liberal in matters concerning morals, unless they hope to capitalize on the publicity of public censure. To the court, the author's intent will usually be the deciding factor, rather than the actual words. However, in an infringement suit of James Cain's novel *Serenade,* when the copyright of the book was challenged by an opposing lawyer on grounds of its immorality, the judge declared that the outcome of the story sublimated the otherwise immoral 'church scene' — even though Cain himself denied indignantly that he had intended for it to be so interpreted.

In times of national tension, the accusation of being 'subversive' also becomes a hazard. College and textbook publishers are peculiarly vulnerable in this field, and there is often a narrow line between what is 'objective' or 'open-minded' and what is 'subversive.'

2. The second point to be decided is the form of the notice of copyright. Arguments in favor of the author's having the copyright in his own name are: (a) Under UCC copyright notices are used not only in the United States, but in many other countries. It is undesirable that a book should be copyrighted in one country under one publisher's proprietorship and under another elsewhere; (b) a suit against infringers can be instigated only by the owner of the copyright; (c) if the publisher holds the copyright the author cannot license the various other rights except through the publisher; (d) even if the publisher assigns the copyright to the author, the notice will be inconsistent with the fact; (e) if the publisher becomes bankrupt a copyright in the name of the author is not transferable to the receiver and consequently copies cannot be sold without the author's consent.

On the other hand, if one author is solely responsible for the material and is publishing in the United States only, and with a well-established house, it makes little difference whether the copyright is taken in his own name or in that of the publisher as copyright proprietor, if it is stated in the contract that the copyright is to be held in trust for the author. In this case, however, when the book goes out of print and rights revert to the author, he should have the copyright reassigned to him, and the assignment recorded.

Contributions to magazines are usually copyrighted by the proprietor and reassigned to the author on request. Reassignment is especially important with regard to material that is later to be published in book form. Unless there has been an outright sale of all rights, a publisher who takes out a copyright for an author will later reassign it to him if the author so desires. However, the author may have the copyright in his own name even in a contribution to a periodical if a separate copyright notice is carried. Most magazine publishers have little liking for the practice, but will usually comply under pressure.

Some publishers of leading magazines insist on having complete ownership of all their material, licensing back to the author or book publisher reprint rights, book rights, or rights in any other fields they do not wish to exploit. In this case, when the material is used in any other media, even though it is enlarged or modified, it must continue to carry the copyright notice of its original magazine publication, along with that of the new version, if there is a new copyright.

On books written by joint authors, legally the copyright may be registered in both names, but this is not advisable: either author may then license the work without consulting the other, which sometimes causes considerable confusion. It is better for one author to take out the copyright and hold it in trust for his collaborator — technically, they are 'tenants in common' — or for the publisher to take out the copyright in trust for both authors. One collaborator may grant a license, but both must be party to an assignment. Renewal can be made by one author for the benefit of (in trust for) the other.

There is no clause in the Copyright Act stating that a copyright may not be held under a pseudonym. The Copyright Office formerly discouraged the practice. Few pen names are deceptive for any length of time if the author is successful as a writer. Modern librarians ferret out the real name as quickly as possible, and the courts refuse to recognize any violation of privacy in attaching a man's name to his works, even though he does not wish it. If the author decides to copyright under his pen name in spite of these arguments, or a married woman wishes to copyright under her maiden name, the Copyright Office will accept the registration, but allows the real name to be given in the application also, if desired. Presumably a book copyrighted under a pen name should be renewed under the author's real name, but there too a cross-reference should be made to the name of registration. In some foreign countries in which the duration of copyright extends for a given number of years after the death of the author, the use of a pen name may reduce the term of protection.

Suppose an author wishes to be anonymous. He may preserve his anonymity if he wishes with the co-operation of his publisher. The Copyright Office 'requests' his name, but does not demand it. The copyright is necessarily in the name of the proprietor, who if challenged in court must trace his claim to the author.

Suppose an illustrator contributes a major part to the copyrighted work. The author of the text copyrights the book as a whole, holding the copyright for the illustrations in trust for the artist. Or, the publisher copyrights the book in trust for both author and illustrator. Or the illustrations may have been done 'for hire' and therefore should be copyrighted by either publisher or author (according to the fact) as an employer.

3. Before publication the author has certain definite common-law rights (q.v.) in his work. He not only owns the physical manuscript but may do with it what he wishes without jeopardizing his rights. He may read it aloud in public, pass it among his friends, submit it to publishers or to authorities for criticism, make copies to give to his friends at Christmas, have it privately printed and bound, so long as he does not allow it to be sold or distributed to the public.

He has the right to first publication: he may choose who his publisher will be, when it shall be published (within very round numbers), or, if he wishes, that it shall never be published at all.

He has the right to license certain uses of it without sacrificing his common-law right in the original. He may sell movie rights, dramatization rights, translation rights, all requiring a copyright of the resultant independent product, without copyrighting his own first version. If he goes bankrupt, his unpublished manuscript is safe from his creditors. He may sell the manuscript itself, reserving his own common-law rights of publication; or he may sell it or assign it with no reservation, in which case the common-law rights go with it to the new owner. Common-law rights are lost only by authorized publication or dedication to the public. After publication, if the work has been published in accordance with the Copyright Act, it is protected by statutory copyright.

The exclusive rights reserved to the author are enumerated in the Copyright Act and cannot be repeated too often.

If it is a 'literary' work:

66

1. To print, reprint, publish, copy, and sell it.

2. To translate it or make any other version of it (but see translations under *Universal Copyright Convention,* page 171).

3. To dramatize it, or make any other version of it.

4. To deliver, authorize the delivery of, read, or present it in public for profit.

5. To make or have made any transcript or record of it by which, in whole or in part, it may in any manner or by any method be exhibited, delivered, presented, produced, or reproduced.

6. To play or perform it in public for profit, and to exhibit, represent, produce, or reproduce it in any manner or by any method whatsoever.

If it is a dramatic work, in addition to 1, 2, 4, 5, and 6 above:

7. To convert it into a novel or other non-dramatic work.

8. To perform or represent it publicly.

9. To sell any manuscript or record of it if it is unpublished.

If it is a musical work, in addition to 1, 5, and 6:

10. To arrange or adapt it.

11. To perform it publicly for profit (but see *Publication,* page 150).

12. To make any arrangement or setting of it, or its melody, in any system of notation or any form of record from which it can be read or reproduced (but see also *Music,* page 129).

If it is a model or design for a work of art, in addition to 1 and 5:

13. To complete, execute, and finish it.

Under (1) are included first and second serial rights, reprint, abridgment, foreign reprint rights, quotations in anthologies, compilations, or even in smaller sections in general books.

Under (2) are included all foreign-language rights, and adaptations, digests, and versions for other media.

Under (3) are included theatrical, dramatization, and motion-picture rights.

Under (4), (5), and (6) are included recording, radio, and television rights.

All of these rights are separately controlled by license. In all contracts the author should see that the rights he licenses are carefully enumerated and that all other rights are reserved to him.

The transference of all rights (by unqualified sale, will, or bequest) is an assignment (q.v.), which cuts the author off from his work forever. Thus a story sold for an outright fee, without any qualification, gives the publisher full title to the work, including reprint rights, book rights, moving-picture and dramatic rights. For his own protection the author should insist on a written agreement specifying what rights he grants and what he reserves for himself.

The author's final right is that of renewal (q.v.). He should keep a list of the dates of copyright for all his works, whether published separately or in periodicals, whether the copyright is in his own name or in his proprietor's name. If he feels he will not live to renew his works himself, he should file this list with his will to go on his death to his widow or executor. (See also *Common-Law Rights; Moral Rights; Unpublished Works.*)

Books

'All original writings, be they an advertisement, a short poem, a direction sheet for a card game, or an item appearing in a column of a newspaper . . . are classified as books. The term "book" is a general term which distinguishes writings from such other copyright subjects as pictures, paintings, music, motion picture films, and the like.' *

BOOKS, AS DEFINED ABOVE — or as in Mr. DeWolf's book, 'any article consisting of words not otherwise classifiable' — constitute the class for which copyright laws were originally formulated. A survey of the diverse material that is included in this class is given on pages 74–5. Wide as is the scope of the term for copyright purposes, there is some material normally considered 'books' that does not come under it. A drama, even though it never sees the stage and has its only public as a book, is not a book but a drama (Class D). A beautifully bound gift volume of Christmas carols with their original melodies is not a book, but music (Class E).

'Books' (Class A) must be published before they can be registered for copyright. They must be 'reproduced in copies for sale' or for general distribution, whether by printing, lithography, typewriting, mimeographing, or any other means of reproduction. They must have a title (although the title is not subject to copyright), a copyright notice, and a definite date of publication. Before publication, they are protected by the author's common-law rights; if they are sent to the Copyright Office for registration, they will only be returned.

The primary concern of most American publishers is with books first published in the United States.* If they are 'original' (see page 62) and if their authors are entitled to copyright, books having their first publication here acquire copyright protection as soon as they are published with the proper copyright notice. There are only three legal requirements: they must be manufactured according to the provisions of the Copyright Act

---

* William B. Woods, in a Master's Report on Sebring Pottery Co. *v.* Steubenville Pottery Co., et al., 12.11.34.

† For other books, see *Ad Interim Copyright, Alien Authors, International Copyright Relations, Newspapers and Periodicals,* and *Universal Copyright Convention.*

(see *Manufacturing Clause*); they must bear on the title page or on the back of the title page the word Copyright, Copr., or © (for UCC protection, © must be used), the year, and the name of the copyright proprietor; if the author is not a United States citizen or a person living in this country at the time of publication, he must be a citizen of a country with which the United States has a reciprocal copyright agreement.*

To register the copyright, it is necessary to send to the Copyright Office (a) application form A, on the back of which is an affidavit; (b) the registration fee of $4; (c) two copies of the best edition.

(a) Application form A is given on page 208. It calls for:

1. The copyright claimant or claimants. This will be either the author(s) or proprietor(s). If the latter, it must be someone to whom the common-law rights of the author have passed legally — by assignment (contract, if it is so worded), outright sale, inheritance, or will. The name(s) must be given exactly as in the copyright notice. Check against the book itself, for if the application and the notice are different, the application will be either rejected or sent back for correction.

2. The title — again exactly as it appears on the title page, not the 'short title' used on the spine, jacket, or running head. Include subtitle, volume number, edition, if on the title page as part of the title (e.g. *Courage. A Symposium on Heroism in Korea. Volume II, third edition, revised*).

3. The authors. If possible, give name, address, and pseudonym if any, of all authors, including illustrators, translators, collaborators, etc. Citizenship *must* be given. The other information is not only useful for cataloguing purposes but is especially valuable to the publisher and the author in cases of litigation and at the time of renewal. The employer is legally the 'author' of a work done for hire. Be sure to check either 'yes' or 'no' after 'Domiciled in U.S.A.'

4. Date and place of publication. The information wanted is that pertaining to the American-manufactured edition being registered; if the book being registered is an American edition of one previously registered for ad interim protection, give the American publication date, not the English.

5. Books that in some form have had earlier publication (revised editions, translations, serials republished in book form, United States editions of ad interim books). The information to be supplied here is (a) whether the book is a new edition, translation, expanded serial, etc., and on what the new copyright is claimed (e.g. 'extensive revision and two new chapters' or 'additional material amounting to approximately 50 pages'). If it has been registered for ad interim (but not under UCC) give the information

* See pages 101 and 107.

requested in (b). The original edition of a foreign UCC book is registered on Form A-B Foreign.

The publisher's most frequent question, how much material is required to justify registration as a revision, can be answered only indirectly: mere reprints are not enough; typographical, stylistic, and factual corrections are not enough; the addition of minor facts bringing the book up to date is not enough — e.g. death rates, new personnel, additions to the bibliography — rearrangement or regrouping of chapters or volumes is not enough. The material is significant not so much for its quantity as for its importance. If in filling out the application form the applicant has to search for material to record, he is probably not justified in claiming a new copyright. If there is any doubt about the validity of the claim for new copyright, the earlier publication date should be included in the notice, lest the whole copyright be lost if the new copyright is challenged in court. This writer recommends the inclusion of the earlier date in any case, although it is not required by law. If the copyright claimant is painstaking in not deceiving the public, the courts are much more likely, as innumerable cases have demonstrated, to protect his rights when he brings suit against an infringer who bases his case on a technical flaw.

In books that were originally published serially, but to which new material has been added, the new material is hard to designate, as usually it is a matter of general expansion rather than separate chapters or annotations. The best method, especially in fiction, is to estimate what the additional material amounts to in pages. If the serial version consisted of approximately 50,000 words and the book about 75,000, the entry on line (5a) may properly be: 'New characterization, narration, and incident equivalent to about 80 pages.' If the serial copyright was held by the magazine, it must be assigned to the new owner and be recorded before publication or the notice of the magazine must be carried. The notice should (but is not legally required to) carry both dates if the serial appeared in an earlier year. The name of the earlier copyright holder need not appear in the notice if the assignment has been recorded.

No new registration is required for an American edition of a work claiming protection under UCC; the foreign edition may be registered on Form A-B Foreign, but such registration is optional (see *Universal Copyright Convention*).

5. The affidavit. The affidavit on the reverse of the application should then be filled out and notarized (see *Affidavits*).

Application form A should be used not only for what are usually considered 'books,' but also for the first publication of the following works:

A poem or song without music, even if it is only on a card or in a leaflet, if it is published separately.

A greeting card, illustrated or not, if it is 'original.'

The printed text to explain how to use a game, a device, plan or system, a deck of cards, et cetera, if it is on a separate sheet or leaflet and has the proper copyright notice.

A published version of a motion-picture, television, or radio scenario, synopsis, or script.

(b) The registration fee of $4 and the application, may be sent with the books for deposit, or may be sent separately, but it should be a check or money order, not currency or stamps.

(c) Two copies for deposit should be forwarded to the Copyright Office 'promptly' after publication. If there are both college and trade editions of the book, or popular and limited editions, to be published simultaneously, the best edition must be sent. It is not necessary to send both editions unless there are major differences in the text or illustrations (i.e. the fact that the cheaper edition omits some of the text or illustrations does not necessitate a duplicate deposit). If a better edition is published later, no second registration or deposit is required if no new material subject to copyright is added.

The copyright notice in a book by an American citizen or national or a book first published in this country must be on the title page or the page immediately following. Other books protected under UCC may have the notice in any reasonably distinguishable place. The c in a circle, ©, may now be used rather than the word Copyright in any notice.

Choreography
(DANCES)

ALTHOUGH THERE IS no specified classification under which to register choreographic works (the Copyright Act contains no provision for copyrighting dances), ballets, pantomimes, and other dances that are dramatic (i.e. 'tell a story' either by music or acting) may be protected, before or after publication, under Class D, dramatic and dramatico-musical compositions. The material submitted must be fully worked out, with an accompanying description if the action is diagrammatic, so that it will be clear that it is dramatic. Ballets and other dances in motion pictures, as well as those transcribed from televised performances, may be registered under Class L or M.

Dances that are not dramatic (dance steps, ball room dances, eurythmics, et cetera) are not subject to copyright unless they are recorded on film or are published as a 'book' (q.v.).

Whether performance rights are protected by registering choreography for copyright is questionable, however the work may be classified. But until the law is specific or there have been enough court decisions to build up precedence, copyright is the only protection available.

Classification

THERE ARE 13 CLASSIFICATIONS, according to the Copyright Act, into which copyrightable material may fall. Each classification has special forms for its applications (see page 47), and time is saved both for the publisher and for the Copyright Office if the proper form is used. Wrong classification does not jeopardize the copyright, nor are classes always water tight. However, if there is doubt about the proper classification of any material, time will be saved by consulting the Copyright Office before filing the application for registration. The general classes are:

(A) Books (A-B Ad Interim; A-B Foreign)
(B) Periodicals, including newspapers (BB, contribution to a periodical)
(C) Lectures
(D) Dramatic or dramatico-musical compositions
(E) Music, with or without words (E Foreign)
(F) Maps
(G) Works of art, models or designs for works of art (GG, published 3-dimensional work of art)
(H) Reproductions of works of art
(I) Scientific or technical drawings or plastic works
(J) Photographs
(K) Prints and pictorial illustrations (KK, commercial prints and labels)
(L) Motion-picture photoplays
(M) Motion pictures, other than plays

Classification A, 'Books' (q.v.), includes almost any embodiment of an idea in readable form, with the exception of dramatic works and music. Dictionaries, gazetteers, composite and cyclopedic works and compilations; leaflets, charts, tables, and pamphlets; abridgments, translations, codes, picture books; all of these are books. A collection of lyrics from an opera or operetta in the public domain is a book (but not a complete libretto, with or without music). A collection of cartoons is a book. A comic 'strip' (sequence of cartoons) telling a story is a book. A book need not be a bound volume. A single poem on a card is a 'book.' So is a map, if it has descriptive commentary on the back. A 'book' may be a printed explanation how to use a slide rule. (But the slide rule itself is not, nor are blank books, check books, record books, devices, or instruments or tools.) In general, a book

74

is the written expression of the author's idea or labor. It need not be original — perhaps it is a collection of other people's writings, or a telephone book. It need not have literary value; it may be a series of cartoons interspersed with wisecracks. One 'book' for which the Copyright Office issued a certificate of registration was a birth certificate embellished with a picture of the hospital, some well-nourished cherubim, and a line of inspiring verse. But a drama, play, or musical comedy published in book form should not be copyrighted as a book, but as a drama (Class D); a book of songs with their musical score is not a book, but music (Class E); a book of paper dolls is conceivably a print (Class K); but a scenario of a motion picture with descriptions of the settings, production, et cetera, published in book form is a book.

A-B Ad Interim is for books and periodicals in English manufactured and first published abroad *not* claiming UCC protection (see *Ad Interim*).

A-B Foreign is for books and periodicals manufactured and first published abroad and *not* subject to ad interim protection — books claiming protection under UCC may be registered on this form.

A book must be published (see *Publication*) before it is subject to statutory copyright. In manuscript form it is protected at common law.

(B) Periodicals include newspapers, magazines, reviews, proceedings of societies, and publications that appear regularly under the same title — in general, all those periodical publications that are normally accepted as second-class mail. (Serial publications about which there is any doubt — for example, the yearly transactions of an institution or an association — should be registered as 'books.') Each issue of a periodical must be registered separately. The title as such is not subject to copyright, but may be entered in the Patent Office as a trade mark. Periodicals cannot be registered before publication. (See *Newspapers and Periodicals*.) A periodical or a contribution to one in a foreign language published abroad is registered on application form A-B Foreign. A contribution to a periodical manufactured in the United States is registered on Form BB.

(C) The classification 'Lectures, sermons, addresses for oral delivery' (q.v.) refers to unpublished manuscripts that are to be read or recited in public. If these are printed and published in book form, they become 'books.' Monologues (as opposed to plays) and some radio and television scripts may also be classified under this heading (see *Radio and Television*).

(D) Dramatic and dramatico-musical compositions include all types of drama (plays, pantomime, musical comedies, opera, operettas, dramatic scripts for radio and television broadcasting), with dialogue and action or only action, intended for performance. Dances, motion pictures, animal

75

shows, and circus tricks are not included (but dance-dramas and ballets are). Mere narration is not drama. The one essential of this class is that there should be some sort of plot or story told through action and usually dialogue. (See *Dramas and Music Dramas.*)

(E) Musical compositions include both vocal and instrumental works, with or without words, so long as they are not intended to be acted. If *The Mikado* had just been composed and were subject to copyright, it would be Class D: a comic opera. But if it were registered separately, the sheet of the lyrics and music 'Tit Willow' from *The Mikado,* or a volume of the score would be Class E: musical composition. The acting version of *The Mikado,* words only, would be Class D: drama. The lyrics from *The Mikado,* published separately, would be Class A: a book. Adaptations of music in public domain are classed under E. (See *Music.*) Form E Foreign is used for music of foreign origin.

(F) Maps may be 'of the earth or of the heavens,' colored maps, outline maps, pictorial maps, relief maps, or globes. So long as they are published separately, without any extensive text or commentary, they should be registered under F. (An elaborate 'key' or text matter places them in Class A.) Unpublished relief maps may be registered under Class I (see below), but other unpublished maps are not subject to statutory copyright. They are protected at common law. For any map to be subject to copyright, it must have some original element, not be just an adaptation of material already in the public domain.

(G) Works of art include paintings, drawings, sculpture, jewelry, enamels, glassware, and tapestries, and may be copyrighted before or after publication ('publication' in this context means placing on sale or public exhibition without restriction, or public distribution). If they are 'published' without a copyright notice, they fall into the public domain. Published three-dimensional works of art are registered under GG. (See *Art; Architecture.*)

(H) Reproductions — including imprints, impressions, or casts — of a work of art may be copyrighted only after they are 'published.' This classification includes engravings, etchings, woodcuts, casts — any reproduction that contains in itself 'an artistic element distinct from that of the original.' The original may be in the public domain or may have its own copyright. In the latter case, the copyright claimant of the reproduction must be able to trace his title to the original artist. (See *Art.*)

(I) Drawings or plastic works that are scientific or technical may be registered for copyright either before or after publication. Included are diagrams and models, architect's plans, designs for engineering projects, and relief maps. (See *Art; Architecture.*)

76

(J) Photographs (q.v.) have been ruled subject to copyright in that they reflect the 'personality' of the photographer. However, the copyright does not prevent anyone else from taking a picture from the same angle. Half tones or other photo-engravings are not included under this heading. Photographs appearing in a book or periodical either are protected by the overall copyright or are a 'contribution' (BB) or a print (K).

(K) Prints and pictorial illustrations include printed pictures, lithographs, photo-engravings, greeting cards, and postals. The classification overlaps G and H, but most pictures belong under K. They need not illustrate the text of a book, but must 'illustrate something.' This class also includes commercial prints and labels (KK), which formerly were registered with the Patent Office. A commercial print is any single-page pictorial work and/or written text, used to advertise merchandise. It may be published in a periodical or separately on a sheet or folder. The 'label' is the pictorial or written identification, either stamped on the article itself or attached to it. Any Class K work reproduced by lithography or photo-engraving must be manufactured in the United States unless it represents a scientific or artistic original located abroad. (See *Advertisements; Art; Illustrations.*)

(L) Motion-picture photoplays may or may not be accompanied by sound, and need not be based upon an existing stage play to be included in this class. Included are features, serials, comedy 'shorts' (even without plots), and cartoons for screen and television. (See *Motion Pictures.*)

(M) Motion pictures other than photoplays include newsreels, travelogues, educational and scientific subjects. (See *Motion Pictures.*)

CLASSIFICATION OF TYPICAL COPYRIGHT MATERIAL

Abridgments (A)
Acting versions of old plays (D)
Adaptations (A)
Advertisements (A or KK)
Anthologies (A)
Architectural work and plans (G or I)
Articles for magazines and newspapers (A or BB)
Artistic work (G or I)
Books (A)
Busts (G, H)
Cards with text (and illustrations) (A or K)
Casts of works of art (H)
Catalogues (A)

Charts, 'Tabulated Information' (A)
Choreographic works (published, A; if dramatic, D)
Circulars (A or KK)
Compilations (A)
Contributions to newspapers and periodicals (A or BB)
Cyclopedic works (A)
Designs for works of art (G)
Designs for scientific or technical works (I)
Diagrams (I)
Directories (A)
Dramatic works and dramatizations (D)

Drawings (G)
Encyclopedias (A)
Engravings (H, K)
Etchings (H)
Explanatory texts (A)
Gazetteers (A)
Half tones (K)
Instruction sheets (A)
Lectures (unpublished, C; published, A)
Letters (published, A)
Lithographs (K)
Maps (F; if with much text, A)
Models (G or I)
Motion pictures (L–M)
Music (E)
Newspapers (B)
Oral works (unpublished, C)
Paintings (G)
Periodicals (B)
Pictorial illustrations (K)
Photographs (J)
Photo-engravings (K)
Plastic works (I)
Poems (A)
Postal cards (A, J, or K)

Posters (K)
Prints and labels (commercial) (KK)
Prints and pictorial illustrations (K)
Proceedings (A or B)
Quarterlies (B)
Radio scripts (unpublished, C or D; published, A or D)
Relief maps (I)
Sculpture (E)
Sermons (unpublished, C; published, A)
Songs (with music, E; no music, A)
Statues and statuettes (G, H)
Tables (A)
Technical and scientific drawings (I)
Television scripts (unpublished, C or D)
Trade catalogues (A or KK)
Translations of 'books' (A); of dramas (D)
Verses (A)
UCC books (A-B Foreign)
Unpublished works (if not 'books,' C, D, E, G, I, J)
Woodcuts (H)

Common-Law Rights

COMMON LAW IS THE UNWRITTEN LAW of the land that receives its force from tradition and universal acceptance. In relation to the author, it is based on the premise that a writer, artist, or musician has a personal property in his work. After publication — and in some cases before publication — the author can secure his rights by statutory copyright. But from the moment his ideas are placed on paper he may protect his right in them at common law. As the Copyright Act puts it, he is able to 'prevent the copying, publication, or use of [his] unpublished work without his consent, and to obtain damages therefor.'

This is really more extensive protection than that offered by statutory copyright. There is no time limit to common-law right. It ends only on publication, dedication to the public, or authorized deliberate registration for statutory protection. Mark Twain's heirs were able to prevent the publication of one of his manuscripts though the manuscript itself had been sold at auction. Thus it is unsafe to publish letters, diaries, or other previously unpublished writings of persons long dead without the specific consent of their heirs.

There is no such thing as 'fair use' of an unpublished literary work (the situation is somewhat different for unpublished lectures, dramas, and music). The quotation of even a few lines of an unpublished manuscript would probably be condemned in court if the author brought suit. Many authors worry about submitting their manuscripts to publishers, lest they be stolen. It is true that publishers and producers sometimes realize that an unpublishable or unusable manuscript contains an idea that is potentially successful, and that they sometimes solicit or commission a work on the same subject after the manuscript at hand has been rejected. This may not be ethical, but it is legal. An idea is not subject to copyright, nor is it protected at common law. But if the idea has been 'worked out' or has been fully expressed, the author can claim damages against a second author who copies the sequence of its development and its expression. The courts have repeatedly protected motion-picture, radio, and television projects, which are too tenuous to be copyrighted, against infringement by companies to which they have been submitted.

The advantages of statutory copyright over common-law protection, if the author can make his choice, are that the former has a registration certificate to be used as evidence in court, if necessary; that any suit for infringement will be tried in the federal courts, regardless of the citizenship of the author; and that in certain cases the minimum and maximum damages for infringement are fixed.

Common-law rights belong to every resident author, regardless of citizenship. Under UCC, unpublished works of nationals of each Contracting State enjoy in each other Contracting State the same protection as the other State accords to such works of its own nationals.

In a recent case the court defined an author's common-law right as follows: 'It is the sole right to decide by whom, when, where, and in what form his manuscript shall be published for the first time; to restrain others from publishing it without his permission and from using it without his authority; and to recover damages from those publishing it without his permission or using it without his authority.'

An enumeration of the author's rights at common law is given in the section on the Author. Generally speaking, he may do anything he wants with his manuscript, short of authorizing its publication or dedicating it to the public, without invalidating his common-law rights. He owns the physical manuscript; it cannot be seized even by his creditors. He may read it in public, copy it for his friends, license others to translate it or make other versions of it, assign it and/or its rights at common law to another, sell it, broadcast it, set it to music, or what-have-you. He has the right to decide on its first publication. If it should be published without his consent, he could bring action, stop further sale or issuance of copies by injunction, and collect damages. His common-law rights would be unaffected and any copyright that is registered without his authority is invalid.

The author's common-law rights in his work cease under the following conditions:

1. Outright sale of the manuscript with no qualifications or reservations.
2. Authorized publication with notice.
3. Registration for copyright of the unpublished manuscript, if it is a lecture, sermon, address, or radio script, drama, musical composition, or work of art.
4. Dedication to the public (i.e. authorized publication without notice, or unrestricted distribution of copies; see *Public Domain*).
5. Abandonment — i.e. allowing a play to be performed many times by various groups of people without registering a protest; failing to protest unauthorized publication of a literary work with no copyright notice; allowing records of music to be widely sold or distributed; if not protected by UCC,

failing to secure United States copyright although copyright in a foreign country has been secured.

It must be stressed again: A letter, book, short story, poem, periodical, contribution to a periodical, newspaper, or contribution to a newspaper, or motion-picture, radio, or television idea cannot be registered for copyright until it is published. Before that it is protected at common law. Unpublished plays, lectures, music, works of art can rely on protection at common law or can elect statutory copyright.

Compilations
(ANTHOLOGIES)

A COMPILATION, NO MATTER WHAT its subject matter consists of, with the possible exception of music and drama, is a 'book.' The compilation may be of engravings, reproductions of works of art, songs without music, verse, photos, short stories, news articles, radio scripts, prose fiction or non-fiction, aphorisms, familiar quotations — the list is endless. The material need not be 'new'; it may be taken from works already in the public domain, or from other copyrighted works with the permission of the copyright owner. It is not the actual material that is being registered for copyright, but the personal contribution of the compiler: the arrangement of the material, the editorial equipment, the taste in the final selection. Hence it is that the form — i.e. 'book' — is registered for protection, even though the subject may be pictures with or without text, newspapers, clippings, or cartoons. If any material included is in copyright, it should carry a separate copyright notice. In granting permission for copyright material to be used in anthologies publishers usually ask that credit be given to author, book, and publisher, usually with exact wording of the credit line and copyright notice. The notices should be on the first page of the quoted material or grouped on the copyright page. If there is too much for that page the only solution seems to be to continue on the page immediately following, with no intervening material. Under UCC the placement of the notice is less important, but works by American authors and those first published here must conform to our law.

Often the compiler finds that he must make slight changes in the text to achieve a unity for the volume as a whole, or to utilize his space to best advantage. The substance of the material must never be changed in quotations, and even changes in spelling, punctuation, and capitalization or minor deletions should have the authorization of the copyright holder. If the author holds the copyright, the compiler must get his permission for changes, not that of the publisher.

Frequently material included in anthologies and other compilations has also appeared in earlier collections. The compiler should always be sure that he has obtained permission for his material from the real copyright owner, if the work is not in the public domain, not the copyright owner of

82

another anthology. In requesting permission he should also ask for world rights, if there is any possibility of selling his work abroad, and that it be granted for any other editions of the same material — i.e. a school edition, a de luxe edition, serialization, and the like. It may be necessary to apply to various foreign publishers to clear rights for different countries.

Compilations cannot expect to have copyright protection unless they have some element of 'originality.' This is stated in many foreign copyright laws more explicitly than in our own. Infringers of compilations often seek to justify their action by pointing out the common source of their product and that of the work claimed to be infringed. Certainly if the subject matter is taken from the public domain, a copyright will not prevent another compiler from using the same material and even in substantially the same order, if no special plan or method is apparent. The second compiler must be able to prove, however, that in each case he has gone back to the original source.

When a compilation is registered for copyright the Copyright Office has no responsibility to examine the deposit copy to decide whether (a) it is really entitled to copyright protection or (b) proper acknowledgment has been made to the copyright holders of copyright material included. These responsibilities are the compiler's and publisher's, and the mere acquisition of a certificate of copyright will be of no legal use to him if the volume is not entitled to protection.

Deposit

Works first published in the United States: send 2 copies.
Unpublished works: send 1 copy.

Foreign published works: send 1 copy and fee or 2 copies and catalogue card in lieu of fee.

Unpublished works of art (E) *or scientific drawings or plastic work* (I): *send photograph or other identifying reproduction.*

Published 3-dimensional works of art (GG): *send as many photographs (preferably 8 x 10 inches) as necessary, with (Option A) 2 copies (or foreign, 1); or (Option B) 2 copies (foreign, 1) with label (supplied by the Copyright Office on request) for return at sender's expense; or (Option C) no copies, but later deposit may be necessary in case of infringement.*

Unpublished motion pictures (L-M): *send title and description, with 1 print from each scene or act (if non-dramatic, at least 2 prints from different sections).*

Published motion pictures (L-M): *In addition to 2 complete copies (foreign, 1) a synopsis, press book, continuity, or other descriptive identifying matter.*

IN GENERAL, THE LAW REQUIRES for deposit at the Copyright Office two copies of domestic published works; one copy of unpublished works and works published abroad but bearing a United States copyright notice (but see below); an identifying reproduction of unpublished art works and motion pictures. Of the published works, the Copyright Act stipulates that the deposit copies must be 'complete' and of the 'best edition.' A proof copy will not do, nor will a 'school edition' if a trade edition or a de luxe edition is published simultaneously. If a de luxe edition is published later, it need not be sent, but if it is released at the same time as the trade edition it must be regarded as 'the best.'

When a contribution to a periodical or newspaper bears a separate copyright notice, one complete copy of the issue in which it appears must be deposited (not just a clipping). This applies also to serial publications, of which a copy of each number must be deposited separately, with the appropriate fee. If a contribution to a composite work (an article for an encyclopedia or symposium) bears a separate copyright, the pages involved should be sent for deposit. (There is no ruling in the Copyright Act on the mode of deposit of contributions to composite works, but the practice of the

Copyright Office is to accept the sheets containing the article, with application form A.)

Of works not reproduced for sale (unpublished works) the deposit copy must be 'clean, legible, and fastened securely together.' It must also have a title, corresponding to the title given in the application for registration.

Although only one copy of works of foreign origin (i. e. published abroad and not by a U.S. citizen or national) is required for deposit, since 1949 foreign copyright claimants have had the option of depositing two copies and a catalogue card instead of the fee. A model of the card is supplied by the Copyright Office with instructions for filling it out (see page 213). The filing of deposit copies and cards must, according to law, take place within six months of publication.

Deposit copies can be sent through the mail free of charge; publishers may prepare receipt forms to be filled in and signed by the postmaster:

United States Post Office

(*Place*)

(*Date*) _____19___

Received from (*name and address of publisher*)
One package addressed to The Register of Copyrights, Washington, D.C. said to contain two copies of the following work.

(*Author, Title, Publisher*)

_____

Postmaster

per _____

Over the postmaster's signature, this receipt serves as evidence of the publisher's intent to deposit two copies in accordance with the law. Local post offices will furnish franking labels free of charge. The application forms may be sent separately with the fee or may be sent with the deposit copy, also postage free, if they are attached to the package or placed immediately inside, i.e. not hidden in the leaves of the book.

All deposit copies and other communications should be addressed to

The Register of Copyrights
Library of Congress
Washington 25, D.C.

If deposit copies cannot be or are not sent immediately on publication, they should be sent as soon afterward as possible. If they are not deposited 'promptly' the copyright is not invalid, as was the case under the former law, but the Register of Copyrights may send the publisher or copyright claimant a request for them. If copies are then not supplied within three months (or six months if they are published outside the limits of the United

States) the copyright claimant is liable to a fine of $100 and twice the retail price of the best edition, and the copyright is lost.

Under UCC deposit is one of the formalities waived for the works of citizens and nationals of Contracting States and works first published in them if not by American citizens or residents. Anyone bringing action for infringement, however, may be required to make deposit before action is maintained. It should also be remembered that even for UCC books, the formality may be required in order to take advantage of the renewal term. If registration is desired for a foreign UCC book, it is made on Form A-B Foreign with the deposit of one copy and the fee or, if within six months of publication, two copies and a catalogue card.

One of the most important cases involving deposit copies is that of Pearson et al. *v.* The Washingtonian Publishing Co. Inc., in which infringement took place before copies were deposited. The courts first ruled that Drew Pearson, the plaintiff, had no legal basis for suit, since he deposited the copy of his paper that was infringed *after* he found it had been copied. It was finally established, however, that failure to deposit promptly is not fatal to the copyright until three months after the Copyright Office has demanded deposit, and that action for infringement can be taken immediately upon deposit, even though the infringement has already taken place.

The two justifications for the requiring of deposits of copyright works are (1) to have the material officially on hand in case of infringement, and (2) to enrich the Library of Congress. Although few other leading countries in the world — especially those who are members of the International Copyright Union — have much sympathy with the idea of making 'formalities' such as registration and deposit requisite for copyright, many do follow our custom of building up their official and major university libraries in this way. England requires a total of six copies of important books — for the British Museum, Oxford (Bodleian) and Cambridge University Libraries, the University of Edinburgh, Trinity College, Dublin, and the National Library of Wales. The copy for the British Museum is obligatory on publication, the others on demand. Failure to deposit does not invalidate the copyright, but results in a fine.

The Library of Congress decides upon the disposal of books deposited for copyright. Some are placed in its permanent collection; others are put in a reserve collection to be sold or exchanged with other Government libraries. Deposits of some classes of works may be destroyed periodically after public notice.

Dramas and Music Dramas

Published, Form D, *deposit 2 copies, fee $4.*
Unpublished, Form D, *deposit 1 complete copy (typed, handwritten, mimeographed), fee $4.*

DRAMATIC WORKS INCLUDE ALL TYPES of 'plays': tragedy, comedy, farce, pantomime, closet drama, marionette, extravaganza. Also included are radio and television plays or scripts, if they are completely worked out and not just a suggested outline.

Dramatico-musical works include musical comedies, operas, operettas, dance dramas, and reviews. Both text and music of dramatico-musical works must be deposited. If a musical comedy is copyrighted as a whole, all songs included are also copyrighted. Any songs that have already been published and copyrighted should bear their respective copyright notices, with the year date of first publication, and should not be registered a second time.

Dances, unless they are essentially dramatic — i.e. 'tell a story' — animal shows, sleight-of-hand performances, circus acts, scenery, and moving-picture scripts are not dramas and are not subject to copyright. Motion-picture scenarios (scripts) are protected at common law until they are used as the basis for motion pictures, which may then be registered for copyright. If the scenarios are printed and published they may be copyrighted as a 'book.'

A dramatic work, unlike a 'book,' may be copyrighted in manuscript form (D) before publication. However, if it is published later, a new registration must be made. In this case, the 28-year copyright term starts with the date of the registration of the unpublished manuscript, not with publication. Copies of published dramas should be deposited as soon as they are available.

Published dramas, even though in book form, are not copyrighted as 'books' but as dramas. This means that even if by a United States citizen or national they do not have to be manufactured in this country, and also that they may not be performed in public without permission, whether for profit or not. Thus they have greater protection than books or music. To

87

secure United States copyright, they must carry a copyright notice, even if published abroad.

Unpublished dramatic works are protected at common law (q.v.) until publication or until they are registered for copyright. Before publication the author may choose between common-law protection and statutory protection — that is, whether to copyright or not.

Public performance, broadcasting, and telecasting do not constitute publication; only the public distribution or sale of copies does. However, repeated unauthorized performances of which the copyright owner knows and does not protest have been termed a kind of publication, or abandonment of copyright.

The copyright holder of a drama has the exclusive right to novelize his work or convert it into any other form, such as a series of cartoons, a radio drama, a motion picture. His exclusive right of public performance includes amateur performances by schools, churches, and clubs, and all forms of radio and television presentation.

Copyrighted non-dramatic works can be dramatized only by the authority of the copyright holder. This applies to novels, short stories, cartoons, moving pictures, songs, poems, and copyrighted news articles, in so far as the latter represent the original ideas or expressions of their authors (see page 135). New acting versions of dramas in the public domain may be copyrighted, but the copyright protects only the new material. A statement of what comprises the new material should appear on the application form.

News as such and all other works in the public domain can be dramatized by anyone, without permission. However, such dramatization, even after it is copyrighted, does not secure to the copyright holder exclusive right to the source material used.

Dramatic copyrights are infringed by substantial copying, either of words or dramatic sequences. Ideas and incidents cannot be copyrighted, nor can stage business. The use of the same fundamental plot is not infringement, if there is difference in the leading characters, episodes, action, dialogue, and locale.

Titles of dramas cannot be copyrighted, but the holder of a copyrighted drama may protect his title in some instances on the grounds of unfair competition (q.v.). While it is current, he may protect it against use for another drama or a moving picture, even on an unrelated subject.

Duration

THE DURATION OF A COPYRIGHT for a work first published in the United States is 28 years, starting from its first publication date. At the end of that time it can be renewed for 28 years (see *Renewals*). The 28-year statutory copyright of an unpublished work is understood to begin at the time of its registration at the Copyright Office. When a work is published serially, the copyright starts with the dates of its serial publication, thus making a series of copyright terms. If it is later published in book form, and new material is added for which a second copyright is secured, the new material is protected for 28 years from the date of publication of the book version. Thus in determining whether or not the copyright of a book is still in effect, it is unsafe to estimate from the first copyright date on the notice, if there is more than one. From the point of view of the copyright claimant, it is also dangerous to take out a second copyright for a work unless the new material is appreciable. The courts are not sympathetic toward attempts to prolong copyright by the registration of a new copyright for every minor change. A reprint with only typographical corrections is not entitled to a new copyright (see *New Editions*, etc.).

A copyright is presumably invalidated if the year given in the notice is later than the year of publication. Although the Copyright Office occasionally registers works with postdated notices, the courts have declared that postdated copyrights are invalid. If the year in the notice is earlier than the actual publication, the copyright is not invalidated, as in this case the public benefits. But the term of the copyright starts on the last day of the year recorded in the notice, rather than on the day the work was published.

In most foreign countries copyright endures for the author's life plus 50 years. This is usually longer than the term in the United States, since our renewal term is really a new copyright period and often is lost through the failure of the proper person to make application within the time limit fixed by the law. Thus the illogical situation often occurs that an American book is in the public domain in the United States, but is technically still in copyright in England and other Berne Convention countries. Attempts to revise our law to make it conform to that of the majority of the countries of the International Copyright Union have been defeated on the grounds that the author who has been injudicious in disposing of his property in the first term should have an opportunity to protect himself in the second term. This is more fully discussed under *Renewals*.

The copyright on a book 'first published' (or simultaneously published) in any country is protected there according to the laws of that country. Under UCC the duration of protection is that of the Contracting State in which it claims protection. In the case of simultaneous publication in two or more Contracting States (and publication within 30 days is 'simultaneous,' under UCC) the work may be treated as though it were first published in the state offering the shortest term. Hence if a book is published simultaneously in the United States and Canada and the author lives say twenty years after it is published, it may be considered first published in the United States. In no case in UCC countries, except for certain restricted classes of work, can protection be less than 25 years after the author's death, or in countries such as the United States that reckon copyright protection from publication, 25 years from the date of first publication (see *Universal Copyright Convention*).

Unpublished works by American authors that have been registered for copyright in the United States are protected in British countries only for the life of their American copyright. If they are 'first published' in Canada or Great Britain, they are protected there for 50 years after the death of the author. The Buenos Aires Convention ruled that the copyright term of any book should in no case be longer in any country than in the country of origin, but that individual members could apply such domestic terms as they desired. Copyright duration in various countries is given in the table on pages 107–9.

The copyright term of a book published in the United States that was first published abroad starts with its *first* publication wherever it was. The term for a work copyrighted in manuscript and that is later published starts from its registration rather than its publication date.

The fact that a book goes out of print does not affect the term of its copyright. Even though it sold but a few copies and went out of print within a month of publication, its copyright will continue throughout the full term of 28 years, subject to renewal during the final year. It is never safe to assume that a copyright has lapsed because (a) the book is out of print; (b) no copies are available; (c) the author is no longer living; (d) the publisher is no longer in business; (e) no descendants or heirs of the author can be located; (f) no one answers your letters requesting permission to reprint.

Fair Use

'FAIR USE' OF COPYRIGHT MATERIAL has been defined by the courts as that extra-legal use that is usual, reasonable, and customary. There is no rule-of-thumb of how many 'lines' may be considered fair use, though many publishers set up such limitations for their own guidance. Actually two lines of poetry copied without permission might constitute infringement, and two pages of other material might be legitimate 'fair use.' In the following cases quotation, either direct or by paraphrasing, is considered legitimate and the permission of the copyright owner is not required:

1. Dramatic and literary criticism: Any 'writing of an author,' once it is published, is subject to fair criticism, serious or otherwise, and for this purpose, it is permissible to quote from it and describe it by words, pictures, or in any other manner.

2. Mimicry, editorial comment, parodies:

> I'll never see, where'er I roam,
> A tree as lovely as a pome . . .

does not infringe the copyright of Kilmer's 'Trees'; nor does Betty Smith's

> I'd drather say I hated fleas
> Then be like youse what runs down trees

infringe Jan Struther's parody, quoted above. Nor does this quotation, for purposes of illustration, infringe the copyright of *The Saturday Review of Literature,* from the 16 September 1944 issue of which these two parodies are quoted. (However, see *Quotations.*) Parodies on the stage, screen, radio, or television are somewhat more hazardous, and substantial amounts of the original material should not be used without permission.

3. Incidental or background use: This has been described by the courts as that casual use of quotation, usually music or verse, to create an atmosphere. McEvoy's use of the lyric 'You Can't Stop Me From Lovin' You' to create an atmosphere in his short story, 'Are You Listening?', published in *Collier's,* was judged by the court to be fair use, and not an infringement. *The New Yorker*'s use of the whole chorus (without music) of 'Poor Pauline' in its obituary article on Pearl White was also declared fair use.

4. The use of dictionaries, compilations, law digests, and citations for checking and comparison: Any work of this sort must depend to a certain extent on other books in the field. However, using another's compilation without checking or verifying sources is copying, a practice often revealed by the carry over of the errors of the earlier work into the new.

5. The use of existing scholarly, legal, medical, and scientific works in the writing of new ones: Here again the serious scholar must take cognizance of the work done by his predecessors and colleagues. Earlier works can be commented on and discussed, and quoted at sufficient length to make the comments intelligible.

6. The use in 'companions' and 'guide books' of synopses of literary, dramatic, musical, or motion-picture works: A case in which a composer sued the author of a book of opera stories for including a synopsis of his work came before the courts. The judge pointed out that a synopsis is not an 'abridgment,' and that the composer's rights were in no way infringed. However, if the synopsis can be used as a substitute for the original, it is 'unfair competition.'

7. A spring-board use, or what Ladas, in his book on International Copyright, calls a 'jumping-off use.' It is the use of one work as the inspiration and incentive for a second one. In fiction, Thayer's use of Dumas' *The Three Musketeers* is an example; in nonfiction, the carrying on of scholarship by later scholars.

A question frequently used to determine whether a quotation from a copyrighted work is 'fair' or not is whether it injures or impairs the value of the original. A dramatization of two characters called Nutt and Jeff was found to infringe the copyright of *Mutt and Jeff,* since if one saw the former he would be less likely to spend money to see the latter. On the other hand, an adverse review of a book of poems in which verses are cited to illustrate the reviewer's criticism is not an infringement, even though it may be injurious to the sale of the book.

Other tests of fair use are:

1. Whether the quotation is a 'material and substantial part' of the original: The length does not matter so much as does its relative importance. Were the 'Ode on a Grecian Urn' still in copyright, and its author alive, Keats might well object to the unauthorized appropriation by someone else of its last two lines.

2. The extent and relative value of the extracts: A quotation of 200 words in a 2000-word article would not be fair use, whereas a similar quotation in a 500-page tome might be fair and incidental — provided that credit was given to the author.

92

3. Whether the quoted portions might be used as a substitute for the original: This was the crux of the Sayers case against Sigmund Spaeth (see page 154) and conversely was used in McEvoy's defense in the case cited earlier in this article.

4. The nature and purpose for which it is used: A famous statesman's photograph in which the cover of a magazine is seen lying on the table beside him is not an infringement of the copyright of the magazine or of the artist who drew the cover, the court has declared. A statement from Richard DeWolf's book, *An Outline of Copyright Law,* has frequently been quoted ('fair use'!) by the courts in regard to cases involving fair use:

It is convenient to distinguish between permissible use of a copyrighted work, which the law does not forbid, and 'fair use' strictly speaking, which is a use technically forbidden by the law, but allowed as reasonable and customary.

Those two words — reasonable and customary — are the criteria of fair use.

A final word of caution: If the quotation from another source is clearly 'fair use' it is not necessary to ask the proprietor's permission. If permission is asked and refused, however, it would be most unwise to use the material, whether the use would be fair or not. The common practice of asking permission and giving extensive credit lines for every quotation of over 50 words (or other rule-of-thumb length) not only is confusing to the public but is a far departure from promoting 'the Progress of Science and the Useful Arts.' Meaningless also is the notice some publishers print in the beginning of their books forbidding unauthorized quotation of more than a limited number of words. (A similar notice but with opposite intent, authorizing permission to quote up to, say, 500 words without permission, is more meaningful.) What can be considered fair use must rest on the intent and judgment of the user.

Fees

(See page 157 for permission fees.)

For registration of copyright, $4 (except for a print or label, classification KK, of an article of merchandise, $6).
For recording a copyright renewal, $2.
For an additional copyright certificate, $1.
For recording an assignment $3, for not over 6 pages (see Assignment).
For search in the copyright records, etc., $3 for each hour of time used.

EVERY SEPARATE REGISTRATION requires a new fee. If the prints or cartoons in a collection are all copyrighted separately, each must have its own application form and fee.

Registration fees cannot be mailed postage free but may be enclosed in a stamped envelope with the deposit copy. Time will be saved by sending the necessary fee, as nearly as it can be estimated, with all applications, assignments, or requests for search. The most frequent causes of delay and for further correspondence with the Copyright Office in regard to fees are the failure to make the checks or money orders payable to the Register of Copyrights, and failure to send a sufficient amount to cover the charges. Coins, stamps, or currency should never be sent, because of possible loss in the mails, and the fact that there is no way to trace them.

Deposit accounts may be placed with the Copyright Office by publishers or agents who have many copyright transactions. These are especially convenient for newspapers and magazine publishers. It is then unnecessary to send a separate fee with each application, and time is saved both for the publisher and the Copyright Office. Book publishers who register 25 or more books yearly will also find it convenient. The initial deposit may be from $50 to $1000. For a newspaper or periodical, the deposit account usually covers one year's fees. If at any time the depositor wishes to discontinue the account, the Copyright Office refunds the existing balance. Statements are issued to deposit account holders by the Copyright Office at regular intervals.

Illustrations

ILLUSTRATIONS, CUTS, OR PICTURES in a book are protected by the copyright of the book. Even if the pictures are not attached to the binding, but are in a separate pocket or folder, they are protected by the book copyright. It is safer, however, in this case, to have each carry a copyright notice of its own — one with the proprietor's initials, at least. If the artist wishes a separate copyright, the illustrations should each carry a separate copyright notice in his name and have a separate registration (Form K). Two complete copies of the book must be deposited for each registration.

Books of pictures, illustrations, cartoons, et cetera, with or without words, are books (Class A).

Illustrated publicity catalogues may be books (A); advertising bulletins, individual advertisements of merchandise in periodicals, or cuts in a catalogue may be A, BB, or KK (see *Advertisements*).

If the artist's pictures are published in a periodical and copyrighted only as part of the whole, he should stipulate in his contract or letter of sale exactly what rights he grants to the publisher. If the publisher has magazine rights only, or right of use in a specific book, the artist remains the real copyright owner, and the publisher holds the copyright in trust for him. If desirable, the copyright can be assigned back to the artist immediately after publication.

Unless there has been a written assignment, duly recorded, republished illustrations must carry the copyright notice of the original registration.

The cover of a book or magazine is usually not considered to be subject to copyright. However, if it is in itself an artistic work and is closely related to the subject matter of the text, it is entitled to protection as an illustration. In this case, however, it should carry a copyright notice on it, and not rely on that on the copyright page of the book.

If the artist wishes to take out his own copyright on pictures published in a newspaper or periodical he must include a separate copyright notice, and he must register them on Form BB (see page 215). He then deposits one complete copy of the issue in which they are published, and sends a deposit fee of $4.

Often, a book publisher hires an artist to illustrate a book for a specific

95

fee, and thus buys the material outright. If the artist is on the publisher's staff, it is usually agreed that the illustrations are 'done for hire.' If the book is copyrighted in the publisher's name he then has renewal rights on the illustrations. If the artist wishes to retain his renewal (and other) rights, he should ask that when the application for registration is made his name be entered on line (3) after the author's name, with 'Illustrator' in parenthesis following it.

In books by United States citizens and nationals containing lithographs and photo-engravings and illustrations reproduced by lithography or photo-engraving, all such processes must be performed in the United States unless the illustrations represent works of art or science that are located abroad.

Infringement

THE RESTRAINT OF UNLAWFUL USE of copyright material is the most frequent cause of copyright litigation. By the Copyright Act, the author — or copyright owner — is guaranteed certain definite and exclusive rights. For books, newspapers, periodicals, and all contributions to them (Classes A and B) these are the rights:

1. To print, reprint, publish, copy, and vend.
2. To translate or make other versions.
3. To dramatize.
4. To deliver or present in public for profit.
5. To make any transcription or record by which it can be exhibited, presented, or reproduced.
6. To play or perform it for profit, and to exhibit, represent, or reproduce it in any manner or any method whatsoever.

To print is not only to print in type, but also to multigraph or write by any other mechanical means. *To publish* means 'to reproduce in copies for sale or public distribution.' *To copy* includes any wholesale rewriting of the material, whether literal copying or not. Slight changes to disguise the source will not lessen the culpability of the infringer. *To vend* refers to the control by the copyright owner not only of the first sale but also of leases, licenses, and assignments.

To translate or make other versions includes translating, abridging, revising, and making versions for other media.

To dramatize includes the reworking of non-dramatic material into dialogue and/or action.

By (5) and (6), added to the law in 1952, literary works are protected against unauthorized oral delivery for profit and unauthorized use by recordings, radio, and television.

Any of these uses of copyright material without the express permission of the copyright owner constitutes infringement and, if wilful, is punishable by fine, imprisonment, or both. Everyone who takes part in infringement is liable, jointly or severally — the printer, the author, the publisher, the bookseller, the sponsor, the company. Unpublished material and intangibles such as reputation, fully developed ideas, good will, are protected against unfair use at common law.

It is not always immediately apparent whether there has been infringement or not. Similarities of plot, character, scene, and expression suggest copying, but they may be the result of the use of common source material, such as history, news, or works in the public domain. 'Access' must usually be proved before there can be judgment for infringement. If A has never read B's book, or had it read to him, or seen or heard any version of it, he cannot have infringed it, since it is impossible to copy something to which you have never had access. However, if he read it years ago, he may have copied it unconsciously, from memory. If so, he is legally culpable. Such was the case of an infringement by a well-known and well-meaning song writer. In a recent case the court pointed out that when two works are so much alike that 'coincidence' is impossible, no proof of access is necessary.

Infringement may sometimes be detected through similarity of expression, from errors in quotations when second-hand sources are used, through similarity of chapter headings and subheadings. This was true in a guide book to restaurants and hotels that infringed *Adventures in Good Eating*. The courts have ruled that there may be infringement through the labor-saving use of a rival's gathering of material, even though the results differ.

Ideas are not copyrightable, and in most cases similarity of idea is not infringement. But when a copyrighted advertisement describing a contest was duplicated by another advertisement the first was protected on the grounds that the copyright owner had 'a property right in a particular combination of ideas where the combination is reduced to concrete form.'

Only material that has some claim to originality can be infringed. (Miller, in his *Re-examination of Literary Piracy,* quotes W. R. Inge's quip that originality is nothing but undetected plagiarism.) If a scene or situation has so little novelty that it occurs in many novels or plays, there can be no infringement of it. This was found to be the case in regard of the Irish-Jewish love tribulations of *Abie's Irish Rose,* when Anne Nichols unsuccessfully sued Universal Pictures Corporation, contending that *The Cohens and the Kellys* infringed her play. To constitute infringement, copying must be 'material and substantial.'

Copying without the copyright owner's permission is infringement even when it is in a different medium. A doll copied from a well-known character in a copyrighted child's book was an infringement, even though the doll itself was not copyrightable. A copyrighted painting might be 'copied' by a photograph of it. Wholesale copying is never 'fair use,' whatever its purpose. A telephone book was infringed by a later version in which the material was rearranged according to the exchanges instead of the subscribers' names.

A person's high professional reputation does not necessarily preclude him from infringing the works of others. Sometimes he does so unconsciously, through quoting from memory; sometimes he doesn't understand the copyright law and thinks that if he acknowledges the source no permission is needed. Scholars of the first rank have been found to infringe the work of colleagues whom they respect and admire. In a case involving the infringement of a biography of Hans Christian Andersen it was stated, 'Intention is immaterial if infringement occurs. . . . Nor does the fact that the defendants acknowledge the source . . . excuse infringement.' The cautious publisher will check the manuscripts of his authors, no matter how high their standing in the academic or professional world.

Infringement is not avoided by altering the plot or adding characters or incidents. A copyrighted map is infringed even though additional boundaries, cities, or colors are included. Nonfiction books are infringed when their citations are used without further checking by a second author, although there is no infringement in using a book for reference, comparison, or checking. Here again the duplication of error is a common way of detecting unfair copying.

When Classified Geographic, Inc., cut up copies of the *National Geographic Magazine* and, after classifying the articles by topics, sold the resulting compilation in a new binding, it infringed on the original copyright owner's right to 'publish and sell,' even though there was no disguise of the source of the material. When a second-hand book dealer printed the missing parts of old books and inserted them before sale, he infringed the copyright holder's right to print. When a moving-picture company dramatized a novel without permission of the copyright proprietor — in this case, the publisher — even though it had the author's permission, it infringed a former dramatization authorized by the publisher to whom the author had previously granted movie rights. The actual amount that is infringed is not the decisive factor. In one case the court stated, 'In order to constitute an infringement of the copyright of a book it is not necessary that the whole or even a large portion of the book shall have been copied. It is sufficient if a material or substantial part shall have been copied, even though it be a small unit of the whole.'

To win a suit for infringement the copyright owner must prove (1) that his work actually was copied, and (usually) (2) that he has suffered damages. Usually, also, he must prove access. If he brings suit ill-advisedly, simply because another has been successful with material similar to his that had little or mediocre success, he may find himself with court costs to pay and

99

little else for his pains. Similarities that may suggest copying to him may be the result of using a common source. The resemblance must be close enough to be detected by the unprejudiced mind without legal analysis.

Plays and novels on similar subjects or with a common background or locale often use the same atmospheric material. Cases of this type have come before the courts where the subject matter is the gangster, women's reformatories, the personal idiosyncrasies of Alexander Woollcott, and even an unhappy second wife (the case against Du Maurier's *Rebecca*). It is usually found that the similarities are entirely incidental. On the other hand, a fictional biography of Clara Barton was found to be really infringed by a so-called 'factual' biography that appropriated some of the fictional incidents of the first book. Although one should not be too suspicious of other books on the same subject, it is equally foolish to be too naïve and unsuspecting.

Penalties for infringement are clearly defined in the Copyright Act (page 235). Since this is a book of practice, they will not be discussed here. In any case of suspected infringement, a copyright lawyer should be consulted at once.

International Copyright Relations

UNITED STATES COPYRIGHT PROTECTION is extended to an alien author only when he is domiciled in this country at the time of first publication of his work or when he is a citizen of a country with which the United States has a reciprocal copyright agreement established through convention, proclamation, or treaty with one notable exception; it is now extended to the work of an author who is a citizen or national of any UCC country and whose work is first published with a UCC notice, and to the work of an author, of whatever citizenship, first published with notice in a UCC country. Conceivably, and ideally, UCC will someday be ratified by all the leading nations of the world. As of this writing some sixteen nations have deposited their articles of ratification (see page 107 and *Universal Copyright Convention,* page 171). The works of citizens and nationals of those countries and works first published in those countries, provided each carries the UCC notice on first publication, are automatically protected here for 28 years after publication * without further formality of registration, United States manufacture, deposit, or fee, unless the author is a United States citizen or is domiciled in the United States at the time of publication. Hence the work of a citizen of Albania (with whom we have no copyright agreement) would be protected here without further formality if it were first published in Spain (a UCC Contracting State). The same work would not be protected if it were first published in Italy (with whom we have an agreement but which is not in 1955 a UCC Contracting State). If the Albanian (or a Spaniard) were domiciled in the United States at the time of first publication, the work would be protected here only if it conformed to all our formalities including United States manufacture.

It does not necessarily follow from the fact that the United States has a reciprocal copyright agreement with another country that all works copyrighted in that country are automatically protected here, or that ours are protected there. For example, a British copyright protects a book in Great Britain and in all the countries of the International Copyright Union, but until Great Britain ratifies the Universal Copyright Convention, if the book is in the English language the copyright has no effect in the United

* For the possible exceptions on the length of protection, see page 171.

101

States unless there is an American edition too, carrying a United States copyright notice, or it is registered for ad interim copyright. 'All rights reserved,' 'Copyright reserved,' and other similar statements placed on the copyright page of books of foreign origin may protect South American copyright, but have no significance under United States copyright law. The only effective notice for books so far as the United States is concerned is © or Copr. or Copyright, the year date, and the name of the copyright holder.

No book in the English language can hold a full-term United States copyright unless it is protected under UCC or it is completely manufactured here. A foreign work lacking UCC or United States copyright has only two forces working against its possible infringement: first, the moral pressure, the pressure of public opinion, that ostracizes the publisher who steals the unprotected property of others; second, the fact that the United States Copyright Office will not knowingly register a copyright for a piratical edition, and that United States judges refuse to allow a piratical publisher to defend his stolen goods in our courts. In other words, from the strictly legal point of view, if a work is in the public domain, anyone is free to print it; if it is not, it can be defended only by the legal copyright owner.

An American author or publisher who wants to publish, reprint, or quote from a foreign publication that has no copyright here — perhaps because it was published before UCC — but is protected in its country of origin is morally bound to get permission from the original owner and usually pays at least a 'courtesy' fee for the use accorded him. This is not just nobility on the part of American authors and publishers. In return they expect, and in most cases receive, like treatment from foreign authors and publishers.

Works by authors of countries with which we have no copyright relations * may secure copyright only if the authors are residents of the United States at the time of first publication of the work in question or the work is *first* published in UCC State. Citizens of proclaimed countries may secure copyright by conforming to the requirements of our law (ad interim registration within six months and American manufacture within 5 years of books in English; publication with notice; registration, deposit, and fee) or first or simultaneous publication in a UCC country. Foreign books in the public domain in this country before the enactment of the law of 1909 or before UCC cannot be copyrighted now by the publication of 'new editions' unless those editions are true revisions, with additional material of importance. Even then it is only the new material that will be protected.

Since a translation is a 'new work' in the terms of the Copyright Act, a translation of a book of foreign origin may be copyrighted, even though the

* See chart, page 107.

original was not. The copyrighting of the authorized translation in this country would not, however, preclude the possibility of another translation, which could also be copyrighted, if the original work is in the public domain here.

When an American wants to copyright his work in a foreign country, the situation is a little different. Most of the leading countries of Europe belong to the International Copyright Union and many have indicated their interest in UCC. In a UCC country our books are given substantially the same protection as is granted to nationals of that country. Under the Berne Convention one of the conditions of membership is that any work first published or simultaneously published in a country belonging to the Union is protected in all Union countries. Hence our books may gain international copyright by simultaneous publication in a Union country (see page 110). England is usually the country of choice.

British publication requires the delivery of one copy of the best edition to the British Museum within one month of publication. Failure to make deposit does not invalidate the copyright, but it makes the British publisher liable to a fine. Within a year of publication, five other libraries may demand copies; for these the regular trade edition suffices. It is also required that publication be 'actual,' not merely colorable — that is, that books be actually placed on sale and on hand to supply the demand. In one case it was conceded that the 12 copies available at the British publishers were enough to fulfil this stipulation. An unpublished work is automatically protected in Great Britain when it is registered for copyright in the United States, since in British countries all works are protected by statutory copyright rather than at common law. However, the term of the protection of unpublished works is governed by the American copyright term, not the usual British term. Unpublished works that cannot be copyrighted before publication under our law (books, periodicals, etc.) have no copyright status in England.

British copyright extends for the author's life plus 50 years, but after 25 years any publisher may produce the work if he applies for a license and agrees to pay the statutory royalty to the copyright owner. With a few exceptions copyright is assumed to belong to the author, not the proprietor. In the case of cyclopedic works — or works that in the terms of our law are 'done for hire' — the copyright extends for fifty years from publication. This applies also to anonymous, posthumous, and pseudonymous works, if the pseudonym is not generally identified. Since no formalities are required for copyright in Great Britain, and all writings are automatically protected during the author's life and for 50 years after his death, a copyright notice is unessential except for UCC protection. When an American book is 'first published' in Great Britain it is protected for the author's lifetime plus 50

103

years. When a British book is published in the United States it is protected for 28 years plus 28 years (see *Duration*). Hence Americans usually fare better under the British law than they do at home or than British subjects fare here. An American book may be in copyright in Great Britain for years after it is in the public domain here.

Canada has several provisions not in the Copyright Law of Great Britain. Although she automatically extends copyright protection to all United States books complying with our copyright law (first publication in the United States), she has added a clause to her law that if a book is not actually produced and published in Canada, any Canadian may apply for a license to reprint it. The American copyright owner is then given six months to produce a Canadian edition; if he does not, the license is granted, with an arrangement for royalties to be paid to the copyright owner. Up to the present time, this clause has never been used, since if Canadian sales justify an edition there, the American publisher is quick to co-operate.

United States copyrights may be registered in Canada (Ottawa), but registration is not obligatory. However, a certificate of registration is prima-facie evidence of copyright. The Canadian Government does not supply application blanks; in the Canadian Copyright Law, however, the following form is given:

APPLICATION FOR REGISTRATION OF COPYRIGHT IN A PUBLISHED WORK

I, ...
of the city of . . . .
in the state of . . . .
. . . . *Hereby declare*
That I am the owner of the Copyright in the original literary work entitled
" . . . . *"*
by . . . . *of* . . . .
and that the said work was first published by the issue of copies thereof to the public on the . . . . *day of* . . . . *19. . . . ,*
in the . . . . *of* . . . .
and I hereby request you to register the Copyright of the said work in my name in accordance with the provisions of the Copyright Act, 1921.

I herewith forward the fee of $2.00 for registration of the said Copyright and the further fee of $1.00 for certificate of such registration.

Dated at . . . . *the* . . . . *day of* . . . . *19. .*
Signature of applicant . . . .
To the Commissioner of Patents,
    Copyright Office,
        Ottawa

The 'author, owner, or publisher' of, or 'other person interested in,' the copyright may cause it to be registered; the application may be made in 'the name of the author or his legal representatives, by any person purporting to be agent of such author or legal representatives.' Within one month after publication two copies of the first edition of every book manufactured in Canada, or written or illustrated by a Canadian, or about Canada, should be deposited in the Library of Parliament in Ottawa; but failure to deposit does not invalidate the copyright or subject the publisher to penalty.

In most Latin American countries, compliance with the copyright law of the country of first publication protects * the work in other countries of the Buenos Aires Convention of 1910 (of which the United States is a signatory): Argentina, Brazil, Chile, Colombia, Costa Rica, Dominican Republic, Ecuador, Guatemala, Haiti, Honduras, Nicaragua, Panama, Paraguay, Peru, and Uruguay.† The terms became binding as each country ratified, so the date of ratification is important in deciding the status of the works of each country. It is required that to secure copyright each work must carry a notice to the effect that copyright is reserved, in English or any other language. (Our copyright notice presumably fulfils this requirement, but for complete safety it is well to add *All rights reserved*.) There are also various requirements of registration and deposit (see pp. 107–9) in the country of first publication. The duration of the copyright protection need not exceed that of the country of origin, but otherwise is governed by the laws of each country.

To quote from DeWolf's book,

It appears that works of American citizens or residents copyrighted under our law automatically obtain protection in the other countries above named which have ratified the convention [Buenos Aires]. No doubt it will be prudent, however, in case copyright is to be claimed in any of these countries, to arrange in advance of publication with an agent acquainted with the local laws and conditions in the country where protection is sought.‡

At the Havana Convention of 1928, a revision was added that the notice should include the name of the copyright proprietor and the year and country of first publication, but to date this revision has been ratified by only a handful of states (not the United States).

In 1937, in a case having to do with the infringement of a song copyrighted in the Dominican Republic by a New York recording company, it was decided that the Buenos Aires Convention does not apply to recordings, unless there is a separate agreement between the countries concerned. (Un-

* Reciprocal protection of mechanical reproduction rights is not effective in all countries; see page 107.

† The status of Bolivia is dubious. According to a circular issued by the Copyright Office (1955), 'Bolivia considers that it is a party to the 1910 Convention,' but there seems to be no record of its ratification.

‡ Richard C. DeWolf, *An Outline of Copyright Law*, Boston, 1925.

fortunately, the question of the failure to include a copyright notice was not discussed.) As a similar decision was reached by a higher court in 1948, the principle seems established.

A third revision of the Buenos Aires Convention was made at the Washington Convention (Pan-American Copyright Convention) of 1946. It is much more detailed in its provisions, and includes protection of radio, television, motion-picture, and recording rights. The notice called for (not required, but to be 'encouraged' by the adhering States) is Copyright (or Copr. or ©), the year of first publication, the name and address of the copyright owner, and the place of origin of the work, and it 'should appear' on the reverse of the title page in literary works. Another clause of interest reads (Article XIV): 'When a copyrighted work has become internationally famous and its title has thereby acquired such a distinctive character as to become identified with that work alone, that title cannot be attached to another work without the consent of the author.' But it goes on to say that this would not apply to works so different in kind that there would be no possibility of confusion. The Washington Convention has been ratified by 14 South American States, including Mexico, but not yet by the United States.

Copyright relations between the United States and the Philippines have been governed since 1948 by reciprocal proclamations as of that year. The Philippine law was modelled largely on ours, and requires notice and deposit, as well as several minor formalities. In 1954 an amendment was pending that would require also Philippine manufacture, but in view of the fact that in 1951 the Philippines ratified the Brussels Revision of the Berne Convention and in 1955 UCC, it is doubtful that the manufacturing clause will ever become effective.

Following is a list of the major countries of the world, with an indication of our copyright relations with each. Those preceded by an asterisk are members of the International Copyright Union, those followed by a © are States of UCC. The year dates are those in which reciprocal copyright agreements with the United States became effective. Those marked 'O.K.' grant to citizens of the United States the same copyright privileges extended to their own citizens upon compliance with the local copyright law, in return for which United States copyright privilege is extended to their nationals upon compliance with all the conditions of the United States Copyright laws. This often means first or simultaneous publication. If there are local copyright conditions for nationals, they are indicated in parentheses.*

* The Copyright Office issues circulars on the protection of U. S. copyrighted works abroad, copyright relations with Latin America (including addresses of Latin American copyright offices), and copyright protection under UCC.

International Copyright Relations

	Duration of Copyright	Treaty or Proclamation [1]	Foreign Status of U. S. Copyright Material
Andorra ©		none	UCC
Argentina	life + 30	1934m B. A. 1950	O. K.
*Australia	life + 50(l)	1918m	simultaneous publication
*Austria	life + 50	1907, 1909, 1920m	O. K.
*Belgium	life + 50	1891, 1909m	O. K.
Bolivia	life + 30	B. A. 1914?	none (?)
*Brazil	life + 60	B. A. 1915	O. K.
*Bulgaria	life + 30	none	(Berne)
Cambodia ©		none	UCC
*Canada (applies also to Newfoundland)	life + 50(l)	1924m	O. K.
Chile ©	life + 20	1896, 1909, 1925m B. A. 1955	O. K. + UCC
China	30 years	1904, 1948	(translations protected for 10 years; registration, deposit)
Colombia	life + 80	B. A. 1936	O. K.
Costa Rica ©	life + 50	Mexico 1908, B. A. 1916	O. K. + UCC
Cuba	life + 80	1903, 1909, 1911m	register within 1 year; deposit
*Czechoslovakia	life + 50	1927m	O. K.
*Denmark	life + 50	1893, 1909, 1920m	O. K.
Dominican Republic	life + 30	Mexico 1908, B. A. 1912	O. K.
Ecuador	life + 50	B. A. 1914	O. K.
Egypt		none	none
El Salvador	life + 25	Mexico 1908	deposit
Ethiopia		none	none
*Finland	life + 50	1929m	O. K.
*France ©	life + 50	1891, 1909, 1918m	O. K.
*German Federal Republic ©	life + 50		UCC

* Indicates member of International Copyright Union, in which copyright is extended to a book first published in any Union country.[1]
© Indicates Contracting State of Universal Copyright Convention, 1955.
B. A. = Buenos Aires Convention.
m = reciprocal agreement also on recording music.
l = compulsory license after 25 years.

[1] Proclamations not applicable to literary copyright are not included.

107

	Duration of Copyright	Treaty or Proclamation	Foreign Status of U. S. Copyright Material
*Great Britain and possessions	life + 50(1)	1891, 1909, 1915m	simultaneous publication
*Greece	life + 50	1932m	O. K.
Guatemala	perpetual	Mexico 1908, B. A. 1912 †	O. K.
Haiti ©	life (+ widow's life) + 20 years for any children	B. A. 1919	O. K. + UCC
*Holy See (see Vatican City)			
Honduras	10–20 years	Mexico 1908, B. A. 1914	O. K.
*Hungary	life + 50	1912m, 1947	must comply with formalities
*Iceland	life + 50	none	(Berne)
*India	life + 50	1947m	O. K.
*Ireland	life + 50(1)	1929m	first publication
*Israel ©		1948m	O. K. + UCC
*Italy	life + 50	1892, 1909, 1915m, 1947	O. K. (deposit 1 copy)
*Japan	life + 30	1906, 1908, 1952m	O. K. until 1956
Korea		1908 (abrogated)	none
Laos ©		none	O. K. + UCC
*Lebanon	life + 50	none	(Berne)
Liberia	life + 20	none	none
*Liechtenstein	life + 30	none	(Berne)
*Luxembourg ©	life + 50	1910m	O. K. + UCC
Mexico	life + 20	1896, 1909	register, notice
*Monaco ©	life + 50	1952m	O. K. + UCC
*Morocco(French)	life + 50	none	(Berne)
*The Netherlands and possessions	life + 50	1899, 1909, 1922m	first publication
*New Zealand	life + 50(1)	1916m	first or simultaneous publication
Nicaragua	perpetual	Mexico 1908, B. A. 1913	O. K.
*Norway	life + 50	1905, 1909, 1910m	O. K.
*Pakistan ©		none	UCC
Panama	life + 20	B. A. 1913	O. K.
Paraguay	life	B. A. 1917	O. K.
Peru	life + 20	B. A. 1920	O. K.
*Philippines ©	28 + 28	1948m	(notice, deposit, and registration) UCC
*Poland	life + 50	1927m	O. K.
*Portugal	perpetual	1893, 1909	O. K.
*Rumania	life + 30	1928, 1947	O. K.
*Siam (Thailand)	life + 30	1921, 1938	first publication
*Spain ©	life + 80	1895, 1909, 1934m	O. K. + UCC
*Sweden	life + 30	1911, 1920m	O. K. (first publication)
*Switzerland	life + 30	1891, 1909, 1923m	O. K.

† 28 December 1912; hence 1913 is a more reliable date to use for determining copyright status.

	Duration of Copyright	Treaty or Proclamation	Foreign Status of U. S. Copyright Material
*Syria	life + 50	none	(Berne)
*Tunisia	life + 50	1912	first publication
*Turkey	life + 30	none	(Berne)
*Union of South Africa	life + 50(1)	1924m	simultaneous publication within 60 days
Uruguay	life + 40	B. A. 1919	O. K.
U. S. S. R.	life + 15	none	none
*Vatican City ©	life + 50	none	UCC
Venezuela	life + 30	none	none
*Yugoslavia	life + life of spouse, + children until 25	none	(Berne)

The International Copyright Union
(BERNE CONVENTION FOR THE PROTECTION OF LITERARY AND ARTISTIC WORKS

WITH A FEW EXCEPTIONS the leading countries of the world belong to the International Copyright Union. The United States is one exception; others are Russia, China, and all of the Latin American countries except Brazil.

There are two basic principles of the Union:

That the author who is a citizen of any unionist country or who first publishes his work in a unionist country, shall be granted in all countries of the Union the rights each country grants its own nationals.

That copyright in unionist countries shall not depend on any further formalities, such as deposit, notice, or registration.

The significance of this for the United States is that it is first or simultaneous publication in a unionist country that counts, regardless of the nationality of the author. By publishing in the United States and a unionist country simultaneously, an American author is protected in all countries of the Union. At the Brussels Convention in 1948 the International Copyright Union redefined simultaneous publication as publication within 30 days — not within two weeks, as does the British Copyright Law. Publication is defined as 'copies issued and made available in sufficient quantities to the public.' * Presentation, performance, recital, broadcasting (radio and television), exhibition, and construction (of architecture) are specifically stated not to be publication.

In many ways the Berne Convention, as it is popularly called, gives greater protection than the United States Copyright Law or UCC (see pages 111 f.). Also it is more explicit in come clauses than our law, and in every way than UCC. Between Berne countries its provisions, when differing from UCC provisions, are decisive, and it has the added advantage of a long period of successful operation. For these reasons many American publishers feel that even when full membership of the countries of the world is obtained by UCC, simultaneous publication in a Berne Convention country will be desirable to gain more extensive protection for works originating in the United States. Whether this feeling is justifiable or not remains to be seen; but until UCC is firmly established and is ratified by the majority of the leading nations,

* Holland has long maintained that publication implies manufacture.

110

the use of Berne through the back door of simultaneous publication would seem a safeguard for an American work likely to be tempting to foreign commercial exploiters.

When time of transportation makes it impossible to effect simultaneous publication here and in England, the best solution would seem to be to publish simultaneously in Canada. Since Canada is a member of the International Copyright Union, simultaneous publication there would secure copyright in all unionist countries. Since, however, Canada provides that unless a book is actually printed in Canada any Canadian firm may apply for a license to issue a Canadian edition, to be granted unless the original publisher elects to issue one himself within six months, the ultimate copyright status of the book is endangered.

The real solution may still be for the United States to become a member of the Union. The chief obstacles — our manufacturing clause (q.v.) and our formalities of copyright notice, deposit, and fee — have been somewhat relaxed in our ratification of UCC. Many people feel that it would be best to give up the manufacturing clause altogether. The next ten years or so should prove whether our fear of foreign competition has any real basis.

In most of the recent cases regarding copyright infringement under the International Copyright Union, Holland has been (from our point of view) the infringing country. But the fact that any one country does not respect international copyright is no indictment of the Union as a whole. By our joining it, American authors would at least be spared this bogy of what constitutes foreign 'publication' and what does not.

A Summary of Various Provisions of the Berne Convention

The International Copyright Union is based on a series of Conventions, of which the revised Convention signed in Brussels on 26 June 1948 is the most recent. (The text of the Brussels Convention is given on page 248.)

The purpose of the Union, simply, is to protect 'the rights of authors in their literary and artistic work.' The works protected include all those listed in the United States Copyright Act, and in addition choreographic works, pantomime, and architecture, about which our own Act is not clear. Works of applied art and industrial designs and models are protected if they are included in the copyright legislation in the country of their origin.

The individual countries also determine the extent to which political speeches, lectures, sermons, et cetera, can be reported without permission, but the author always retains the exclusive right to his lectures in a published collection.

Works published for the first time in any unionist country have the same

111

protection in all unionist countries as do those of nationals, without compliance with further formalities (such as deposit, registration, or copyright notice). However, the work must conform to the law of the unionist country 'of its origin.' For unpublished works, the country of origin means the country of which the author is a citizen or, in the case of architecture, the country in which it is located; for published works, the country of first publication, or, in the case of simultaneous publication, the country in which the copyright term is shortest. If a work is published simultaneously in a unionist and a non-unionist country, the unionist country is the country of origin.

'Published works,' as was stated earlier, are works that have been 'issued' and are available in sufficient quantities to the public. In other words, performance, recital, broadcasting by radio and television, exhibition, or construction (of architecture) does not imply publication.

Authors of non-unionist countries who publish their works for the first time in a Union country enjoy the same rights as authors of unionist countries, so long as the country of citizenship offers adequate copyright protection. However, if a unionist country finds that a non-unionist country does not offer adequate protection, the unionist country may restrict the rights of authors of that country. The unionist country then reports the fact to the Government of the Swiss Confederation (the administrative branch of the Convention), which thereupon advises all other unionist countries. For example, if a hypothetical country, Graustark, allows free-for-all piracy, France can restrict a Graustarkian author from obtaining French copyright, even though his books are first published in Paris; and all other unionist countries will be advised through the Swiss Confederation.

The Union recognizes the moral rights of an author to his work, and provides that even after assigning his work to another, the author may proclaim his authorship and object to any distortion, mutilation, or other modification of the work that would injure his honor or his reputation. The legislative means of guaranteeing these moral rights are left to the individual Union countries.

The copyright duration granted by the Union is the author's life plus 50 years, but if a unionist country has a longer term, the copyright duration of the country of origin is the maximum to be observed. The copyright terms of various countries are indicated in the list on pages 107–9. In a collaboration, the copyright term extends from the death of the last survivor; anonymous and pseudonymous works (if the author is really not known) are protected for 50 years after publication; posthumous works for 50 years after publication.

Translation rights are guaranteed (though individual countries may make certain restrictions about the time limit in regard to their national language), as are also reprint rights of novels, stories, poetry, and literary, scientific, or artistic articles originally published in newspapers and periodicals. Current religious, economic, and political articles may be reprinted throughout the Union unless such reprinting is expressly reserved by notice in the newspaper or periodical in which they appear. When they are reprinted, the source must be clearly indicated. Daily news is not restrictable.

Quotations used in literary, scholarly, scientific, or artistic works are regulated by the laws of the countries of origin of the book from which the quotation is taken and the work in which it is quoted.

Musicians and dramatists are granted performing, presentation, and recording rights, and protected against unauthorized performance or translation of their works. It is not necessary for published dramatic and musical works to carry any notice of the reservation of performance rights. Radio, television, and moving-picture rights are also granted to all 'authors,' to be regulated by the individual countries. However, in no case can the author's moral rights be ignored nor can he be deprived of remuneration for his work.

The Union expressly directs its protection against the unlawful making of 'other versions,' such as adaptations to a different medium, without authorization, credit, and remuneration. Literary authors have the exclusive right of authorizing 'public recital.'

'Authorship,' unless proved untrue, is assumed from the title page, and copyright is assumed to belong to the author. In the case of anonymous works and of pseudonymous works if the author is really unknown, the publisher is regarded as representing the author.

Countries outside the Union that assure these rights may accede to the Union on their request. The protection immediately applies to all works on which the copyright has not expired (i.e. it is retroactive).

Lectures
(SERMONS, RADIO ADDRESSES, ET CETERA)

Unpublished writings intended for oral delivery: Form C *(see page* 216*), deposit* 1 *copy, fee* $4.

UNDER THIS GENERAL CLASSIFICATION come monologues and radio and television scripts (not plays), sermons, even poems if they are intended for public recital and not for publication.

The deposit copy of material in this class should be clean, legible, and securely fastened together. It should have a title, corresponding with that on the application form, for identification purposes. In a series of lectures or radio programs, each performance must usually be copyrighted separately.

The author of a lecture, or of any other writing intended to be delivered orally, has the exclusive right of public rendition of his work. However, the Copyright Act says that his right is 'public delivery for profit.' Unlike dramatic work, it is not infringed by delivery to a non-paying audience. The author may copyright it or not; if he does not, it will be protected at common law.

The public delivery of a lecture is not publication, nor is radio or television broadcast. It can be published only by reproducing it in copies for sale or distribution — in which case it becomes a 'book.' The lecturer may deliver his work (for profit or not) as many times as he likes, and copyright it when he will. His hearers may make notes for their own use, but they cannot sell, publish, or copyright them, nor can they lecture from them for their own profit. A lecture constituting a memory course was infringed by another lecture using the same combination of ideas and treatment. It is not necessary to prove word-for-word duplication to win a case against an infringer.

If the 'lecturer' does copyright his work, and it is later published in book form, the lecture becomes a book (registered on Form A). The copyright term runs from the original copyright date of the lecture unless the material has been amplified or reworked; then both dates should be given in the notice.

A lecturer may use ideas expressed in other works; his property right rests in the expression and treatment of the ideas.

114

Letters

LETTERS ARE SUBJECT to statutory copyright only if published; then they constitute a book (Class A). Unless and until they are published they belong to the writer and may be protected by him at common law.

The publisher should beware of publishing any letters, not submitted by the person who wrote them, without written permission of all persons concerned. The rights of letter writers have for over 200 years been threshed out in court both in England and the United States. Alexander Pope sued the piratical and 'obscene' publisher, Edmund Curll, in 1741, over an edition of his letters that he said Curll was publishing without his permission. Though later biographers have disproved Pope's sincerity in the suit, the principle on which the action was based remains secure. Almost invariably the sympathy and decision of the court favor the author.

Whether the letters are business or personal, of literary merit or dull or trivial, the author — if he dies, his heirs — possesses the exclusive right in them unless he allows them to be read without restriction in public or to be published without copyright, in which case, of course, they are dedicated to the public. A telegram is in effect a letter. Sending a message by telegram is not publication and does not put the message into the public domain.

The addressee has a material right in letters he receives. Except in certain circumstances he may preserve them or not, give them away or sell them, will them if he likes, or read them to his friends in private. (The exception is the 'confidential' letter, so noted, in which there is a 'spiritual right' of privacy, vested either in the author, the addressee, or a third person. Love letters and fiduciary letters are in this class.) The recipient cannot read letters in public, however, without the author's express permission, or over the radio or television. In no case can he publish them for his own profit or benefit without the author's or heir's permission. The author of a letter can sometimes require the recipient to allow him to make a copy within a reasonable time — if the letter has not been destroyed.

Again, let the publisher — or any businessman — beware of quoting letters for advertising or publicity purposes without permission. A professor may say in an acknowledging letter that the textbook of which he has just received a sample copy is the best book on the subject he has ever read —

115

but if this is quoted in a circular without his permission, he has grounds for a suit. On the other hand, if a disgruntled author chooses to incorporate in his autobiography letters illustrative of his squabbles with various publishers, he is liable to a suit. Under common law it is necessary to have the addressee's permission, as well as the author's.

The only exception to the rule of the author's right in his own letters are letters of an agent to an employer, and of men in public office writing in official capacity. The Government can publish or refuse to allow to be published the letters of any of its officials written in an official capacity. The contents of a soldier's letter to his children, written just before he was killed in action in Korea, were ruled to belong to his estate so far as profits from their use by motion picture and music rights were concerned, although the material object, that is the physical letter itself, was the property of the two minor daughters to whom it was written. Also, any letters may be introduced in court without the owner's permission if it is necessary to prove legal points, justify action, or vindicate character.

License

IF AN AUTHOR WISHES TO TRANSFER to someone else (his publisher, a creditor, his wife, etc.) his complete ownership of a copyright, he assigns his title to the copyright and has the assignment recorded in the Copyright Office (see page 57); if he wishes to sell or transfer only a single right, such as that of dramatization or translation, he licenses the right in question, stating in a written document whether the license is exclusive, and whether it is limited in time, quantity, or territory. Whereas assignment is the complete transfer of ownership, licensing simply legalizes the doing of certain things that otherwise can be done only by the copyright owner. But the exclusive and perpetual grant of any right has been ruled to be a sale of personal property rather than a license. Motion picture rights and the publication rights of artists are thus often 'sold,' whether the author or artist realizes it or not.

Licenses may be distributed to many people, exclusively or non-exclusively. Some of the rights to be licensed are: book rights, serial rights (first and second), translation rights, dramatization rights, movie rights, radio rights, television rights, reprint rights, territorial rights. Although the Copyright Act makes no provision for the recording of licenses, the Copyright Office will record them in the same way assignments are recorded, and it is generally advisable to have this done.

The copyright owner assigning his copyright, whether he is the author or someone having otherwise acquired it, does so categorically and irrevocably. The assignee may reassign it or do what he pleases with it. A licensee has only an individual right in the use he has acquired: i.e. a license is not transferable unless so stipulated in the contract.

A licensee cannot sue on his own behalf; any suit for infringement must be made jointly with, or individually by, the copyright holder. When Nina Wilcox Putnam 'sold and assigned' 'all rights in and of' her article 'The Coastal Route to Florida' to the Curtis Publishing Company, she lost all ownership of the story. Although the publisher after publication 'reassigned' in writing to her all rights except American serial rights, actually the second transfer was not an assignment at all, but a license, since the assignment must be for everything or nothing. Hence the author became a mere licensee and could not sue for infringement.

Many authors agree in their contracts that the copyright shall be taken out in the publisher's name.* If, however, the author stipulates that the copyright shall be taken out in his own name, the publisher becomes the licensee of those rights that are granted to him in the contract, and the author retains and controls all other rights. For example, a poet would 'license' the printing of his poem in an anthology or compilation; this grants its use in future editions of that anthology, enlarged or modified, but not elsewhere. An artist may license the use of his drawing in a magazine, by having it carry a separate notice (in this case, ©, with the name of the artist). He would then retain all rights to his work except for magazine publication, unless his agreement included general reprint or other rights.

Foreign rights are usually transferred by license, although they may be by assignment. In the former case the foreign publisher may be allowed to bring out a limited number of copies of the translation, salable in a given territory, within a specified time, usually for a fixed fee or guaranteed royalty.

If a licensee publishes without a copyright notice the work in which he has rights, the copyright may be lost unless it can be proved that he has acted contrary to the terms of the contract. Thus, if a copyrighted novel *Wind Storm* were dramatized, and the dramatization published without a copyright notice, although the copyright on the novel would remain valid, anyone could use the dramatization as source material for a movie, a short story, or even another dramatization or another novel. Even 'Superman' lost the copyright on some of his exploits through faulty notice on licensed publication.

It is of utmost importance that every license should be explicit:

That it be exclusive or non-exclusive;
That it be limited or unlimited territorially;
That its duration, limited or unlimited, be stated;
That the licensee guarantee to copyright any resultant work in accordance with
    the terms of the Copyright Act.

* This is now done less often because of International Copyright complications —
i.e. the undesirability of having a book copyrighted by one publisher in England, another in Canada, a third in the United States, etc. In most foreign countries book-publishing contracts are licenses, not assignments.

Magazine Articles, Short Stories, Poems
CONTRIBUTIONS TO PERIODICALS AND NEWSPAPERS

To register a separate copyright: Form BB (see page 215), deposit 1 complete copy of the periodical, fee $4.

WHEN AN AUTHOR SELLS a story, article, or poem to a magazine or newspaper, his contribution, if it has never before been published, is usually copyrighted as part of the periodical. With the possible exception of his contribution's being expanded into book form, changing its design and expression fundamentally, any further use made of it must carry the date of the first copyright (i.e. that of the publication of the magazine) and unless the copyright is assigned and recorded in Washington it must carry the magazine's copyright notice. In other words, its copyright term originates with its first publication, and to retain its effectiveness must be renewed between the twenty-seventh and twenty-eighth year after that date.

The magazine can assign to authors (or others) the copyright of the individual contributions without vitiating the copyright of the periodical as a whole. This is the one exception to the 'indivisibility' of copyrights. However, the assignment must be made without reservation so far as that contribution is concerned, or the author is only a licensee. If, on the other hand, the author sells (licenses) his material with reservations — i.e. does not assign all rights — the copyright of the magazine does not protect his contribution. The proper procedure is to 'assign and transfer all rights, including the right to copyright the material,' with an added agreement that the magazine will reassign the copyright after publication.

If the author wishes his contribution to be copyrighted in his own name in the first place, he must arrange with his publisher to have a separate copyright line, placed under its title or at the foot of the first page on which it appears: 'Copyright (or Copr. or ©) 1955 by John Doe.' He then files an application for registration (Form BB) immediately on publication, depositing as soon as it is available a complete copy of the newspaper or magazine. It is not sufficient to file only the pages on which it appears. The fee is $4. In the case of a work published serially, each installment must have a separate registration.

If the copyright is not assigned to the author or is not taken out in the author's name, it remains in the name of the publisher-proprietor, and is presumably in trust for the author, except when the author has originally sold it outright to the publisher, waiving all rights. In that case the proprietor becomes the 'de facto,' not merely titular, assignee of the author, and can do what he likes with the material, licensing it or reassigning it at will.

It should be stressed that even though the magazine publisher is only the trustee of the author, future use of the contribution must carry the copyright in the publisher's name, unless the copyright has subsequently been assigned and the assignment recorded. If there is no assignment, any later publisher of the material must have the consent of the original magazine publisher. If the magazine publisher wishes to retain periodical or serial rights after the material is republished in book form, he should reassign the copyright to the author or the book publisher, obtaining a license to those rights he wishes to reserve. Although the book must then carry the copyright date of the earlier publication, if the assignment is recorded the name of the new copyright owner or proprietor may be used in the notice. (See also *Newspapers and Periodicals.*)

Manufacturing Clause

THE MANUFACTURING CLAUSE, modified when the United States became a Contracting State of the Universal Copyright Convention, still applies to works of U.S. citizens and 'domiciliaries,' to works 'first published' in the United States, and to the works of citizens and nationals of all other countries not signatories of UCC, unless first published in a UCC country. In essence, it stipulates that all books and periodicals in the English language, in order to secure full-term copyright protection in the United States, must be printed and bound within the limits of this country; or if they are produced from plates, the type must be set and the plates made here; or if by lithography or photo-engraving, those processes must be performed here. The restriction also applies to illustrations, unless they are scientific or artistic, the originals of which are located abroad. The exceptions are as follows:

1. Works in raised character (Braille) for the use of the blind.

2. Works produced in the United States by other processes than those enumerated above.

3. Works first published abroad, imported within 5 years of publication, that have obtained ad interim copyright (q.v., which then are allowed up to 1500 copies, if they bear proper copyright notice, but must be manufactured here within 5 years in order to obtain full-term protection).

4. Works of foreign origin by a citizen or subject of a UCC Contracting State, and works first published in UCC states (if not by a U.S. citizen or resident), if first published bearing the required UCC notice: ©, the name of the copyright proprietor, and the date.

It should be remembered that under the 1955 modification, although United States citizens and nationals may take advantage of ad interim copyright if their works are first published elsewhere, they cannot take advantage of UCC protection; that is, after 5 years, they must have United States manufacture to secure full-term copyright.

Foreign-language books published in other countries with which we have copyright agreements need not be reprinted here to obtain copyright, but they must carry a notice of copyright if sold in this country. Published plays in English and music (Classes D and E) are exempt from the manufacturing clause. Periodicals and newspapers printed in English must conform to the manufacturing requirements, but no affidavit is required. During the existence of an American copyright of a book in English, even an authorized edition manufactured elsewhere cannot be imported, unless protected by UCC and not of American origin or by an American author. If it is, by the consent of the proprietor, the United States copyright is invalidated and the notice must be obliterated. Notice of abandonment of copyright (dedication to the public) should be promptly sent to the Copyright Office.

An affidavit certifying that the book has been manufactured in conformance with the terms of the Copyright Act must accompany the application for registration of American books in classification A. An affidavit form is printed on the reverse of the application supplied by the Copyright Office (see *Affidavits*).

Maps

Form F (see page 220), *deposit* 2 *copies, fee* $4.

A MAP CANNOT BE COPYRIGHTED under classification F until it is published. However, a relief map may be classified as a 'scientific or technical drawing' and copyrighted before publication on application form 1 (fee $4, deposit a photograph or other identifying reproduction). Other unpublished maps are protected at common law.

For protection in the United States the notice on a map consists of the word Copyright or Copr. or © and the full legal name of the copyright claimant. However, the copyright sign, ©, and the initials or monogram of the claimant may be used if the name of the claimant appears clearly on some accessible part of the map. For protection under UCC, however, ©, the full name, and the year are necessary. So that they may be identified, the two deposit copies should bear a title corresponding to that given in the application. If the map is by a foreign author and published in a foreign country, only one copy need be deposited.

Detachable maps in book pockets are protected as a 'component part' of the copyrighted book, but it is advisable to have them carry a separate notice.

Copyrighted maps are infringed by copying even though the copy is altered slightly or not all details of the original map are shown.

To be eligible for copyright, a map must have some element of originality or show creative labor. The general outlines of the geographical units of the world are now largely in the public domain. A map taken from a government geological survey cannot be copyrighted even though it is modified to disguise its source. Hence although 'new editions' of maps may be copyrighted as a new work, mere adaptations of maps already available are not entitled to copyright. Some independent survey must be made. Government maps are all in the public domain.

If a map has a detailed 'key' or legend, or much explanatory material, either on the face or back, it should be copyrighted as a 'book' (A). This is true especially if its claim to originality lies in its literary rather than its graphic detail.

Moral Rights

IN MOST CIVIL-LAW COUNTRIES an author's 'moral right' in his literary or artistic work is recognized, and the work is protected against degradation, mutilation, and abuse. However, the author's claim to this right is not mentioned in our Copyright Act. In the cases in which it has been invoked it has usually been considered expedient to justify it by recourse to state laws or common law involving contract, unfair competition, fraud, or right of privacy. In the International Copyright Union, even after the assignment of copyright, the author has a certain 'moral control' over his work: he may claim authorship, and prevent the deformation or modification of his work in any way that would injure his honor or reputation. There is no mention of moral rights in UCC.

With the widespread adaptation of literary, artistic, and musical works to motion pictures, radio, and television, such rights are gaining increased recognition here. Theodore Dreiser brought suit in connection with the motion-picture version of *An American Tragedy,* but failed to find support largely because it was proved that he had not taken the opportunity offered him to discuss the scenario and make comment and suggestion.

However, Mrs. Prouty, the author of *Stella Dallas,* won the support of the court when she contended that her rights had been infringed by a radio program that used the title *Stella Dallas* for episodes that served to cheapen her novel. Although the defense contended that there was no 'competition,' the judge declared that the real offense lay in the injury to the author and the deception of the public. Oliver Curwood was upheld in his objection to having his name given to a story (motion picture) he did not write.

In order to insure protection of his moral rights, the author should incorporate into all licenses and contracts a clause indicating the extent of changes to be made for condensation (digest), stage, radio, television, or movie versions, and (if possible) that the final version is to be subject to his approval.

Understandably, moving-picture companies are the chief objectors to legalizing 'moral rights' — in fact, the clause in the Berne Convention causes them great unhappiness. They contend that when the author sells his work to be used in a new medium, the purchaser should have a free hand to exploit

124

it. In the circumstances, probably only the most successful and most sought-after authors are able to insist on an effective approval clause.

An author who publishes his work under a *nom de plume,* without copyright, cannot prevent its being republished under his own name, nor can he prevent the *nom de plume's* being used in connection with it (see page 168). In some states, however, he might be able to prove violation of privacy.

If an author assigns his title — i.e. transfers all ownership in his work — he has no further recourse whatsoever, except possibly to protect himself against libel. An artist who paints a mural for a stipulated fee, with no reservation of rights, cannot object if changes are made in his work after it has been completed.

125

Motion Pictures

Motion pictures, published: Form L-M, *deposit 2 complete copies and description, fee $4.*

Motion picture plays, unpublished: Form L-M, *deposit title, description, and 1 print from each act or scene, fee $4.*

Nonfiction motion pictures, unpublished: Form L-M, *deposit title, description, not less than 2 prints from different parts, fee $4.*

THE REGISTRATION OF MOTION PICTURES applies to the complete photographic film from which the picture is exhibited. Scenarios — the script or synopsis of a motion picture — are regarded by the Copyright Law as 'books' (q.v.), and hence cannot secure copyright until they are published. (Before publication they are protected at common law.) If the scenario is completely worked out with dialogue, stage directions, and other necessary material for production (i.e. in dramatic rather than narrative form), it may be classified as a 'dramatic composition' and can be copyrighted in manuscript on Form D (see *Drama*).

If a copyrighted unpublished motion picture (L or M) is later published, it must be registered again on the proper form (L-M) with the proper deposit and fee. The notice on the published picture should be that of the original date of the unpublished film.

The 'description' accompanying the deposit copies and application may be a synopsis, a press book, a continuity, or any other identifying matter. The deposit copies of a published motion picture (the reels themselves) may be kept by the Library of Congress just as are the deposit copies of books. If the copyright claimant wishes, however, he may arrange for their return by signing a contract with the Librarian of Congress. For information about this, he should write to the Exchange and Gift Division, Library of Congress, Washington, D.C.

The notice on a published film consists of Copr., Copyright, or ©, the year, and the name of the owner (© must be used for UCC protection). It should appear under or near the title heading and need appear only once. It protects all the reels of which the picture is comprised.

A single private or 'preview' showing of a motion picture on the screen is not 'publication,' but releasing of films for public commercial showing, on

126

a contractual basis, probably is. For many years the courts held that the general exhibition of motion pictures was performance but not publication, but in more recent cases the opposite view has been taken. In Blanc v. Lantz et al., 1949, the judge stated: 'The distribution and exhibition of these films in commercial theatres throughout the world in my opinion constitutes so general a publication of the contents of the film and its sound track as to result in the loss of the common-law copyright. The fact that the copies of the film were leased rather than sold does not prevent the distribution from constituting a "publication." ' (See also the UCC definition of publication, page 153.)

Copyrighted movies are infringed by being shown without permission (usually times and places are specified in a contractual license) even if not for profit. 'Flashing on the screen' has been declared by the courts a kind of 'copying,' so even private exhibition is infringement.

In motion pictures, the use of the title of a contemporary copyrighted novel is forbidden (not in the Copyright Law, but as unfair competition), even though a title itself cannot be copyrighted. The difference in practice here arises from the fact that the author of the copyrighted book might want to make a dramatization or motion picture of his novel, which would lose its value if another motion picture had already been released under its title. Even movies with closely similar titles are prohibited if they are competitive. The owner of a copyrighted poem, 'The Ballad of Yukon Jake,' who was arranging a motion-picture version of it, was able to collect damages when another movie was produced called *Yukon Jake,* even though the plots were dissimilar. In the case involving *The Gold Diggers of Paris,* the court ruled that the name would have to be changed 'unless they place upon every piece of advertising used in connection with the picture, and upon the motion picture film also, the words, in type as large as "Gold Diggers": "A production of Majestic Pictures Corporation, not based on Avery Hopwood's play or on the motion picture of Warner Bros. Pictures, Inc.," or some equivalent words . . .'

If the title is taken from a work in the public domain, the situation is somewhat different. Here anyone may use the title in any way he pleases, so long as he does not deceive the public.

When motion-picture producers want to use a title that has been used for a recent novel, short story, or poem, they usually offer to buy it, getting a release from the author and publisher. It should be stipulated in the agreement that it is the title only to which rights are given, and exclusively for motion picture use.

Motion-picture, dramatic, television, and dramatico-musical rights are

127

often hopelessly entangled and great care should be taken over contracts granting them. The 'new work' involved in preparing a novel, for example, for production in each medium entitles that medium to a new and separate copyright. *Madame Butterfly* had a separate copyright, and a different copyright owner, as novel, drama, opera, and motion picture, and 50 years after the original publication of the story in a magazine the court was still trying to disentangle the various rights. The Copyright Act is explicit: it is the new contribution in each form that is protected; but careless licensing of exclusive and non-exclusive rights inevitably results in confusion and often in litigation.

Authors of novels, plays, comic strips, dramas, songs, poems — and even artists and photographers — are prone to see infringement of their copyright in successful films more than in any other medium. Sometimes they are justified, but more often they read into the motion pictures a plot or character they believe to be their own but that really has no relation to their work. Frequently a man who has realized perhaps a few hundred dollars on his story is incensed and envious when he sees a movie on a similar theme reaping profits of Hollywood magnitude. Before bringing suit, however, he would do well to get a disinterested legal opinion. Moving-picture producers have good legal advice at every turn. The suing author or small publisher is liable to find himself paying costs, with only a sense of deflation for his trouble.

This does not mean that many suits against infringing motion pictures have not been decided in court in the author's or publisher's favor, nor that the author should fail to protect his own work by copyright. If there is a flaw in his copyright, and his book is potential movie material, he may be assured that the flaw will be discovered, to his disadvantage. If there is real evidence of infringement, the aggrieved party should by all means bring legal action, and should engage the best copyright lawyer available.

Music

Published: in the United States, Form E, deposit 2 copies, fee $4; foreign (pub-
lished with copyright notice), Form E Foreign, deposit 1 copy, fee $4,
or 2 copies and catalogue card, no fee.
Unpublished: in the United States, Form E, deposit 1 copy, fee $4; foreign,
Form E Foreign, deposit 1 copy, fee $4.

THE COPYRIGHT NOTICE FOR MUSIC must be on the title page or
the first page of music. It consists of Copyright or Copr. or ⓒ (ⓒ must be
used for UCC), the year of publication (or the earlier year of registration
of the unpublished music), and the name of the copyright claimant.

With regard to music, publication means 'sold or publicly distributed,'
not public rendition. Allowing a musical composition to be played in public
will not imperil the composer's rights at common law, but allowing it to
be recorded, and the records to be sold or distributed without restriction,
presumably will, according to recent decisions.

To secure copyright under classification E, words, if any, must be actually
set to music, not submitted separately or on a separate paper. A lyric without
music may be registered for copyright only after publication as a 'book'
(Form A). If it is later set to music it may be registered in Class E, but it
should carry both dates.

A complete copy of unpublished music must be submitted for deposit with
Form E, but the composer should not send the only copy, as the deposit
copy will not be returned. The copy should contain both a title and the
author's name.

The copyright term on unpublished music starts with deposit. If the
music is later published a new registration and deposit must be made, but
the date of the first registration is retained.

In registering new copyright material (i.e. substantial revision) the copyright claimant should be sure to indicate the new matter for which the new
copyright is claimed. The title and date of the previous registration, if any,
must also be given.

Music (Class E) is not required to be manufactured here, and music of
foreign origin may be registered for United States copyright either before

or after publication (Form E Foreign). The foreign copyright claimant of published music has the option of depositing 1 copy of the work and a $4 fee, or 2 copies and a catalogue card (see page 213). Under UCC of course, no registration is required, but since no expense is involved most foreign publishers will register for their own convenience.

Songs or dances with words and music, published in book form, even though illustrated, are 'music,' not a book. A book of folk dances, a hymnal (with music), a book of college songs are all Class E. The libretto of an operetta or musical comedy is dramatico-music or drama (Class D), not music. A collection of lyrics from a musical comedy or operetta, or a hymnal with words only, is a book, not music.

The rights granted to the copyright holder for a musical composition are: to print, reprint, publish, copy, and vend; to dramatize; to arrange or adapt to other musical forms; to perform publicly for profit; to license its use on records . . .* Operation on juke boxes is not 'public performance for profit' unless a fee is charged for admission as of this writing, but several proposals have been made to amend this.

Adaptations of music in the public domain may be copyrighted if the variations of rhythm, harmony, accent, or tempo are original and of musical workmanship. Minor changes, such as any competent musician might make, do not justify a copyright. Merely setting an alto to an old hymn would not justify a copyright. A Russian composition to which the English words were adapted received a copyright, but it applied to the words only. Anyone else was free to use the music.

Arrangements can be copyrighted, such as that of a song or dance for an orchestra, or the arrangement of an old folk song with new words and modern rhythm. In modern music, the author of the words and the composer are considered co-authors, and either can renew.

There is probably more altercation about musical infringement than any other subject in copyright law. Fortunately, book publishers and authors rarely need concern themselves about this field. Occasionally, a story will quote a bar or two of music as 'background' or atmosphere. Although the courts have declared this fair use, the book or magazine publisher will add to his own feeling of security if he has the copyright owner's permission.

Another field in which the paths of music and book publishers cross is that of books about music or composers, in which music is quoted. The publisher will do well to get permission for any quotation over several bars.

---

* The licensing of music for use on mechanical instruments is detailed in Section 1 (e) of the Copyright Law. Notice of use is recorded in the Copyright Office on Form U.

He could probably defend his position in court if he failed to do so, by demonstrating that such use was for illustration or criticism, but by securing permission in advance he eliminates the possibility of having to defend himself.

Be sure of the real ownership, and of the copyright date, of any lyrics included in an anthology. They are not necessarily in the public domain because the music to which they are set is old. Also, assignments of musical copyright are more general than assignments in other categories. If in doubt, have a search made (see page 164).

New Editions, Revisions, Reprints, and Reissues

Form A, deposit 2 copies, fee $4. Affidavit required.

IF A NEW EDITION of a published work is to carry a new copyright date, there must be new material justifying protection. Slight factual, stylistic, and typographical corrections are not enough, nor is the redistribution of the material by volumes or chapters. On application form A, the copyright claimant is asked to state what the new copyright matter is. New textual material, rearranged or improved editorial annotations, new appendices, new illustrations, new introductory matter, even a new or enlarged index of a long and scholarly work will justify a new copyright. It is the quality and importance of the revision and addition that matter, rather than the amount. A short story or magazine article enlarged into book length with new material and perhaps illustrations may be copyrighted with a new date as a reissued book, but mere 'colorable' additions, designed to prolong the life of the copyright, are not acceptable.

Only the publication date of the new edition is legally required to appear on the copyright page if a new copyright is obtained, as the Copyright Act regards works republished with new material as 'new works.' It is safer, however, to list the older dates, too, in order to avoid any semblance of 'deceiving the public.' Moreover, if the new material should later be judged by the court to be insufficient to justify a new copyright, notice would have been served that the basic material was protected by the earlier copyright. If the earlier editions differed in title or authorship, it is well to state the fact clearly on the copyright page: 'Fourth edition, © 1956 by Jane Doe Marston and Richard Roe; first, second, and third editions, Copyright 1948, 1952, 1955 by Jane Doe.

The Copyright Office has no obligation to examine the claim for a new copyright. However, if it appears on its face to be false, the Office can refuse to issue a certificate of registration.

A reprint is a new printing or reissue in which there is no new material added. It can be made only by the authority of the copyright owner either given in the original contract or by a new agreement. The fact that a book is out of print does not mean that it is in the public domain. If the original publisher has gone out of business, a search should be made through the Copyright Office to determine if possible the present copyright owner. Even this is not always conclusive, as some copyrights are only registered when threatened with infringement. It should be remembered that publication with notice establishes copyright, whether the copyright is registered or not. Unless an assignment of copyright has been made, the reprint must carry the notice of the original edition.

A mere reprint is not registerable for a new copyright, since it has no new copyrightable material. If there is a change of title, second registration is not required, but it is to the author's and publisher's advantage to notify the Copyright Office of the new title so that a cross reference can be made in the title file. Under a ruling of the Federal Trade Commission, a reprint or abridgment with a new title must carry the original title in 'an equally conspicuous place.' If it is an abridgment, the word 'abridged' must also appear on the front cover and the title page (see *Abridgments and Adaptations*).

It should be remembered that anything originally published as a 'book' (Class A) — a poem, a short story, an instruction sheet, a magazine article, and so on — if brought out in enlarged or modified form, is a 'reissued book.' This applies also to new editions or versions of 'books' in the public domain. In registering any new copyright, a statement of the new material must be given.

Newspapers and Periodicals

Form B (*see page* 214), *deposit* 2 *copies, fee* $4. (*Foreign, Form* A-B *Foreign.*)

THIS CLASSIFICATION INCLUDES magazines, daily and weekly newspapers, reviews, serial publications, journals, bulletins and proceedings of societies and conventions that appear more than once every year (the Copyright Office circular reads 'at regular intervals') and under the same title, and other material of this type ordinarily registered as second-class mail.

No newspaper or periodical (Class B publication) can be copyrighted until it is published.

Material in this class by United States citizens and nationals or first published here must be manufactured in the United States, but no affidavit is required. However, if there is any doubt whether the work to be registered is a periodical or book, it is safer to call it a book and send the affidavit (Form A). The lack of an affidavit cannot then serve as an argument to justify an infringement. Periodicals of foreign origin in the English language may, of course, take advantage of ad interim protection.

The publication date is that on which the issue is actually placed on sale or publicly distributed, not necessarily that recorded on the front cover (the date of issue). In other words, a monthly is usually placed on sale from three weeks to a month before the date that appears on the issue. The January issue is usually published (placed on sale) in the preceding December. The date in the copyright notice should then be of the old year, not the new.

Separate registration is required for each issue or number of a periodical, and a copyright notice must appear in each issue.

Under the United States law the notice must appear on the title page, the first page of the text, or under the title heading, which by general agreement seems to include the mast head. Foreign periodicals claiming protection under UCC are not limited to these places, but must have it so located as to give reasonable notice of copyright.

The title itself cannot be registered for copyright, but protection against similar titles of newspapers and periodicals in direct competition is more often accorded by the courts than in the case of a mere 'book,' especially

134

when the format as well as the title is copied (see *Unfair Competition*). The title of a periodical or newspaper may be registered as a 'trade mark,' but this registration does not protect the contents.

The copyright on any issue of a periodical protects all the separate articles contained in the issue if ownership has been transferred to it. The magazine may then assign the copyright of an individual article as if he held a separate copyright for it. The publisher may be thought of as holding the separate copyrights for each component part — often in trust for the various authors and artists. On request he will usually assign to the contributor the copyright on the individual piece.

If any contributions are to be copyrighted separately, they must carry a separate copyright notice (register on application Form BB, or if an advertisement of an article of merchandise on KK). If they appear later in book form, the notice must bear the copyright date of the periodical publication. If there has been no separate notice, it must also bear the name of the copyright owner of the periodical unless he has assigned the copyright to the author (or new publisher) and the assignment has been registered in the Copyright Office. Book publishers are often careless about having this assignment made before publication. Should the work ever come before the court, however, they stand the chance of losing the whole copyright, since no work can be claimed simultaneously by two different copyright holders, and the Copyright Act specifies that the assignee's name may be used only *after* the assignment is recorded. It is not the duty of the Register of Copyrights to check this, but of the author and the publisher.

Material that has previously been published must carry the original notice if reprinted in a periodical ('second serialization'). So usually should abridgments and condensations of copyrighted material. The notice should appear on the first page of the contribution. There must also be a clear statement that the material is an abridgment or condensation.

Sometimes the publishers of periodicals fail to change the year in the copyright notice of the January or February issue. This antedating of the notice does not invalidate the copyright, but will probably shorten the actual term of copyright, the usual practice in such cases being that of dating the copyright term from the last day of the year of notice rather than from its actual date of publication.

News as such is not subject to copyright, since it is 'fact' and therefore belongs to the public. However, if it involves 'authorship' in the way of editorial comment, conjecture, deductions, and descriptions, it is subject to copyright. If a newswriter publishes an account as news, although it is really his own invention, the copyright of the newspaper will not protect it, as the public has been deceived. Copyrighted lectures, dramas, sermons, et cetera (or those protected at common law) may be 'reported' in newspapers without infringement and without being thrown into the public domain. Others may then quote from the parts so reported, but only those parts. If the whole lecture is reprinted, and it is copyrighted, it must be by the authority of the copyright owner and must carry a separate notice.

Newspapers are protected by laws on unfair competition against piracy of their news by immediate competitors. They are not protected against other uses of the factual news itself, whether by other papers, broadcasts by radios, or fictionalizing or dramatizing by individual authors. Editorials, special articles, stories, recipes, cartoons, photographs, et cetera, published in newspapers are all protected by the copyright for the issue, but often carry a separate copyright line.

Notice

ANY PERSON ENTITLED TO DO SO may secure copyright for his work by publishing it with the notice of copyright required by the Copyright Act. The notice must appear in every copy published or offered for sale in the United States,* and must be in the English language. Books imported under ad interim copyright must carry a notice, although the deposit copies sent to the Copyright Office with the application need not.

For published literary, musical, or dramatic works, the notice must contain the word Copyright, Copr., or ©, the year of publication, and the name of the copyright proprietor:

© or Copyright 1945 by John Doe, Inc.

For UCC protection, © must be used rather than the other alternatives. Whether the date comes before or after the name is unimportant (see page 140).

For various types of art works (Classes F to K), © and the initials, symbol, or monogram of the copyright proprietor will suffice for U.S. protection (but not UCC), if his full name appears elsewhere on the work.

Minor variations, such as the inclusion or the omission of the commas before and after the year, or of 'by,' do not affect the validity of the notice. The omission of the date in Classes A, B, D, L, or M, does invalidate it, as does any variation of the symbol — c in a triangle or square, for example — in any of the classes.

In 'books' (q.v.) and published dramas by United States citizens and nationals — in fact in all books not relying on UCC protection — the notice must appear on the title page or the reverse of the title page (the page following it); in newspapers and periodicals, on the title page, or the first page of text of each separate number, or under the title heading (commonly interpreted to include the masthead, wherever it appears); in musical works, either on the title page or the first page of the music. UCC protection is secured if the notice is placed 'in such manner and location as to give reasonable notice of claim of copyright.'

---

* The law is not clear whether books published abroad (other than in UCC States) in a foreign language, and copyrighted but not offered for sale here, require a notice. One court decision has been in the affirmative, one in the negative.

137

In an anthology or compilation, the notice of the individual copyrighted parts should appear on the copyright page of the volume or on the first page of each selection. If there are too many for the copyright page, conceivably they can extend to the page following if no advertisement or text appears between them, but this practice has never been confirmed by court decision.

Advertising material may appear before the title page, providing the title page itself precedes the first real page of text. If there is no title page, the notice may appear on the front cover if the cover bears a title. A notice on the back cover is not effective.

One copyright notice in each volume or in each issue of a newspaper or periodical suffices, providing it is properly placed.

The year must be the actual year of publication (q.v.). If a book is published on Christmas 1955 and carries a 1956 copyright notice the Copyright Office may legally refuse to register it if the fact is known; even if it does, the copyright, if challenged, will be declared invalid. A January issue of a periodical published (actually distributed for sale) in December must carry the year of the December distribution. If the year given in the notice antedates actual publication, that is, if it is dated 1955 but not actually published until 1956, the copyright is not invalidated but the copyright period begins on the last day of the year of notice rather than on the actual publication date. (The copyright is not invalidated because, in this case, the public is the actual gainer.)

A story or poem published and copyrighted in a magazine and later republished in a book collection must carry its first copyright date unless it has substantial new material and a second registration. Even then it is wise to carry the original date in addition to the new one. If a copyright is assigned and recorded, the assignee may substitute his name in the notice. Unless it is recorded, he cannot do so. This applies not only to assignments by publisher to author, and vice versa, but also assignments between publishers, as when one publisher buys out another and takes over all existing copyrights, or when a book is reprinted by another house. Furthermore, unless the 'assignment' is a true assignment (i.e. without reservations), not merely a license, the original notice must be carried.

The American edition of a book originally published abroad, on which ad interim copyright was secured, carries the year of first publication abroad. This is not stated explicitly in the Copyright Act, but is the accepted interpretation of § 23.

The name in the notice must be the legal name of the copyright holder. It need not be the full name, if it is an individual; the surname and initials are

138

enough. A trade name is valid if it is legal in the state in which the work is published. In most states, a person can adopt any name he chooses without legal proceedings. However, if a pen name is used, and used for writing only (i.e. if the author does not have any bank account or business account under that name), some difficulty might conceivably arise. Although most copyright lawyers maintain that it is perfectly legal to use a pen name in the notice, and that nothing in the Copyright Act actually forbids it, the Copyright Office formerly discouraged the practice. If one is used, the application form should give both the pen name and the real name: Sylvia Duplaix (Jane Doe).

On publication, the name in the notice must be of a living person, if it is of an individual and not a corporation. If the author dies before publication, the notice must be in the name of his executor, administrator, or legatee as stated in the author's will, if the contract called for the copyright in the author's name. The publisher cannot substitute his own name as proprietor unless he can show that an assignment was made by the author before his death.

If a notice is omitted by accident in some copies, the copyright is not invalidated so long as the proprietor has made an effort to comply with the law. If it is omitted in all copies, or is wrongly placed, or incomplete, the copyright is invalid if the book has been published. If only a few copies have been released, the publisher may recall them and have a proper notice inserted. This can be done by a rubber stamp or even pen and ink. If too many copies have been distributed to do this, the copyright is lost. Later publication with proper notice will not remedy the situation. It is of no use to appeal to the Copyright Office in such a case, since the Office is bound by the terms of the law. Even if a certificate of registration should be issued, it would be declared invalid if its validity were ever challenged in court.

The Copyright Office is constantly forced to return deposit copies and applications because of the inadequacy of the copyright notice. The most frequent irregularities are:

1. Omission of the notice altogether. (If this is discovered *after* publication, and is omitted in all copies, the copyright is lost forever.)

2. Wrong year date of publication. (If the year antedates publication, it will probably be accepted with the understanding that the copyright period starts with the last day of the preceding year; if it postdates publication the copyright is probably lost if publication has already taken place, even though the Copyright Office may unknowingly issue a certificate.)

3. Name of copyright owner is omitted. (The word Copyright or © and

139

the date, without the name of the copyright owner, has no legal significance in this country, although it is sometimes used in books of foreign manufacture that do not have a United States copyright.)

4. The notice is misplaced.

5. The wrong copyright symbol is used. (The symbol is ©, not any variation or decorative design modelled on C. Any other symbol such as C in a triangle, C in a square, or just the initial C is invalid.)

6. The name, initials, monogram, mark, or symbol of the copyright owner is lacking, in works in Classes F to K.

7. The copyright owner's name is not given (Classes A, B, D, etc.) but only initials.

8. The date of assignment is given instead of the publication date.

On the form letter the Copyright Office incloses with material being returned because of faulty notice appears the following warning:

If publication occurs, by distribution of copies or in some other manner, without notice or with an inadequate notice, the right to secure copyright is lost and cannot be regained. In such cases it would serve no purpose to add the notice to copies distributed at a later date.

Except for UCC protection, few if any European countries require any copyright notice. The purpose of it, in the eyes of the framers of the United States Copyright Act, is to protect the 'innocent infringer.' All States belonging to the Buenos Aires Convention require a 'statement of reservation of property right' in any language. Since there is some question whether our copyright notice fulfils this requirement, many publishers feel that it is safer to include on a second line, 'All rights reserved.' This seems especially advisable if the copyright symbol © is used. Further amplification, such as 'no more than _____ words may be quoted without permission' may give some comfort to the publisher, but has little legal — or practical — significance.

Some people are bothered by the fact that Article III of UCC describes the notice as 'the symbol © accompanied by the name of the copyright proprietor and the year of first publication' whereas the usual order of the U.S. notice is ©, the year, and the name. Actually there is no discrepancy. In both requirements it is the *elements* of the notice that are defined, not the order. Although §19 of the United States Copyright Law reads 'The notice of copyright required by section 10 of this title shall consist of the word "copyright," the abbreviation "Copr.", or the symbol ©, accompanied by the name of the copyright proprietor, and . . . the year in which the copyright was secured by publication,' the last sentence of the same section gives the example 'Copyright, 19 —, by A. B.' Seemingly the order is unimportant.

Photographs

Published: Form J, deposit 2 copies, fee $4 (1 copy if by a foreign author and published in a foreign country, or 2 copies and a catalogue card).
Unpublished: Form J, deposit 1 copy, fee $4.

'A photograph which through arrangement of light, color, and grouping presents an attractive and pleasing picture . . . [is] entitled to separate copyright.' (Condé Nast. Pub. Inc. v. Vogue School of Fashion Modelling, Inc., 1952.)

PHOTOGRAPHS ARE REGISTERED for copyright on Form J, which calls for (1) the name and address of the copyright claimant; (2) the title of the photograph (which it must have, and which must be written on it in some place, for purposes of identification); (3) the name, address, domicile, and citizenship of the 'author' (i.e. the photographer or, if made 'for hire,' the employer); (4) if published, the place and date of publication; (5) information about new matter if there has been previous registration or publication.

Publication here means the distribution of copies of the photograph, for sale or otherwise, not the reproduction of the photograph in a book, newspaper, or magazine. (In the latter case it is protected by the copyright of the work in which it appears, or may be copyrighted separately, either as a 'book,' a 'print,' or a 'contribution.')

For registration purposes, every photograph should have a title, which must appear on the photograph.

For U.S. protection, published photographs should bear a copyright notice (q.v.): © with the initials of the copyright owner will suffice if the full name of the owner appears on the back of the photograph. The year need not be given. For possible UCC protection, the prescribed full notice must be given (but see pages 142 and 171).

If a copyrighted unpublished photograph is later published, a new registration should be made under J, with the proper deposit and fee. The copyright period begins with the date of the first copyright, and the notice should bear the date of the first registration.

Half tones and other photo-engravings are 'prints' or 'pictorial illustra-

141

tions' (Class K), not photographs (Class J). But postcards made from photographs are Class J or possibly K.

Since in some foreign countries photographs are not subject to copyright, UCC does not include them in the list of works for which protection is mandatory. In any State in which they are protected, however, the period of protection must be at least ten years. (See UCC Article IV, § 3.)

The ownership of copyright is somewhat different in the case of photographs from what it is in most copyrightable matter. When a commercial photographer takes a picture of Mrs. Jones for which she pays him, Mrs. Jones, not the photographer, is entitled to the copyright unless there is an agreement to the contrary: Mrs. Jones, the subject, is the 'employer,' and the photographer is working for hire. No use of the photograph may be made without Mrs. Jones's consent before it is published; but if she is an actress or public personality and uses it for publicity (i.e. distributes or publishes it without copyright notice) it can be used by anyone who wishes to use it, for purposes other than advertising or trade. Many states have laws protecting the right of privacy, by which no commercial use may be made of a portrait or picture of a living person without the person's consent. If a photograph of a child is being used, the written consent of the parent or guardian should be obtained. One copyright authority warns that the consent of the owner of an animal must be obtained if the photograph of the animal is to be published — otherwise the copyright will belong to the animal's owner, not the photographer.

Photographs not 'made for hire' may be copyrighted by the photographer even though they are of public buildings, statues, or other subjects in public domain. In 1936 the courts ruled that a photographer who takes a picture of a person (with that person's consent) or object at his own solicitation and expense and for his own benefit is entitled to the copyright. Of course, A's copyright does not prevent B from photographing the same subject, even from the same angle, if he wishes. Actually, the two photographs would differ slightly even if both photographers were experts. The lighting, the focus, the timing all help to individualize the resulting picture.

It is, however, possible to infringe by taking a second photograph of a subject of which the first has been copyrighted, although it is not usual. Such a case is reported in the *Copyright Decisions of* 1909–1914 (Gross et al. *v.* Seligman et al.): An artist took a photograph of a model, and having copyrighted it under the title 'Grace of Youth,' sold it to a distributor, copyright and all. Two years later he photographed the same model in a pose that was identical except for the fact that in the second photograph 'the model wore a smile and held a cherry stem between her teeth,' while

142

in the original she posed with her face in repose; the backgrounds were not identical, and there were some slight changes in the contours of her figure, but otherwise the photographs were the same.

The court ruled that this was not simply a case of taking two separate photographs of the same person; it was a deliberate attempt to make what, to the ordinary person, would seem to be the same picture. The court added, 'In this undertaking we think he succeeded.' The second photograph therefore constituted an infringement of the first.

Posthumous Works

THE COPYRIGHT OF POSTHUMOUS WORKS, i.e. works published after the author's death, can be registered in the name of the publisher, as proprietor, if this is in accordance with the contract for publication signed by the author before his death or by his legal heirs after his death. If the contract calls for a copyright in the author's name, and the author dies before publication, the copyright notice must be in the name of his estate or his administrator or his legatee. It cannot be in the name of the deceased author, even though he died on the day before publication. If the copyright notice is already printed with the author's name as proprietor, it should be corrected before publication; otherwise copyright registration will be refused. Even though the Copyright Office, unaware of the author's death, issued a certificate, if the copyright were ever challenged in court it would be declared invalid.

In the United States the unpublished works of a deceased author, if they have never been registered for copyright, may be indefinitely protected at common law if the author's legal heirs so desire. A newly discovered unpublished diary of a soldier in the Civil War, dead over fifty years, could be legally published only by the authorization of the soldier's legal heirs. Common-law rights cease only on authorized publication, registration, or dedication to the public by the author's legatee.

Works published posthumously and originally copyrighted by the proprietor are renewable by the copyright proprietor, not the author's next of kin or heirs, as are other works. (See *Renewals*.)

In some foreign countries posthumous works are protected for a given number of years after publication, not the usual 50 years after the author's death. In such cases the term of protection under UCC is that provided in Article IV, § 4: 'No Contracting State shall be obliged to grant protection to a work for a period longer than that fixed for the class of works to which the work in question belongs . . . in the case of published works by the law of the Contracting State in which the work has been first published.'

144

Proprietor

THE COPYRIGHT PROPRIETOR is the person in whose name the copyright is registered. He is the author or the assignee of the author; in the latter case he must trace his title to the author. However, the proprietor may hold only the legal title to the copyright, if the author remains the equitable (real) owner; i.e. he may take out the copyright for the author 'in trust.' This is usually the case when books are copyrighted in the name of the publisher, unless the whole manuscript was bought outright or assigned to him. Unless this is so, the proprietor, for all his 'legal title,' is really only a licensee of the author, and in case of a suit against infringers he must not only trace his title to the author but must have the author join him in the suit.

A proprietor's actual position depends on the terms of the contract. If he has book publishing and/or serial rights only, he is a licensee. If he has magazine rights only, he is a licensee. In every case he has only those rights specifically granted him by contract or agreement. But if the contract is an assignment of all rights, and the proprietor takes out the copyright, he remains the true owner, even though he later transfers all except magazine or serial rights back to the author (see page 117). The court ruled in a dispute over whether a magazine was the true proprietor, 'property cannot "revert" from one person to another unless the person from whom it "reverts" holds title to it.'

The proprietor may be the real owner as well as the titular proprietor also if he 'hired' the work to be done for him (as a newspaper or magazine has staff writers on salary); he is then the employer-owner. Often members of religious organizations pledge to donate their works to a common order; then the order (or its representative) is the proprietor-owner. It is worth repeating, however, that a proprietor can be a real owner only by tracing his ownership to an assignment (contract; transfer of *all* rights; outright sale) from the author, or to ownership of the common-law copyright.

The proprietor may be a person or may be a corporation, partnership, company, or organization. However, the proprietor's name under which the copyright is registered must be a real name, or a business name legal in the state in which the work is published. For example, if John Doe was planning a publishing company with James Ray, and filed a copyright application under the name Doe-Ray Publishing Company, but at the time of registration had not actually formed the company with Mr. Ray, he would be using a fictitious and therefore, in New York State, an illegal name.

An actual case similar to the imaginary Doe-Ray case was that of Haas v. Leo Feist, Inc. A man named Deutsch employed Haas and Cahalin, two composers, to write 'You Will Never Know How Much I Really Cared,' and copyrighted the work under the fictitious name of 'Haas and Cahalin Music Company.' The copyright was automatically invalid since the 'company' was non-existent. Later, when the song was infringed, Haas, the composer, was unable to win his suit for damages. The court declared: 'When the law required copyright proprietors to affix their names, it certainly intended only such names as they may use under the law of their domicile.' In a more recent case where the name of a subsidiary corporation was used in the notice rather than that of the true 'proprietor' with whom the contract was signed, the court was more lenient, but a qualifying circumstance was that the officers of the true corporation were the same.

A proprietor has no better status than the author from whom he derives his title. Hence if the author cannot claim copyright protection under our law (i.e. is a non-resident foreigner from a country having no copyright relations with the United States, or, perhaps, has already forfeited his common-law right) neither can the proprietor.

Ordinarily, a proprietor cannot renew copyright in his own name, as the renewal right belongs to the author (see *Renewal*). There are, however, certain exceptions to this:

Copyright of cyclopedic and composite works that were originally copyrighted by the proprietor is renewable by the proprietor. This may apply to books written by one person and illustrated by another, when the two are brought together by a publisher-proprietor and when the importance of the illustrations equals that of the text.

Works 'made for hire' are renewed by the proprietor, as are also in some instances posthumous works (q.v.); periodicals (excepting contributions bearing separate copyright or for which the copyright has been assigned back to the author); cyclopedic works (with the same exception); and works copyrighted by a corporate body that was not an assignee or licensee of the author.

In regard to renewals, 'the proprietor' has been interpreted as referring to the proprietor owning the copyright in the renewal year, not the original proprietor to whom the copyright was granted, if there have been subsequent assignments.

146

Public Domain

ANY PUBLISHED MATERIAL SOLD in this country that does not have a copyright notice is legally in the public domain. This is true whether publication took place in this country or anywhere else. The easy and obvious way to determine whether copyright exists for any book sold in this country is to look for the copyright notice. If there is none — Copyright (or, if published after UCC, ©), the date, and the name of the proprietor — there is no copyright. Even the presence of a notice, however, does not mean that everything in the book is protected by copyright. The copyright may apply only to the editorial comment, the annotation, the selection, the illustrations, or the arrangement.

Also in the public domain are works of which the copyright has expired. In the United States this includes all books published more than 56 years ago and many published more than 28 years ago, for which no renewal was filed. It also includes any book published either here or in a foreign country before 1909 (the date of our present copyright law) that had no United States copyright at that time. It also includes books originally protected under ad interim provisions, but on which the ad interim copyright has expired and no American edition has been manufactured, and those for which the ad interim copyright was vitiated by the importation of more than 1500 copies. If there is any doubt about copyright status, before making any use of any material published with a copyright notice the author or publisher should have a search made by the Copyright Office (see *Search*).

United States Government publications and official state publications are in the public domain, but not necessarily the publications of all government institutions and agencies (e.g. the Smithsonian Institution) or the writings or utterances of all government officials. The works of government officials that are not official publications may be copyrighted. Churchill's published speeches secured copyright protection when gathered together, edited, and published in book form, as did also Roosevelt's. Material that has previously been copyrighted does not lose its copyright by being included in a government publication, even though it bears no copyright notice. However, if it is *first* published in the government bulletin and carries no sepa-

147

rate notice it becomes a part of the public domain. For example, when after the First World War one publisher brought out an illustrated edition of *General Pershing's Official Report,* which had appeared in the newspapers, he could copyright the illustrations only. Another company brought out the same report with other illustrations. When the first company sued, the court declared, 'What the defendants [the second publisher] did was to learn by handling the plaintiff's pamphlet that there was a good market for the report, and so they imitated the plaintiff's attractive get-up therefor. This conduct may be called mean, but it is not punishable under the Copyright Act.'

News — the facts of current life and history — belongs to the public and straight reporting cannot be copyrighted. However, when news accounts carry, in addition to the facts, the author's deductions, descriptions, and comments, they are protected by the copyright of the paper.

Anyone can rework material in the public domain, creating a compilation, abridgment, adaptation, or 'other version,' which if it has sufficient originality may have a copyright of its own. If the changes from the original are immaterial and have not required judgment or skill on the part of the new author or editor, the resultant work will not be subject to copyright. The new work must have at least a 'distinguishable variation.' But no matter how successful a new version of work in the public domain is, it does not have a monopoly on the original material. Disney could not prevent the showing of a French film of *Alice in Wonderland* on the grounds of unfair competition.

A derivative work may be infringed, but to prove infringement it must be shown that the infringing work copied what was original in the first derivative work, not just the material that was in the public domain. Cases involving this type of infringement occur frequently in the field of music, where old songs are adapted to modern taste and, after their popularity is established, are copied by others. In one case a composer copied a Strauss waltz from *Die Fledermaus* and incorporated it in his work with no changes and no acknowledgment. When Romberg later used several bars from the same waltz, and gave credit to Strauss, the first composer sued Romberg for infringement. Naturally, his suit found no legal support.

Often the first edition of a work will go into the public domain long before a later annotated, revised, or elaborated edition will. If the borrower is careful to use only the material that was in the first edition he is safe, even though other editions carry much later copyright dates. A later revision or elaboration cannot prolong the copyright on the original material.

Works can go into the public domain by the author's abandonment of

148

common law or statutory copyright (allowing his rights to be infringed repeatedly without offering protest); by dedication to the public (deliberately authorizing publication without notice); and forfeiture of copyright (omitting the notice through carelessness, neglecting to register after request of the Copyright Office; or failing to conform to the law in other ways). Once a work is in the public domain, nothing can restore the author's rights. (See also *Common Law.*)

UCC is not retroactive in any Contracting State if a work is already permanently in the public domain in that State. A copyright notice in a work published before 1955 (or the date of accession of any particular Contracting State) will not protect a work that was in the public domain in that Contracting State at the time of accession. But a new version based on any such work is entitled to UCC protection of its new and original contribution.

Publication

THE ACTUAL CALENDAR DAY of publication is of the utmost importance in matters of copyright, since in the United States the whole term of protection (28 years plus 28 years' renewal term) starts with this day in all cases of published works. The application for renewal (q.v.) must be filed before midnight of the twenty-eighth year (a day of grace is granted, however, if the final date falls Saturday, Sunday, or a holiday — see page 160).

Books, periodicals, newspapers, maps, prints, and pictorial illustrations cannot be registered for copyright until after publication with the proper notice (q.v.).

Of works reproduced in copies for sale, publication may be defined as the authorized, unrestricted circulation, 'placing on sale, or public distribution of copies or reproductions.' The sale of one copy of an edition of even ten is legitimate publication. However, the work must be actually 'placed on sale' and available for purchase. A gratuitous gift to the public — for example, giving copies of the manuscript to a public institution where they are publicly circulated — may also be publication, but on this question authorities differ. Sending out review copies, or placing sample copies on display, however, is not generally considered publication.

For further amplification, publication is:

1. Selling or distributing printed copies (or a copy) to the general public.
2. Distributing or selling mimeographed, multigraphed, or typed copies to the public, unsolicited or on request.
3. Sending out copies on subscription.
4. Being printed in a newspaper, periodical, or magazine.
5. Being placed in a public library with no restriction against being circulated (this is sometimes disputed).
6. Of art, being displayed in a public place with no restrictions on being copied or photographed.
7. Of music, being widely sold commercially on phonograph records (still sometimes disputed).

8. Of motion pictures, being widely exhibited commercially (still sometimes disputed but generally accepted).
9. Of architecture, being opened to the public for inspection.
10. Of architectural plans, being printed in a book, magazine, etc., or being filed with the city building authorities.

Publication is not:

1. Distribution of a copy or copies (in manuscript, multigraphed, or printed) to a few limited known persons for a specific purpose (e.g. criticism or review) (= limited publication).
2. Public delivery or rendition, whether for profit or not.
3. Submitting a manuscript for criticism, possible publication, or appraisal (= common-law rights).
4. Selling a manuscript (the material object) if authorization to publish is not sold also.
5. Distributing acting versions to actors for rehearsal.
6. Broadcasting or televising.
7. Producing a play or playing music.
8. Exhibition (of art) in a gallery in which copying and photographing are prohibited.
9. Reproduction (of art) in gallery catalogue.
10. Privately exhibiting motion picture film (but wide commercial distribution of film generally is).
11. Displaying of maps.
12. Depositing of unpublished works (for registration) in the Library of Congress (Copyright Office).

In most countries, including the United States, countries of the International Copyright Union, and UCC Contracting States,* copyright of published works depends on protection granted in the place of 'first publication.' To secure copyright protection in the United States it is necessary for a foreign author publishing his book abroad to have it carry a UCC or United States copyright notice on its first appearance. If he publishes it without notice in Italy, for example, and allows copies to be imported for sale into the United States, the book falls automatically into the public domain and can never acquire a valid United States copyright. The only exception is books in the English language first published abroad on which ad interim copyright is secured. But if books in English are imported into the United States, either bound or in 'sheets' and sold here, they are 'published'; and if they carry no notice, even though an American edition is produced later it cannot receive American copyright.

* UCC also protects the works of 'Nationals' wherever published.

A work must always carry the date of its first publication in the copyright notice. If a book was first published in Scotland in December 1954, received ad interim protection, and was subsequently manufactured and published in the United States in February 1955, its copyright notice should read 1954.

If a publisher announces a book for January 1956, has it printed with a 1956 copyright notice, sends his copies to the Copyright Office for deposit with a January 1956 date on the registration, but has sold copies in his own sales room before Christmas 1955, or authorized their sale by book stores before Christmas, he has published his book in December 1955, with a false copyright date, and has lost his copyright irrevocably, should it ever be challenged in court. Even though the Copyright Office is unaware of his Christmas sales and issues him a certificate, should there ever be an infringement and the case be brought to court, his copyright could be declared invalid.

'Limited publication' has been the subject of much controversy and worry among publishers and authors — that is, whether sending out review copies, examination copies, advance orders to book stores, copies to agents to use in selling subsidiary rights, before the formal publication date constitutes *de facto* publication. It seems to this writer that much of the worry is unnecessary. 'Limited publication,' whether recognized by definition or not, has long been an accepted practice. To have copies available on publication in both California and New York, copies must be shipped (and billed) in advance. It is important that the receiver should be notified that the books are not yet published and must not be sold, displayed, or given away until the date of formal publication. They are then not 'distributed' *by the authority of the copyright owner* or his representative before the day set. In review copies and copies sent to agents, it would seem advisable to stamp the publication date and a warning not to distribute in the books themselves, but few publishers are willing to do so. 'Limited publication' of manuscripts has long been accepted by the courts. In White *v.* Kimmell et al., 1952, the court said, 'A limited publication that communicates the contents of a manuscript to a definitely selected group and for a limited purpose, and without the right of diffusion, reproduction, distribution, or sale is considered a "limited publication," which does not result in the loss of the author's common-law right to his manuscript; but that the circulation *must be restricted both as to persons and purpose,* or it cannot be called a private or limited publication.' (Italics ours.) In Stanley *v.* Columbia Broadcasting System (1950) the court defined limited publication as 'the communication of the contents of a work *under restric-*

152

tion.' It seems to this writer that sending copies of a book to *known persons* for a *definite purpose,* and *restricted against general distribution or sale* is limited publication.

Publication in a foreign country to secure copyright under the terms of the Berne Convention cannot be merely 'colorable.' Publication is making copies available to the public. Copies must actually be placed on sale, whether there is a demand for them or not. It is not enough in claiming simultaneous publication in England, for example, to send only six copies for deposit in the British Museum and special libraries. Some copies must be available for sale. In one case it was judged that 12 copies were enough to fulfil the requirements of public demand, but this should not be used as a criterion.

Under UCC, publication is defined as 'reproduction in tangible form and the general distribution to the public of copies of a work from which it can be read or otherwise visibily perceived.' It is assumed that since the sound track is an essential part of the modern motion picture, both picture and sound are protected if the film carries the UCC notice.

General sale and distribution in the United States, without copyright notice, under the United States law is dedication to the public. A work once so published loses irrevocably common-law protection and the right later to gain statutory copyright.

Quotations
(PERMISSIONS)

How MUCH CAN BE QUOTED without the specific permission of the copyright owner?

Probably no other question besets publishers — and the Copyright Office — so frequently. In a form letter the Copyright Office says cautiously but not very helpfully, 'One must use his own best judgment' — which is exactly what the quoting author and publisher want to avoid.

The Copyright Act is silent, the Copyright Office is noncommittal, and for the most part the courts have been evasive in defining just what 'reasonable quotation' is. However, there are a few facts to be gleaned from court decisions, from general publishing practice, and from books of copyright authorities, that will serve as guides for safe action:

1. Fair use (q.v.). The courts have conceded that there is a fair use of quotation from copyright works. For material quoted for critical, satirical, discursive, incidental, and scholarly purposes, permission is the exception rather than the rule, and most authors and publishers welcome it as free publicity. It stimulates rather than competes with the sale of the work from which it is quoted (unless it is adverse criticism, and sometimes even then). However, the author and publisher of a book making what they deem to be fair use of copyright material should be sure that their publication falls into one of the categories listed above. When Sigmund Spaeth defended his use of 'Ta-Ra-Ra-Boom Der E' in his book *Read 'em and Weep,* he said that it was for 'comment and criticism' — certainly fair use. In his preface, however, he recommended the book for use of the amateur performer, which immediately put it into a field competing with the sheet music of the song. It is not necessary to ask permission for what is obviously fair use, and to do so may result in embarrassment. If the original publisher or copyright owner says 'no' or asks an exorbitant fee, the person who wishes to quote dare not go ahead. But, if he does not ask, and he is sure the quotation is 'fair,' there is little likelihood that he will ever have any delay or difficulty.

2. Use in biographies, histories, and other scholarly or scientific works. Many publishers feel that quotations of over a specific number of words should be used only by permission of the copyright owner, that full credit

154

should be given to author, book, and publisher, but that no fee should be required. (If full credit is given for a quotation of limited length, probably no publisher would bring suit or make trouble, even though his permission had not been asked. However, the practice is not recommended.) The actual number of words that can be used in scholarly works without permission is interpreted variously by different publishers. One may say 50, another 200. It is safe to assume, however, that no quotation of over 500 words (about a page to a page and a half of text) should ever be used without permission. In some circumstances publishers feel free to ask a fee for quotations of this length, even when they are to appear in scholarly works and are fully acknowledged. Also, it is inadvisable to use more than three or four lines of poetry without permission, even in this type of work — publishers of music and poetry are often overly zealous in protecting their author's rights.

3. Use in anthologies, compilations, collections, symposia, digests, reprints, readers. No material should be used in works of this type without giving full credit, carrying copyright notice, and having the written permission of the copyright owner. For the quoting author's and publisher's safety, the fee for use should be fixed before the manuscript goes to the printer.

4. Use in periodicals and newspapers. It is dangerous in such media to use any material as an independent article or even a 'fill-in' without permission and credit, with the fee fixed. It might get by, but it also might cause embarrassing litigation and expense.

5. Quotations from foreign sources. As is stated elsewhere (page 147), material not formally copyrighted in the United States (unless protected under UCC) is legally in the public domain (q.v.). There is an ethical obligation, nevertheless, to ask permission for an extensive profit-making use of material still in copyright in other countries, especially for the purposes listed in paragraphs (3) and (4) above. There is less necessity in the case of those works listed in paragraph (2). If the use is for profit, the foreign publisher will probably ask a 'courtesy' fee.

In regard to books in foreign languages published before UCC that have never been offered for sale here, it is not always easy to determine whether they hold a United States copyright or not. It is safest to assume that those published in countries with whom we have reciprocal copyright agreements and that were published after the date of the agreement, are protected, especially books from Buenos Aires Convention countries. If there is any doubt, a search should be made through the Copyright Office (see *Search*), but it must be remembered that many South American books are not registered. If possible the foreign author or publisher, or representative, should be consulted.

If foreign material is used that is in the public domain in the United States but is protected in its country of origin (or under Berne or one of the South American conventions) the copyright proprietor's permission may still be necessary if copies are to be sold for export. It is well to bear in mind that both Canada and the Philippines are Berne Convention countries.

6. 'Limited' use. Any extensive typewritten, multigraphed, or privately printed copy, abridgment, outline, or digest of copyright material for distribution to school, church, club, or similar group should be made only with the consent of the copyright owner. The citation of the source is not enough. Copyrighted works are protected against unauthorized copying in any form, not mere publication. The copy does not have to be 'sold' to be an infringement of the original.

7. Radio and television use. Since 1953 'books' as well as other copyrighted material have been protected against unlicensed public performance, or exhibition, or presentation, for profit. Sponsored programs are obviously 'for profit,' as are sustaining programs if they serve to advertise or promote the network or system on which they are given.

8. Illustrations and art work. The copyright on such material depends on where the illustrations originally appeared. Even though no copyright notice is discovered, the work may be protected by an over-all copyright of the magazine, book, or other medium of its first publication. No illustrative material not definitely known to be in the public domain should be used without permission. Even though the subject of the illustration may be in the public domain (a Greek statue, or the Empire State Building), the reproduction of it — sketch, water color, drawing, etching, photograph, or the like — may be in copyright. Work of foreign origin in this field may enjoy full protection here. Pictures of living people should never be used without the written consent of the subject, because many states have strict laws protecting the right of privacy.

Usually permission to use an illustration applies only to a specific use. If the material is to be reprinted in any other outlet, a new permission must be secured. Credit lines may be set in very small type, at the margin of the illustration, but they must appear with the picture every time it is used, and especially in advertising or publicity.

9. Advertising, publicity, or any other commercial use. Not even one line or the author's name should be used without permission.

Fees: Many publishers have a definite scale of 'permission fees,' usually based on the number of pages and the author's popularity. However, some publishers are avaricious and some authors dislike to be quoted. If the fee for a quotation seems unreasonable, the best thing to do is to find a substitute for the material, if possible, or avoid direct quotation by paraphrase, discussion, and comment. All permissions should be cleared and the fees definitely fixed before the manuscript goes into work. The penalty for going ahead without this precaution is the possibility of being forced to pay whatever fee is demanded, reasonable or not.

In securing permission to use copyrighted works, be sure that the person granting the permission is really the copyright owner or his agent. If the copyright has been assigned, it is the assignee's permission that is needed. If it has been licensed, it is the copyright owner's. In the case of joint authors, one will do, but both is better. In the Sayers case against Sigmund Spaeth, referred to above, Spaeth had received permission from the original publisher of the song he quoted, and gave credit in his book to the author. But the first term of the copyright had expired, and Sayers, the author, had renewed it in his own name. In the *Firebird* case, the publisher gave a motion-picture company permission to use excerpts from the music in a sound film, but Stravinsky himself was not consulted and he claimed that his 'moral rights,' defensible under French law (but not the United States) were infringed.

In the case of any extended reprint or quotation, it is well to have in writing what specific rights are given: periodical publication, trade or text book, any other edition, et cetera. It should also be stated what territorial rights are included: British, Canadian, South American, et cetera, and how the credit line should read.

It is the author's responsibility to clear permissions unless the publisher voluntarily undertakes to do so.

Radio and Television

SINCE RADIO AND TELEVISION were unheard of by the framers of the Copyright Act, no exclusive classifications have been reserved for them. The copyright claimant must either decide which classification is nearest to covering his material, or rely on his common-law rights. Several circulars are issued by the Copyright Office that define the various applicable classifications.

Unpublished radio or television scripts that are not dramatic in form — that is, monologues, educational lessons, news commentary, panel discussions, et cetera — are best registered on Form C. To be acceptable for registration, however, they must be fully worked out, so that the program could actually be produced from them — not just 'ideas' for a program. If a recording on a film is made of a television program, it may be registered as a motion picture (non-dramatic), Form L-M.

Dramatic scripts for radio or television — worked out with dialogue, but again *not* just an idea — may be registered as Class D, drama. Musical and choreographic scripts if they tell a dramatic story also come within this classification. If transcribed on film, they may be registered on L-M.

Other material included in television programs may be copyrighted in their proper classes: music (Class E), art (G or H), and photographs (J). If the program is not filmed each script and the various component non-literary parts must be copyrighted separately.

Although the idea for a program as such, or the title, cannot secure statutory copyright, if the idea is concrete and unusual or the title is imaginative and unusual it may be protected under laws on unfair competition.

If a script writer is employed by a company, usually the terms of his employment make the company legally the 'author' of any work produced (i.e. 'author of work done for hire'). A free-lance script writer, however, is the legal as well as the actual owner of the common-law right in his work. If it is used without his permission after he has offered it for sale he usually can prove damage. If it is registered for copyright even after he sells it, he, not the buyer, is entitled to renew it at the end of 28 years.

Broadcasting and telecasting are not (as of 1955) 'publication' in terms of the Copyright Law. They do not end common-law protection.

158

Since 1953 literary works (i.e. 'books') as well as music, drama, lectures, et cetera, are protected against unauthorized broadcasting and televising, as indeed are all copyrighted works, including works of art, photographs, maps, for example. As such exhibition or performance is not publication, however, it is not necessary to insist on a copyright notice except on film transcriptions that are 'issued in copies for sale.'

Actors' rights in television and radio — popular stars who have gained a wide reputation — have been the subject of much controversy. The courts have not been entirely consistent about what is subject to protection against imitation and infringement and what is not. What protection there is comes, of course, under unfair competition, not copyright.

Renewals

Form R, (see page 226), no deposit, fee $2.

THE APPLICATION FOR RENEWAL of a copyright must be made within the last 12 months of the original term. If a work was first copyrighted 28 February 1930, the application must be in the Copyright Office before midnight 27 February 1958 — not just in the mails. In 1954, however, the Copyright Act was amended to provide a slight leeway in certain instances: 'When the last day for making any deposit or application, or for paying any fee, or for delivering any other material to the Copyright Office falls on Saturday, Sunday, or a holiday within the District of Columbia, such action may be taken on the next succeeding business day.' If the renewal is too late, the copyright expires. Many people misunderstand the wording of the law and believe that copyright renewal may be made any time within the named year, i.e. any time before 31 December 1958. This is definitely wrong. Also, a renewal application submitted 27 February 1957 would be invalid; the renewal privilege is not open until the beginning of the last year of the original term.

Under UCC, since the first term of United States copyright is longer than the minimum required, the formalities from which Contracting States are exempt do not have to be waived for the second term. The Copyright Office is not obligated to renew the copyright on a work that has never been registered there. UCC proprietors who want to be assured of renewal rights would therefore be wise to register the works on Form A-B Foreign immediately after publication.

A copyright renewal is a new grant, not an extension of the original term. The law specifies explicitly who may apply for copyright renewal:

1. the author
2. the widow (widower) or children, if the author is dead (if there are several children, they will be tenants in common)
3. the author's executor, if none of class two is living
4. if none of class two is living, and the author died intestate, the author's next of kin
5. the proprietor only in the cases listed below:

160

a. if the work was posthumous and originally copyrighted by the proprietor
b. if the work is a periodical and originally copyrighted by the proprietor
c. if it is a cyclopedic or composite work and originally copyrighted by the proprietor
d. if the original copyright was held by a corporate body other than an assignee or licensee of the author
e. if the original work was done for hire, and the employer was the original proprietor

The Copyright Office issues renewal application forms (see page 226) on which must be recorded the exact status (in terms of one of the classes listed above) of the person making the renewal. The fee for recording a renewal is $2.

The claimant's full name should be given in the application, not just 'J. Doe' or 'Mrs. John Doe,' but (Mrs.) Jane L. Doe. On the lines 'claiming as' should be written, 'author,' 'widow of the author,' 'child(ren) of the deceased author,' 'next of kin of the deceased author, there being no will,' 'proprietor of the composite work,' or whatever the status may be. The complete title of the book must be given as it was on the original registration, and any later change of title should also be indicated. On line 3 of the form must be given *all* authors of renewable matter: the illustrator, the writer of the lyrics of a song renewed by the composer of the music, any contributing authors of special parts or chapters. On line 4 are requested the original registration number, the date of publication, if it was a published work, or of registration if it was unpublished, and the original copyright claimant(s). No deposit copy is required.

In the case of work done originally for hire, such as writing produced by employees on a weekly salary, if the employer who originally copyrighted the work assigns his copyright, the new proprietor, not the original employer or his heirs, should make application for renewal. In other words, in the case of (5e) above, the present proprietor makes the renewal, not the original employer or proprietor.

A translation must be renewed in the name of the translator, not in that of the author of the original work. (But if the translation was of an unpublished manuscript, and done 'for hire,' the 'proprietor,' if he was the original author, may renew.)

In the case of co-authors, a renewal made by one is sufficient. This applies to composer and lyricist, to author and illustrator, as well as to collaborating writers.

If a dead author's affairs are in the hands of his executor, the executor

161

should make the application if there is no widow(er) or children, not the heirs or next of kin. It has been ruled by the court that the widow is entitled to renew before the next of kin even if she has remarried. If there are both widow and children, renewal may be made by one on behalf of all — even, according to a recent ruling, on behalf of the author's illegitimate children. In other words, though the renewal is made in one name only, all entitled to do so share in the benefits.

If a book is written by one person and illustrated by another, the author's renewal will be considered to renew the artist's work, as a trustee. If the book was originally copyrighted by someone other than the author, and the author is now dead, the renewal made by his widow, heirs, or executor, et cetera, will not cover the illustrations. The illustrator or proprietor will have to renew, depending on the facts of the case (true ownership); the illustrator cannot renew if he did the work 'for hire' — i.e. if he was employed to do them, on salary or for outright payment for all rights.

The renewal of the copyright by the proprietor of a periodical will not cover any individual copyrights that were assigned back to the authors, or on which separate copyrights were obtained. In each of these cases the author is responsible for the renewal.

If a renewal form is made out incorrectly, even though all the facts are given, the Copyright Office need not make the correction. It may return the form to the sender, with necessary information, and a new application must be filed. It is therefore imperative to submit the renewal application in plenty of time to allow for the correction of possible errors.

An author's assignee as such cannot make a renewal, but an author or his widow(er) may, *during the renewal year,* assign the renewed copyright, so that the proprietor may keep the notice in his own name. An author may also contract to assign the renewal after it is made, or to make it for the benefit of someone else. Copies issued after the renewal has been made should probably carry both the original date and the renewal date, although the law is not clear about this. It is suggested that the notice read, "Copyright 1918 by Dash Publishing Company; renewed 1946 by John Doe.' However, if the new copyright is assigned to the publisher *after* renewal, and the assignment is recorded, the notice may read 'Copyright 1918 by Dash Publishing Company; renewed 1946.'

The theory behind the renewal clause is that if the author made a bad bargain in his first copyright, he or his heirs may have a chance to reap some benefit from the second term. Actually it is often difficult to demonstrate how our system is an improvement over that of England, for example, where the term runs during the lifetime of the author and fifty years thereafter. In that system, although the author does not have the opportunity to remedy an earlier error, he is protected against losing his copyright through carelessness or oversight in making the renewal. The dramatization of Henry James's *The Turn of the Screw* (*The Innocents*) is a case in point. The United States copyright on James's work was allowed to lapse but the British copyright was effective. It must be conceded, however, that when the author's heirs make the renewal they are sometimes in a better bargaining position than if there were only one term, since they were not parties to, and therefore bound by, the original contract.

When the renewal year comes, the proprietor, publisher, or anyone interested, if he cannot get in touch with the author or his heirs, may file an application in the name of the person to whom he thinks the claim belongs, even if he is not certain of that person's address (or even of his existence). The Copyright Office will probably renew in the name of any beneficiary eligible under the Copyright Act. If there are two applications, at least the work is saved from going into the public domain, and the rival contestants can settle the matter between themselves.

Search

BEFORE ANY MATERIAL from a published book or periodical is used, in whole or in part, its copyright status should be determined. In the case of material from a book offered for sale in the United States, the simplest way to discover whether it is in copyright is to look for the notice. Generally speaking, if there is no notice, there is no United States copyright. But there is always the possibility that it may be an unauthorized reprint or importation, and to determine this the *Catalogue of Copyright Entries,* published by the Copyright Office and available in most of the larger public libraries, should be consulted.

If there is still doubt about the copyright of any material to be quoted, reprinted, abridged, translated, dramatized, or used in any other way specifically restricted by the Copyright Act, it is advisable to have a search made at the Copyright Office.

When a search is requested, all available facts should be furnished: the title, the author and any *nom de plume* he may have used, the copyright claimant, the publisher, the year date, and what the work is: book, drama, music, art, and so forth. If it was first published in a magazine or periodical, full details about that should be stated when known or ascertainable. It should also be stated if there may have been a change of title. If a search is to be made for an assignment of copyright, the name of the assignor, assignee, or both should be given, as also should be the copyright number if it is known.

The fee for a copyright search is $3 an hour, and the usual search takes about an hour or two at the most. Time will be saved by enclosing a money order for $3 or $6, according to the time it is estimated the search will require.

The fact that the Copyright Office has been unable to discover a copyright record for a particular work is not conclusive evidence that no United States copyright for it exists, especially in the case of very recent material that may not yet have been catalogued, of a foreign work, or of material that appeared first in a newspaper or periodical. Nevertheless, the fact that the author or publisher has attempted through a search to discover the copyright status of material he wished to use may prove evidence of his good faith in case he has unwittingly infringed.

164

Titles

TITLES CANNOT BE COPYRIGHTED. It is true that any work to be registered in the Copyright Office must have a title, but the recording of the title is for purposes of identification of the work, not to register the right of exclusive use to the copyright claimant. One need only look through a volume of the United States *Catalogue of Copyright Entries* to see that title duplication is the rule rather than the exception. The courts have held that the author of a copyrighted work is not entitled to the protection of its title unless it has a 'secondary significance' and has attained such wide recognition that the public would be deceived by its connection with another work, and the first author would be deprived of his rights of exploiting his own writing. That there is not more duplication of titles is the result of the very natural wariness of authors and publishers against having the public confuse a new work with one already on the market.

The opportunist sometimes tries to foist his work on the public as something that it isn't, through deliberate duplication or close similarity of title with a contemporary success. Against such people there is protection, not through copyright law, but through laws against unfair competition and fraud. Injunctions against duplication of this sort have been issued most frequently when they relate to newspapers and magazines, plays and moving pictures, rather than to stories, poems, and novels. Hemingway successfully prevented the use of *Fifth Column Squad* as a title for a motion picture. When the author of the 'Frank Merriwell' comic strips and novels found while his moving-picture version of the material was in production that a rival company was also planning a movie called *Frank Merriwell,* he had the production stopped by court injunction. The judge declared that a title that has become closely identified in the public mind with the work of a particular author may not during the life of the copyright be used to mislead. Even after the copyright of a widely known work lapses anyone using the title would have to explain that the material was not that of the original author. But the author of an unsuccessful play entitled *Shady Lady* could not prove damages against Universal Pictures Company, who produced a movie of that title some twelve years later. It was pointed out that the title had been used a number of other times for stories, novels, and even a motion picture; 'the prior use of the title by others did not bar either the plaintiff or the defendent from using it, because the copyright of a novel or story does not necessarily give the author the exclusive use of the title.'

The cases in which author and publisher may look for court protection of a title may be summarized as follows:

(a) A novel about political bribery entitled *The Toy Shop* published last year and still selling successfully. The copyright owner would probably be able by injunction to force a change of title of:

1. another novel of the same title, published this year
2. a play of the same title *on the same theme*
3. a movie of the same title *on the same theme*
4. a radio serial of the same title *on the same theme*
5. another novel *on the same theme,* with a title so nearly the same that the public would be deceived; *The Toy Shoppe, Toy Shops, Old Toy Shop*
6. if his novel has been successfully dramatized or sold to the movies, any other drama or movie of the same or very similar title, whether on the same theme or not

He would *not* be able to effect a change of title of the following:

1. a novel, play, or movie, even if on a similar theme, brought out years later, after his novel is out of print or no longer selling in any quantity
2. a short story, poem, or child's book (i.e. a work of another *genre*) with the same title
3. a satire or parody of his work, on stage, screen or in literary form, of the same or similar title

(b) The work is a juvenile, short story, or poem entitled *The Toy Shop*. Unless it has been dramatized or sold to the movies, the copyright owner would probably not be able to effect a change of title of any other work unless it was of the same *genre* as his, on a similar theme, and capable of deceiving the public. Even if his work has been dramatized or sold to the movies, he could probably not stop any other drama or movie with the same title unless the theme is so similar that it suggests 'palming off.'

(c) The novel, drama, or movie is entitled *George Washington*.

1. The copyright owner could not prevent the use of the title by anyone else, unless he could prove that the public was being misled into thinking that the competing work was his — i.e. that it is being passed off as the work of another. A competing *Abraham Lincoln* was prevented from being foisted upon the public during the time Drinkwater's *Abraham Lincoln* was having its initial success and with a great deal of publicity was touring the country.

(d) A copyright on a work entitled *Hamlet,* or any other title or phrase in the public domain, or based on any material no longer in copyright, does

166

not prevent anyone else from using the same title. It is in the public domain and none can use it to the exclusion of anyone else.

In general, to prevent someone else's using his title, the copyright owner should be able to show direct unfair competition (q.v.), preventing the full realization of the profits of his work, or that the public has been deliberately deceived or confused.

As already has been implied, the courts are much quicker to see unfair competition and wilful fraud in connection with title duplication of periodicals, newspapers, dramas, and movies.

In the case of motion pictures, no duplication is allowed of any title of a copyrighted work that is not purely descriptive. Producers now register their titles with a central bureau. In the *Shady Lady* case, mentioned above, the title had been registered with the Motion Picture Producers and Distributors of America by Columbia Pictures, and Universal had to get a waiver before they could use it. 'The Gold Diggers' suit is also an illustration of this principle (see page 127). In the case of a descriptive title, however, the copyright owner of a book entitled *The Test Pilot,* made up of a series of articles on factual flying experiences, was unable to prevent Metro-Goldwyn from using the same title for a fictional biographical film. If a movie is based on material in the public domain — a work no longer in copyright — or on history or biography, duplication in title will only be prohibited if the first work has had so great a success that the title has acquired a 'secondary meaning' (as in Drinkwater's *Abraham Lincoln*), so that the public will be deceived. In Ernest Hemingway's case contending that a film title *Fifth Column Squad* constituted unfair competition against his play *The Fifth Column,* the court declared:

It is equally true that, where a play has attained such popularity that its title has acquired a secondary meaning, one associated with or suggestive of the play, a rival producer will not be permitted to use or simulate the title, or any part of it, in such manner as to deceive or mislead the theatre-going public into believing that the later production is a motion-picture version of the earlier play . . . It is not essential to prove actual confusion, deception, or bad faith as a basis for injunctive relief to prevent the use of a name which is likely to lead to confusion.

In the case of newspapers and periodicals, direct competition is the decisive factor: the Philadelphia publisher of *Suburban Life* was able to stop by injunction the issuance of *Philadelphia Suburban Life,* which imitated it in appearance and subject matter.

A change of title does not affect the copyright of the work, but for his own protection against innocent infringers the copyright owner should have the new title recorded and the original title must appear on the jacket, copyright page, and title page of the new edition. This is not a matter of copyright law; it is required under fair trade laws. In an American edition of a foreign book, the original title should appear on the copyright page if it has been changed.

There have been many attempts to prolong the life of a literary copyright by registering a title or a pen name or the name of one of the characters as a trade mark. Sometimes such registration can be made, not through the Copyright Office, but at the Patent Office. Distinctive titles of radio and television programs are so protected (*Information Please, The March of Time*). In no case, however, can a trade mark protect the work itself, or prolong the copyright of a work once it has fallen into the public domain, i.e. after the copyright has expired. Every publisher who has been in business since the 1880's has probably heard of the Mark Twain case. Clemens tried to prevent the use of his trade mark (Mark Twain) on reprints of his works that were no longer in copyright, but the courts refused to sanction this.

An uncoined or non-fictitious title of a periodical is not exclusively the property of the 'first user.' In a dispute between two comic-book publishers the judge ruled: 'Use of a title which has acquired no secondary meaning and which is descriptive of the publication [*Radio News, Motor Record,* etc.] is open to all, and even if a secondary meaning has been acquired, a title can be used by others if additional words and differing combinations satisfactorily distinguish it [*Field and Stream, Forest and Stream*].'

In the 'Nick Carter' case, Street and Smith had registered *Nick Carter* as a trade mark of their detective-story weekly, devoted to various tales about the character Nick Carter. They did not copyright the magazine or the individual stories. When a motion-picture company produced a movie entitled *Nick Carter,* using the same character but in a new plot, Street and Smith had no protection against it. A registered trade mark would protect it against another periodical using the same name, but, as the judge ruled, literary property cannot be protected by a trade mark, or in any other way than by copyright. He went on to quote from the case of Black *v.* Ehrich:

Neither the author nor the proprietor of a literary work has any property in its name. It is a term of description which serves to identify the work; but any other person can, with impunity, adopt it and apply it to any book, or to the trade commodity, provided he does not use it as a false token to induce the public to believe that the thing to which it is applied is the identical thing which it originally designated. If literary property could be protected under the theory that the name by which it is christened is equivalent to a trade mark, there would be no necessity for copyright laws.

168

Unfair Competition

'UNFAIR COMPETITION' IN LITERARY MATTERS is usually characterized by the passing off on the public the product of one person as that of another (fraud and deception and 'getting a free ride' on the results of someone else's labor). It is most often appealed to in matters to which statutory copyright does not apply: titles (q.v.), ideas, stage business. It specifically protects 'property rights,' which in the Metropolitan Opera Association case the court defined as 'the right to acquire property by honest labor or the conduct of lawful business as much as the right to guard property so acquired.' So it has protected the exclusive right of the cartoonist to the use of the characters he has created (Mutt and Jeff); the right to take photographs and motion pictures (the Sharkey-Walker contest); the property right in good name, reputation, good will (Madison Square Garden; the Metropolitan Opera); the exclusive right to broadcast and televise (World Series, boxing matches): 'the granting of relief in cases where there was no fraud on the public, but only a misappropriation for the commercial advantage of one person of a benefit or property right belonging to another.'

The publication of 'Dr. Eliot's Five Foot Shelf of the World's Greatest Books' did not infringe on the copyright of 'Dr. Eliot's Five Foot Shelf of Books,' as there could be no copyright on the title or the idea; the original publishers of 'Dr. Eliot' won their suit, however, under the laws relating to unfair competition. As the court declared, 'the decisive fact is that the defendants are unfairly and fraudulently attempting to trade upon the reputation which the plaintiff has built up for its books.'

A magazine, *Adventure into the Unknown,* was protected against an imitator, *Unknown,* not because of the similarity of the title, but because its cover and format were so similar as to deceive the public. The acting personality of a performer — stage business, gags, mannerisms — is sometimes protected, sometimes not. As long ago as 1928 Charlie Chaplin was able to stop another actor from imitating his name (Charlie Aplin) and mannerisms; some other well-known motion picture, television, and radio 'stars' have also been successful since then, but the rulings of the various courts have been far from uniform. In many foreign countries protection of this sort is more general.

169

The two key questions are (1) whether the original author suffers loss (of sales or prestige); and (2) whether the public is deceived. As the court put it in one case, 'Plaintiff must also show, in an action for unfair competition, that the defendants are trading upon the plaintiff's name and good will and are palming off their goods upon his reputation.' However, although the second element, fraud, is still usually a factor, it is not absolutely requisite for it to be present in order for an author to obtain relief. When (before books were granted 'delivery' rights) a radio company read over the air in five successive programs a complete current 'best seller,' the author sued successfully in the state courts and recovered substantial damages. Certainly in this case the public was not deceived about the author or title.

The deliberate misappropriation of titles is often prevented on the grounds of unfair competition, especially when a movie uses the title of a novel or drama before the original author disposes of his subsidiary rights. 'Unconsummated' contracts are protected if material is rejected but later used. If an author presents a fully worked out idea for a radio or television series, he can often prove unfair competition if a closely similar series is later used by the company who studied and rejected his. So too can an author in many cases protect characters that he has popularized, and also his pen name.

The great differences in state laws on unfair competition make any brief discussion of it unprofitable. Unfair competition has nothing to do with copyright. It has much to do with the individual copyright owner's development and exploitation of his property.

The Universal Copyright Convention (UCC)

So THAT IT MIGHT BE ACCEPTABLE to as many countries as possible without running foul of local domestic legislation, the Universal Copyright Convention contains only the broadest and simplest provisions for the protection of an author's works. Basically it provides as follows: If a work is first published in a Contracting State, or is by a citizen or national of a Contracting State though first published elsewhere, it is protected in all Contracting States providing that at first publication it bears the notice ©, the name of the copyright owner, and the date (year) in some reasonably prominent place (for order of notice, see page 140). No other formalities are required except in case of legal action, and then failure to comply with them does not invalidate the copyright. The protection granted is that which each state grants to its own nationals and to works first published in its territory. The duration of the period of copyright is that granted in the State in which protection is claimed, but with certain exceptions it cannot be less than the life of the author plus 25 years *or* 25 years after first publication. (The exceptions are photographs and works of applied art, which in some States are not protected as artistic works; if they are, the period of protection must be at least 10 years.)

Unpublished works are also protected, either by statutory law, as in Great Britain and in the case of registered lectures, music, and drama in this country, or at common law.

Translations are protected, but a Contracting State may by domestic law limit the term of absolute protection to 7 years; after that if there has been no authorized translation into the national language or languages of that country, any national may secure a non-exclusive license to make a translation, with the proviso that a reasonable proportion of the royalties be allocated to the original author. The Convention is not retroactive to works already in the public domain in any specific Contracting State.

The works of nationals and works first published in any country must conform to domestic law.

This brief summary is over-simplified but it contains the essence of the Convention. An outline is given on pages 25–7, and the text itself in the Appendix, page 242. The following illustrative examples may serve as clarification.

If England has become a Contracting State, *Our Good Queen,* by John Englishman, first published in England in 1956 with proper UCC notice, '© by J. Englishman 1956' in some easily discernible place, will be protected in the United States (without United States manufacture, registration, deposit, or fee) for 28 years — i.e. till 1984. If before 1984 J. Englishman has conformed to our formalities, however, on application it will be entitled to protection for a renewal period also — i.e. till 2012. If it is first published in the United States, or its author is domiciled here, it must conform to all formalities, including manufacture to be entitled to United States copyright.

Our Good President, by Sam Yankee, first published in the United States, must conform to all domestic formalities to obtain United States copyright, but if it carries the UCC (and United States) notice, '© 1955 by Sam Yankee' (on the title page or page immediately following to conform to our law) it is also protected in all UCC countries, in most of them for 50 years after the author's death, though no State is required to protect it longer than it is protected in the United States. If Sam Yankee or his publisher failed to file a renewal application during the twenty-eighth year, no UCC countries would have to protect it after it had fallen into the public domain here (or 25 years after the author's death). If Sam Yankee *first* publishes his book in Canada, however, he must take out ad interim copyright and the book must be manufactured in the United States within 5 years to preserve his full term protection. But it will have protection in other UCC countries for 50 years after his death. It would also have full Berne Convention protection.

If *Our Good President* is simultaneously published (i.e. within 30 days) in the United States and Canada, it must still conform to our formalities for United States protection, but for other countries the one having the shortest period of protection will be the country in which it is 'first published.' If Sam Yankee died the day before publication UCC copyright would end in 50 years, not 56.

If after 7 years *Our Good President* (or *Our Good Queen*) had not been translated in Spanish, Sanchez Castello, a Philippine citizen having asked permission to translate it and been refused (perhaps the author did not like his terms) could obtain a license to translate it and Sam (or John) would receive whatever share of royalty the 'representative' allocated (see page

26); Spain and South American Spanish-speaking countries could import the translation if their local law permitted it — or other Spanish translations could be made by similar arrangement. But all translations would have to bear the original title and author's name.

The Universal Copyright Convention became effective on 16 September 1955. The first 12 Contracting States to deposit their instruments of ratification were Andorra, Haiti, Spain, the United States, Chile, Israel, the Federal Republic of Germany, Cambodia, Pakistan, Laos, Costa Rica, and Monaco; for later signatories see pp. 107–9.

To recapitulate the essential points about UCC:

1. A work of foreign origin, whether in English or a foreign language, if it is first published in a UCC state or is by a national of a UCC country, has full first-term copyright protection in the United States without complying with any of the formalities of registration, fee, or deposit, providing that it carries a UCC copyright notice from first publication.

2. A UCC proprietor may register his work on Form A-B Foreign if he wishes to do so; if registration is made within 6 months of publication, no fee is required if 2 copies and a catalogue card are filed.

3. U.S. citizens and residents cannot take advantage of UCC provisions to acquire U.S. copyright; they must comply with all U.S. regulations.

4. Works in the public domain in the United States at the time any foreign country ratifies UCC do not gain U.S. copyright upon that State's ratification.

5. Works that have been registered for ad interim copyright automatically acquire full first-term U.S. copyright without further formalities immediately after the ratification of UCC by their country of origin.

6. UCC protection comes into force in respect to each State 3 months after that State has deposited its instrument of ratification, acceptance, or accession.

7. A U.S. edition of a work of foreign origin protected under UCC requires no new registration but must carry the notice (©, year date, and copyright claimant) of the original publication.

Unpublished Works

A 'BOOK' (CLASS A) MAY NOT SECURE statutory copyright before publication. Until it is published it is protected at common law (q.v.). The cautious author who sends a copy of his manuscript of a book, short story, poem, or other 'literary' work to the Copyright Office before submitting it to a publisher only has it returned to him, with the advice to offer it for registration after publication with proper notice. It is vital, therefore, that an author should know specifically and definitely what publication consists of, from the point of view of the copyright law.

If the author of a text book has the manuscript of his first draft mimeographed and sells copies of it to his students, or, for that matter, generally distributes copies gratis, he has 'published' his book and is liable to lose his rights through publication without notice. However, he may recite his work in public (if, for example, he is a poet, story teller, or radio performer); he may send copies to his friends; or he may authorize a performance of his play without jeopardizing his rights. Publication, with respect to copyright, is exclusively the reproduction (or recordation) in copies that are sold or publicly distributed.

There are certain types of works which may secure statutory copyright before publication. Lectures, sermons, and similar works intended for oral delivery (including unpublished radio scripts) (Class C); unpublished plays and other dramatic works, or musical dramas (Class D); and unpublished music (Class E) can all be registered for copyright on the appropriate application forms, with the deposit of one copy. Works of art (Class G) and plastic works or drawings (Class I) can be copyrighted by proper registration and the deposit of a photograph or some other identifying reproduction. Unpublished photographs (Class J) may be copyrighted by registration and the deposit of one print. Various types of motion picture films (Classes L and M) may also be copyrighted before publication (but not motion-picture scripts or scenarios). On all classes of unpublished work, the registration fee is $4.

If the author of an unpublished work takes out statutory copyright, his common-law rights cease when his statutory rights begin. His statutory copyright dates 28 years from the registration of his work in the Copyright

174

Office. (This is the interpretation of the Copyright Office and the courts; the law itself is not explicit here.) If his work is published later — a collection of his lectures, for example (Form A), or publication of his play or radio dramas in book form (Form D) — he must register it again under the proper classification and pay a second fee ($4). This second registration does not affect the original date of the copyright, so far as its duration is concerned. However, if substantial new matter is included in the published version, a second copyright covering it should be registered, as it becomes in effect a 'new work.'

In registering an unpublished work, the deposit copy should be neatly typed, written, transcribed, or drawn in clean and legible form, and the pages fastened together. It must be complete, must have the author's name on it, and must have a title of some sort that corresponds to the one in the application. The title (q.v.) is not protected by copyright, but is necessary for purposes of identification. If a different title is used later for publication (or even if it is changed for the public presentation of a play, song, or radio script) it is advisable, but not required, to list the new title with the Copyright Office, for protection against the "innocent infringer.' A formal statement of change of title may be recorded if it seems desirable, just as an assignment is recorded (see *Assignments*).

To repeat, unpublished works, of whatever class, are protected at common law. They may not even be quoted by 'fair use,' as can published works. But once they are published, their rights at common law are lost, and if they are published without notice they are irrevocably in the public domain.

Part III

Questions on Copyright Practice

The questions in this section were submitted by publishers, authors, and agents as those most frequently arising and most vexing in regard to copyright. Duplicates were of course eliminated, but similar questions were included if the variation suggested a further complication. The author wishes to thank the many people whose co-operation made the section possible.

AD INTERIM COPYRIGHT

Who is the copyright claimant of a book being registered for ad interim copyright? (a) The author? (b) The English publisher? (c) The American publisher?

In most cases, the author, since most publishing agreements in England are licenses rather than assignments. If the book is a compilation or a dictionary, however, the true claimant may be the English publisher. It is hard to see how an American publisher could be the copyright claimant on the English edition of a book being registered for ad interim unless the common-law rights in the material were assigned to him before English publication.

Can books protected by UCC also be registered for ad interim copyright? Is there any advantage in registering them?

A book in English first published with proper notice in a UCC state (i.e. 3 months after that state has acceded) cannot secure ad interim copyright here but can be registered on Form A-B Foreign if the proprietor wishes to register it. The advantages are (1) that it can be registered in the first six months after publication without fee if two copies and a catalogue card are deposited; (2) that it is then eligible for renewal in 28 years, with the facts of its original publication on file.

If a book is registered for ad interim and not protected by UCC, what is the proper procedure to follow if more copies are needed after the first 1500 are sold and the American edition is not yet available?

There is no 'proper procedure' that will save the copyright. Either wait for the American edition or abandon copyright — i.e. notify the Copyright Office and have the notice deleted from any further copies that are imported.

179

What date should be used in the notice of an American edition of an ad interim book?

That of its first publication, the year of the foreign edition given in the ad interim application.

How does the change in the law (1955) in respect to ad interim affect American authors?

Formerly importation privileges were extended only to books or periodicals *of foreign origin* first published abroad; the italicized words are not included in the law as amended in 1955. Hence, for example, an American whose novel appears in England and is imported before book publication here need not lose his United States copyright by having British book publication before publication in the United States, so long as the United States edition is published within five years.

AFFIDAVITS

Must an affidavit be signed by an officer of the publishing company?

No, any 'authorized agent' may sign an affidavit.

If a professor mimeographs a text and sells it to his students before book publication, how shall the affidavit be made in registering the mimeographed edition?

Give as the name of the establishment the college office, or the name of the individual who did the work. It was 'published' on the day it was first distributed.

ANTHOLOGIES

Permission rights are usually given for a trade or special edition. If one obtains permission rights for a trade edition and then finds that there is a school market (textbook) for the same work, is one obliged to pay new permissions? Also, if the reverse procedure obtains, is one obliged to pay new permissions?

Unless otherwise specified, permission rights apply to all editions of an existing title. However, the author and publisher may protect themselves when asking for permission by stipulating that the rights requested are also for any future editions of the same title.

In regard to copyrighting plays, if an original play or an original translation of a play is included in an anthology, does the general copyright of the book protect the author's and the publisher's rights? Can a play be copyrighted separately?

If no copyright has previously been registered for the play, the copyright of the anthology will protect it, providing it has never been published before and providing the author has assigned his common-law rights in it to the owner of the copyright of the anthology. If the author wishes to reserve the copyright for himself, he may copyright the play in his own name either before or after publication of the anthology, if he has stipulated that his copyright notice be given in the text. A play, unlike a 'book,' may be copyrighted at any time before publication, whether it has or has not been performed publicly.

Why is there no uniform ruling governing the transfer of copyright and rights in regard to anthologies and collections of short stories?

The granting of permission to use copyright material in an anthology or collection is almost always a license, not an assignment. In other words, the copyright itself is not transferred, but only the right to use the material in a given medium. Hence every case is a special one to be determined by the copyright owner and the author or publisher of the anthology. The three important points to be stated in the written agreement granting the permission (to be signed by both parties) are:

1. In what editions the material is to be used.
2. In what countries it may be published.
3. That the copyright notice as it originally appeared be printed on the copyright page of the volume or on the first page of the text of the material in every case.

ASSIGNMENT

Why is it that a book publisher who is bringing out a book containing material that has previously been published in a magazine is obliged to get an assignment of copyright from the magazine even when the author stipulated that he was selling only magazine rights?

There can be only one existing copyright on any material and the book publisher has no legal right to place a copyright notice on a book containing material that is at the time registered in another's name — i.e. that of the publisher of the magazine. The law reads that the name of the assignee may be substituted in the notice after the assignment has been recorded. (See below.) If the author had had a separate notice on his magazine contribution and also had the book copyrighted in his name, no assignment would be necessary.

When a book publication has been made of a story that has previously appeared in a serial form, and the serial copyrighted as a whole in the name of the publisher, how important is it that the copyright assignment to the author be recorded in Washington prior to the publication of the book, the book copyright reading in the author's name? In other words, the law specifies that after the copyright has been assigned and the assignment recorded, the name of the assignee may be substituted in the copyright notice. If a book is published before this formality can be complied with, what effect has it upon the original serial copyright as well as upon the book copyright?

Legally, the copyright of the book is invalid. In 99 cases out of 100 when this law is broken, it is undetected. The hundredth time the copyright is lost. In other words, if you have something worth stealing, the unscrupulous person will search for every possible way to get it and still remain within the law.

In what instance is it advisable to get an assignment rather than a mere license? What is the value of an assignment that contains exceptions? Does this type of assignment allow the assignee to print the copyright in his own name without mention of the original magazine publisher?

If you have a license, you have only the rights specifically listed in your contract. In case of an infringement, the copyright owner has the right to sue — not you. All subsidiary rights also belong to copyright owner.

An assignment cannot have 'exceptions.' It must be complete, or else it is a license. A licensee cannot print a copyright notice in his own name, as he has no claim to the copyright. He must print the name of the real copyright owner. Thus the name of the magazine publisher who 'assigns' (licenses) back to the author (or to another publisher) only certain rights must appear on every future use of the material.

There is often confusion concerning first, second, and other serial rights and book rights to a manuscript purchased by a magazine.

The rights purchased by a magazine depend entirely on the individual contract. One or two of the leading national magazines buy all rights (i.e. have an outright assignment of copyright) and license the book rights to subsequent publishers. Usually, however, the various serial rights are disposed of separately, the author holding the equitable copyright even though the first serial publication is protected by the copyright of the magazine. In this case, the magazine assigns the copyright to the author after publication, or on demand. Sometimes, however, the magazine reassigns the copyright to the author but preserves 'magazine rights' (i.e. second serial rights). It is most important that such an assignment be carefully worded so that it will not in fact be a mere licence.

Another question frequently raised by writers is what permanent rights authors retain to basic material on central ideas that appear in stories. It

182

has been our observation that many writers attempt to resell ideas of this type, frequently to the embarrassment of editors who have purchased the original material.

It is possible to bind the author by the first contract not to write 'on a similar theme' or for a similar market for a given period. However, unless this is expressly stated, the author is free to use his idea in other forms where he will. Ideas are not subject to copyright.

CLASSIFICATION

I want to register my half-hour television script before I submit it. How should I classify it?

If it is dramatic (dialogue, etc.) as Drama, Class D. If it is monologue, as a Lecture, Class C. But it must be fully worked out — not just an idea for a program. The copyright protects what you register, not a series developed from it.

May a publisher copyright a book as an original work, four-fifths of whose content consists of original commentary, explanation, exercises, pupil drills, and line-cut illustrations which aim to clarify the remaining one-fifth of the content, which is textual material that had previously been published and copyrighted separately by the same publisher?

He may copyright it as a new work, but, to be completely safe, he should carry the notice of the earlier version also, to protect the part that is not new material.

How should a set of cards for teaching code flags be copyrighted? Should the container, which bears a description of the cards, and the page of directions be copyrighted also?

If the cards contain only pictures of the flags — i.e. only material that is in the public domain — they are not subject to copyright. The page of directions is, however, on Form A — as a 'book.' If the arrangement or selection of the cards has an 'original' element, they too are subject to copyright as a 'book.' If you wish to copyright the container also, be sure that it carries the proper notice (© and initials of the copyright owner will suffice, if the full name appears elsewhere). It must then be registered as a 'label' on KK (fee $6.00).

How do you copyright a book which has formerly been printed in article or short-story form and then enlarged to book size by the addition of illustrations?

Use application form A, and indicate the new material that has been added. The copyright notice should preferably include both magazine and book publication dates, with some such line, as 'Illustrated edition of a short story of the same title published in . . . .'

Is a manuscript copyrightable?

An unpublished manuscript of a sermon, lecture, address (Class C); a drama (D) or music (E) may be copyrighted. That of a book, poem, short story, et cetera (Classes A and B) may not.

Can a book be patented?

No. A title or a pseudonym may be registered as a trade mark, and in some cases the idea or subject matter of a book, such as a method of procedure, may receive a patent or a 'design patent.' This is true in the case of advertising catalogues, prints, et cetera.

How should a ballet, to be performed to music in the public domain, be classified?

If it is dramatic (tells a story), as D. If it is merely pictorial, you cannot copyright it unless it is published (printed and publicly sold or distributed) and classified as a book, Class A, or filmed and classified as a motion picture (M).

How should the following works be classified?
  (a) a compilation of English folk songs with music?
  (b) a book of music for children's dances, some still under copyright?
  (c) a book of new (uncopyrighted) college songs?
  (d) a collection of Gilbert and Sullivan lyrics?
  (e) an acting version of a drama in the public domain?
  (f) a separate copyright for a photograph first published in a travel book?
  (g) a new edition with new annotations, illustrations, and introduction of Jane Eyre?

(a), (b), and (c) all E, but in (b) the copyrighted songs should carry a separate notice; (d) would be A, if it were subject to copyright at all — i.e. had some 'originality' in the arrangement or selection; (e) would be D but the new material should be indicated; (f) may be copyrighted as an unpublished photograph (J) before publication of the book and carry its own notice in the book, or, if it has carried a separate notice it may be registered separately after the book is published; (g) would be A.

DEPOSIT

We add, from time to time, certain features to our Bibles, such as the 'Hour of Prayer,' or 'Bible Helps,' or 'Questions and Answers.' May we secure copyright on these by sending sheets of this additional material, or must text be bound in with Bible and Bible sent?

The Copyright Act specifies that a copy of the *best* edition be deposited, which means that the complete volume is required.

Is a copyright no good if you fail to deposit copies?

Failure to deposit does not invalidate the copyright until three months after the Copyright Office has demanded deposit (or six months, for a foreign publication). If deposit is not made on demand, not only is the copyright lost but the copyright proprietor is liable to a fine of $100.00 plus twice the retail price of the best edition. Foreign works protected under UCC, however, need not be deposited unless there is voluntary registration.

DURATION

Does suspension of publication of a copyrighted book during the life of the copyright invalidate the copyright?

Once a book is published, its continued publication has nothing to do with the life of its copyright. A book might be published in May 1956 and go out of print in June of the same year. Its publisher might go bankrupt. Its author might die in December 1957, without widow or child, and leaving no will. In 1984, the author's third cousin, who is his next of kin, may renew the copyright — which will then extend until 2012. If in the year 2000 a publisher brings out a reprint of this book without the copyright renewal claimant's permission, he is infringing and subject to forfeiture of his product and payment of damage.

Under the English Copyright Law, what is the duration of copyright secured by a publisher of a composite work, such as a dictionary or encyclopedia?

'A juristic person' who is the copyright owner of a cyclopedic work controls the copyright for 50 years after publication.

Under UCC will we have to protect foreign works for 50 years after the author's death when we only protect our own for 56 years?

No, unless the copyright is renewed they will be protected here for only 28 years of the first publication; if it is renewed, for 56 years. No Contracttracting State need give greater rights to citizens of other States than it gives to its own citizens or to works first published in it, nor need it protect a work longer than it is protected in the country of origin.

FAIR USE

To what extent may an editor, in writing a story about a columnist, incorporate in that story without danger of copyright infringement the entire

185

column of that day for the purpose of dissecting and analyzing the columnist's views? Does this fall within the doctrine of fair use?

It would not be safe to use an entire column without permission; it is doubtful if it is 'fair use' to quote any single unit in full. It would be much safer to use parts of various columns, breaking them after every 100 words or so with commentary and interpretation — or to get the columnist's permission. Understandably a columnist could prove competition, republication, and definite copying if his whole day's work were reproduced in one piece, for whatever motive.

In a story about songs, may an editor take whole verses from each of several songs and use them for purposes of illustrating differences between the songs current in World War I and those current in World War II, for example?

See preceding query. It is seldom safe to quote a whole stanza without permission, although it is sometimes done without penalty. However, the fact that cases of this type so often come before the courts proves that time and trouble will be saved by getting permission first. Most copyright owners will regard quotation for such purpose good publicity and give permission gladly. If one does not, you may congratulate yourself on having discovered the possible source of an unpleasant copyright case, and find some other song to quote.

How far can one reprint a poem in a critical analysis of poetry of various periods or of various authors? For example, may an editor use as much as one of four stanzas in such a story?

See the questions above regarding the use of a complete 'unit' without permission. If the stanza is broken by interpolation or exposition, it would not be so likely to bring objection. If the article is really a critical analysis of contemporary verse, it would probably be uncontested even if the whole stanza were used, but it is the occasional 'crank,' the 'ninety-ninth' person who creates the hazard. One contemporary author settled out of court for $1000 for using two lines of verse without permission — probably if he had fought the case he would have won, but he would also have a disagreeable time of it. The publishers of poets and musicians are jealous of their wares. It takes but a little effort to ask permission; it is good practice to do so for more than two or three lines of verse.

Is it necessary to get permission or make acknowledgment if in a book for popular consumption I retell in my own words certain facts about, for example, economic conditions in the time of the Revolutionary War gleaned from some study written for the scholars, assuming that I follow my source

186

closely enough for experts in the field to prove my dependence on it?

If you use a copyrighted book for your source material without doing any further research or checking, you are copying, even though you use your own words and not the author's. You are making 'another version' of his work, and that right is granted exclusively to him. Make your 'version,' give credit, and get the author's permission. He'll usually give it with pleasure. If he doesn't, you can always dig back into the sources he used — though it does take considerably longer time.

One of the most frequent problems is how far it is permissible to quote from a current copyrighted book or article a poem or song. Authors frequently insert in their stories — and indeed they make it an integral part of the story sometimes — a quotation of a verse from a song, perhaps a complete stanza of four lines.

The two most pertinent cases involving this sort of quotation are the McEvoy case, quoted on page 91, and the Spaeth case, quoted on page 154. In the first, the courts upheld the author who used a copyrighted song for background use; in the second, they decided against an author who used a full stanza, *with* music, in a book that might conceivably compete with the original author's interests. In another case, that of Karll *v.* The Curtis Publishing Company, the complete chorus was given, but without music, of the Green Bay Packers' football song in an article about the Packers — 'Little Town that Leads 'em' — published in *The Saturday Evening Post.* Credit was given to the author of that song, but even so he brought suit. In giving the decision in favor of the publishers, the court declared, '[To determine fair use] the courts must look to the nature and objects of the selections made, the quantity and value of the materials used, and the degree in which the use may prejudice the sale, diminish the profits, or supersede the objects of the original work.' In this case, the quotation was declared to be 'incidental' and fair use. 'Fair use' is a ticklish subject. Unless you want to run the risk of spending time and money defending your right of 'fair use' (and few publishers do), it is much the safest policy to get the author's consent.

FEES

Will you give a scale of fair fees for permission to reprint material from other publications? If not, could some sort of guide be included?
It is impossible to give a uniform rate of fees to be used by all publishers. In the first place, it would probably be illegal, smacking of 'collusion.' Secondly, a uniform rate would not be desirable or sensible. Why should a text-

book publisher demand the same fee per page as the publisher of a best-selling short story? Or of a first-class popular poet? Also, if a whole unit is used (short story, article, poem, book) the fee is reckoned on the unit, not by the page.

A uniform consistent scale of fees within the individual publishing house, however, is desirable and a time-saver: a rate per page and a rate per unit, with a sliding scale based on (possibly) four contributing factors: (1) the popularity of the author; (2) the date of the copyright; (3) the use being made of the material; (4) the individual author's attitude about being quoted.

Are only certain classes of foreign works (not UCC) given the privilege of depositing two copies instead of one and the fee? No mention is made of this on some of the application forms.

No, the privilege applies to any published work of foreign origin registered within 6 months of publication, if a catalogue card is sent also.

ILLUSTRATIONS

If material (a book) is copyrighted by the author, does that include illustrations contained in the book, too?

A single copyright notice on a book protects all copyrightable material in it. If the text is by one person and the illustrations are by another, the author of the text may be considered as taking out the copyright in trust for the illustrator. For purposes of renewal, however, the illustrator's name must also be entered on the line in the application form calling for author (line 3).

Is the use of photographs on jackets of books regarded as ordinary publishing or as advertising?

Anything on a book jacket is advertising and, if it is not in the public domain, should not be used without written permission. If the book jacket carries no copyright notice, anything on it, such as an illustration from the book, should carry a credit line.

Do rights on photographs survive the subject's death? Can a photograph of any deceased person be used in advertising?

A photograph, if it is unpublished and has never been registered for copyright, is protected by the common-law rights of the subject if it has been taken on order, or of the photographer, if he has acquired the subject's permission by payment or otherwise. These rights pass on to his heirs on his death. If the photograph has been copyrighted, it is protected by the copyright owner (the heir of the original owner, on his death) for the statutory term. Even if the photograph has been 'dedicated to the public' (i.e. published without notice) its use both before and in some states also after the death of the subject depends upon the laws on privacy of the state in which the owner resides or in which it is used. Most states have laws respecting the living individual's 'right of privacy,' though the degree of protection and the interpretation of privacy varies widely.

INTERNATIONAL COPYRIGHT AND BOOKS OF FOREIGN ORIGIN

List all the countries that subscribe to our copyright laws, and any special regulations that cover each country.

Following the article on International Copyright Relations is a list showing countries having reciprocal copyright treaties or agreements with the United States (page 107). In many of these countries if a work is copyrighted in the United States it is protected in the treaty country also. Some, however, require first publication and/or the observance of formalities, as is indicated in the list. UCC countries protect the works of nationals of other UCC countries without further formalities. Any country belonging to the International Copyright Union will respect the copyright of any American book that is published for the first time, or simultaneously with its first American publication, in a unionist country. To secure protection under International Copyright Union the author should arrange through his publisher to have his book simultaneously published in Great Britain or Canada.

The duration of the copyright is governed by the country of origin, but if publication occurs simultaneously in a unionist country and a non-unionist country, the unionist country governs the term. In most countries it extends for 50 years after the author's death.

Most South American countries belong to the Buenos Aires Convention, according to which publication in any signatory country, with a notice of the reservation of rights, protects a book in all signatory countries. Nevertheless almost all countries have individual formalities that authors 'first publishing' there must observe. To make sure of South American rights it is well to deal through an authorized South American agent. The Copyright Office from time to time issues circulars on our copyright status with foreign countries. These may be had on request.

What's to prevent any foreign publisher, whether in a UCC country or not, using a UCC copyright notice? Since the UCC notice is the same as

189

a U.S. notice, how can we tell if a book really has a legitimate copyright here or not?

There is nothing to prevent a foreign publisher's printing '© John Doe 1956' on his books any more than there is to prevent his printing 'Copyright John Doe 1956.' So far as United States copyright is concerned, however, the following facts should be kept in mind:

1. If the work is in English and the country of origin is not a UCC country and no application for ad interim registration has been filed, the notice is false in respect to the United States and presumably customs could bar copies from being imported. If copies did enter the country, however, a work bearing the notice © John Doe 1955 and *Printed in Canada,* by a Canadian citizen, for example, would be in the public domain here if no ad interim registration had been secured, since in 1955 Canada was not a contracting State of UCC.

2. If the work is in a foreign language and the country of origin has a reciprocal copyright relation with us, publication with notice establishes its copyright in the United States; the formalities of registration and deposit are often not observed even now unless the work is expected to have some sale here or is one that is likely to prove marketable in some other medium (translation, motion picture, recording, television, and so forth). A U.S. notice is therefore legitimate, and since © is now a legal U.S. notice, as well as UCC, presumably there could be no objection to its use.

3. The UCC status of any work can be determined by comparing the date of publication and the date of that country's accession to UCC (or the accession of the country of which the author is a national). UCC is not effective until three months after the accession of the state in question.

Please explain what the relation between American copyright and British copyright is and what are the regulations governing British copyright.

Although United States copyright is based on the earlier British law, there are today several fundamental differences.

(a) UNPUBLISHED WORKS:

All unpublished works of British subjects or residents are protected in Britain by statutory copyright rather than at common law. In the United States, 'literary works' are protected at common law until publication and only works capable of public performance and execution (lectures, music, drama, art, et cetera) may be copyrighted before publication. Unpublished works of this type (i.e. those that may be copyrighted here before publication) if copyrighted in the United States, are automatically protected in Great Britain, but only for the duration of their American copyright (28 plus

28 years). If they are later published they must conform to British copyright requirements.

(b) FORMALITIES:

The British Copyright Law requires no formalities, such as notice and registration, but does require the deposit of one copy to the trustees of the British Museum within a month of publication, and, if requested, one copy each to certain other Government and University libraries: Bodleian (Oxford), Cambridge, Edinburgh, Trinity College (Dublin), and Wales. Failure to deposit does not invalidate the copyright but makes the publisher liable to fine.

(c) PUBLICATION:

In Great Britain this is defined as 'the issue of copies to the public,' and for copyright purposes first publication is considered to be the same as simultaneous publication — i.e. within two weeks.

In the United States publication means the sale of copies to the public, or distribution of copies to the public, and if ad interim copyright is secured for a book in English published abroad within 6 months of its first publication, the American edition may be published any time within 5 years from the original publication provided no more than 1500 have been imported.

(d) DURATION:

British copyright, for most published or unpublished works, extends for 50 years after the author's death. For unpublished copyrighted American works, however, the term of our own law applies. American works first (or simultaneously) published in Great Britain are protected (presumably) for 50 years after the author's death, even though their copyright in the United States expires before that time.

(e) RIGHTS:

Radio, performance, and mechanical reproduction rights are secured to literary works in Britain, as are all other rights that are secured in America. Choreography and architecture are given greater protection in Britain than in the United States. Britain also protects some 'moral' rights not recognized here.

(f) INTERNATIONAL COPYRIGHT UNION:

Britain is a member of the International Copyright Union, and also has a copyright agreement with the United States, articulated in 1915. Works first published in the United States are not protected in Great Britain unless they are published there simultaneously or are first published in another unionist country.

Now that UCC is in effect, can we forget about simultaneous publication in

Canada, 'All Rights Reserved,' and other things not demanded by our own law?

Not until every country in which we want publication is a signatory. Canada gives us Berne protection; *All rights reserved* and other formalities are necessary in many non-UCC Latin American countries.

In cases where a publisher formerly imported unbound copies of books, and is now having the book completely manufactured in this country, can the book now be copyrighted or does the fact of previous importation prevent copyright?

If the foreign edition was sold in this country without copyright notice, it is now in the public domain — i.e. cannot be registered for copyright. If it was protected by ad interim copyright, however, and the five-year period has not elapsed (or the country of origin has become a signatory of UCC) the copyright will be extended to full term.

It has been our experience that British publishers expect courtesy fees for the use in this country of non-copyright material which is protected in the British Empire. It occurs to me that this may not be known to some of the publishers in the United States.

Foreign publishers do usually ask fees for the use of material in copyright in its native country but not in the United States, just as United States publishers sell foreign 'rights' on works that have never been copyrighted outside of this country. There is no 'legal' basis for the fee in either case, but convention serves to prevent the unauthorized use of unprotected works.

Not infrequently a request to quote from some book is referred by the publisher whose name appears on it to publisher in England, from whom a reply cannot be expected in time to keep within publication schedules. Since an English copyright has no legal standing in this country unless there is also an American copyright, is there any reason why I should not go ahead with use of the quotation, provided there will be no sale abroad?

There is certainly no reason if the quotation is not more than a few hundred words, say, and is in a scholarly, scientific, or discursive work. In a work of this type you would of course give credit to author, book, and publisher. For a long quotation, or one in a compilation, anthology, or for commercial use, it would be safer to wait for permission from the English publisher. Even though no sale abroad is anticipated, if copies should sell in Canada, say, the English copyright owner would have a legal claim for damages.

Fairly often a book appears in England and then, a considerable time later, in the United States. Has it any copyright in this country? I am thinking of some of the early books of authors like Kipling and Masefield — the latter's Salt Water Ballads, *for example.*

Before the extension of ad interim protection to 5 years, if the English edition appeared earlier than six months before the American edition, generally speaking there could be no United States copyright. However, there are possible exceptions, such as in the case of books published during the First and Second World Wars, while the time requirements were waived. Any book sold in this country without a copyright notice (U.S. or UCC) can never have a valid copyright here, whether manufactured here or not.

Do you consider that it would be desirable, in securing international copyright, to publish in England or Canada simultaneously as well as relying on UCC?

Until all nations are UCC signatories, it would seem wise to secure Berne protection also by simultaneous publication in a Berne country. It also is wise to carry 'All rights reserved' for Latin American protection.

How can one determine the date of copyright on a book of songs published in Europe before UCC?

If it was published as a 'book' in England or any British country it will probably be listed in *Whittaker's Reference Catalogue of Current Literature,* complete sets of which are available in most large libraries. The publication date is given in the title index. In most European countries a song would be in copyright during the lifetime of the author and (usually) 50 years thereafter, regardless of the time of publication. (See the copyright duration for various countries on page 107.) The collection of songs would be protected during the lifetime of the editor or person making the collection, or, if owned by the publisher, for fifty years after publication.

I have in my possession two books printed in French which appeared originally in Paris around 1800 (*eleven years before our copyright agreement with France*) *and in each there are* 1928 *copyright notices. Can one publish a book in a foreign language without copyrighting it at the time of publication, and then take out a copyright at a future date?*

Copyright is obtained by first or simultaneous publication with notice; the time of United States registration and deposit (if no copy has been demanded by the Copyright Office) is immaterial. The Copyright Office says:

A French book, that is, a book by a French author, originally published in France in 1880, could not under any circumstances be copyrighted. In the first place, no foreign author not domiciled in the United States was entitled to copyright before the Act of 1891, and in the second place, Section 7 of the present Act expressly provides that no copyright shall subsist in any work which was published in this country or any foreign country before July 1, 1909, and was not already copyrighted. There is a penalty provided in Section 29 of the Act for placing a copyright notice with fraudulent intent upon a work which is not copyrighted, and also a penalty for knowingly issuing, selling, or importing any article bearing a notice of copyright which has not been copyrighted. It is always difficult to prove fraudulent intent, but I think it might not be too difficult to prove knowledge of the law as against a person who put a copyright notice on a work by a French author published in 1880 in France.

Of course the copy bearing a 1928 copyright notice may be a 'reissued book with new copyright material' — i.e. the copyright may protect revisions, editorial equipment, or other material not in the original book.

Please explain how English 50-years-after-death termination affects us with regard to works published more than 56 years ago here. If they are in the public domain here, what about Canada?

A United States Copyright extends for 28 plus 28 years. The fact that a book is still in copyright in England after that period does not continue its legal protection in the United States. The book is in copyright in Canada, however, for the duration of its English copyright term. In the Berne Convention the copyright on a book published simultaneously in two countries need never be longer than in the country of its origin — i.e. the country of which the author is a citizen. But if it is a case of a union country and non-union country, the Union is country of origin. Hence if we publish simultaneously in England or Canada we are protected there and in other International Copyright Union countries for 50 years after the death of the author, even after the work goes into the public domain here.

Will you please mention the copyright requirements and protection in regard to translations, made by an American author, of books originally published in a foreign country and not yet published here? For example, if an American wants to translate, say, an Italian book published in Italy and have that published by an American publishing house, what copyright restrictions apply to his doing the work?

(a) If the book is registered for copyright here, he must get permission for the translation from the copyright owner; ownership of the translation would depend upon the terms of the agreement.

(b) If it has been sold here without copyright notice, it is in the public domain; he may translate and copyright the translation. However, to protect his translation outside the United States he would do well to get the permission of the author or foreign proprietor and to pay a courtesy fee if one is demanded. Even so, his right to translate is not exclusive, since the book is in the public domain.

(c) If the book has never been sold in this country, and he does not

194

know whether it is in copyright here or not, he should be careful. Publication with notice establishes copyright whether the copyright is registered or not. Books not sold in the United States do not need a notice. Most authorities believe that the first publication must have a notice, but the rule is not established. The would-be translator should not only get in touch with the foreign publisher but should also have a search made by the Copyright Office. If he is sure there is no copyright, he can then go ahead, as under (b) above.

NEW EDITIONS, REPRINTS, AND REISSUED BOOKS

What extent of revision or enlargement is needed to recopyright a book whose copyright has not expired? that is, claim a new copyright in a re-issued work?

The important thing is that there be new material of sufficient importance to justify a copyright in itself (see page 132). Looked at from the point of view of the would-be infringer, would there be any appreciable benefit in using the second edition rather than the first edition, without fee, when its copyright expires?

Can a mimeographed edition of a foreign book secure copyright if published here simultaneously with the foreign book? Will it satisfy the terms of the Copyright Law if ad interim copyright has previously been secured?

Yes, if it is actually published here — i.e. sold or distributed to the general public — and the formalities of notice, registration, and deposit are all duly observed. The means of reproduction (manufacture) are not important so long as it is manufactured in this country.

How may an individual secure international copyright for his work if he does not have a foreign publisher?

In UCC countries, publication with proper notice is all that is necessary. In Berne countries not belonging to UCC a book must be published simultaneously in an International Copyright Union country. If he cannot arrange for this through his American publisher his only recourse is to have it published in England or Canada for a fee, privately. This can usually be arranged through any of the better literary agents handling foreign rights, but it is apt to be expensive. The usual procedure is to sell a small number of sheets of the American edition, and have a new title page tipped in.

What is the procedure and how is the copyright notice handled where a new edition of a book is published with an entirely different title from that used in the original edition?

If there is no new copyright material in the new edition justifying a new copyright registration, there is no legal requirement to advise the Copyright Office. However, according to a ruling of the Federal Trade Commission the original title must appear wherever the new title is used — the cover, the title page, the beginning of the story, the jacket, et cetera. On the copyright page the notice should read:

Copyright 1940 by John Jones
Originally published under the title *The Apple Tree*

In order to keep the official record straight, it is advisable to inform the Copyright Office of the change of title.

If there is new copyright material, the law requires only one notice. However, the publisher protects himself by having the notice on the copyright page read:

Copyright 1944 and 1946 by John Jones
Originally published under the title *The Apple Tree*

If it was originally published serially the notice might read:

Copyright 1952 by John Jones
Published serially in *Westerly Quarterly* under the title _____.

How do you copyright a book which has formerly been printed in article or story form and then enlarged to book size?

If the copyright owner of the magazine publication is different from that of the book, the copyright should be assigned and the assignment recorded. Otherwise the notice should read:

Copyright 1946 by Blank Publishing Company
Based on a short story 'Winter Rain,' copyright 1945 by Magazine Publishers,
    Inc.

I've had a great deal of difficulty in securing permission to reprint the work of deceased authors, in cases where their books have gone out of print. In one recent instance the publisher of a particular book no longer had a single copy on his shelves, and knew nothing about the book. Is it safe to reprint in such cases without specific permission, would you say?

The first thing to do is to have a search made by the Copyright Office to find out if any assignment of copyright has been recorded or if the copyright has been renewed. Even if the publisher is still the legal owner, an effort to find the author or his heirs should be made. If this sounds like unnecessary expense and precaution, remember that it is more expensive to have to defend yourself in a suit for infringement and in addition possibly sacrifice all the time and expense that have gone into the production of a book.

If the copyright of the book may not have expired — that is, if it is less than 56 years from the date on the copyright notice— it is not safe to reprint without permission, even though the original publisher himself seems apathetic.

May a publisher make application for registration of a reissued book in which the revision is solely the substitution of obsolete matter by matter found in a more recent copyrighted book published by the same publisher?

Yes, but the copyright notice should bear the dates of the first edition of both books as well as the year date of the new edition. If two different authors are involved, credit should be given to both.

When a book has been published serially and the formalities of copyright assignment duly complied with before publication of the book, and there is no new matter in the book to be copyrighted that did not appear in the serial (which of course is unusual), should the book be filed for copyright registration upon publication, which in effect might be termed a double registration?

No, but the assignment should be recorded.

If revisions are made and new copyright is not applied for within a year, can copyright on new edition be secured after a lapse of a year or two?

Yes, if the notice in the new edition bore a new copyright date. Copyright does not depend on deposit or registration, but on publication with notice. If the Copyright Office had learned of the publication and demanded (as it has a right to do) the deposit of copies and registration, then if you had not complied you would be subject to fine and the copyright would be invalid.

How do you copyright a doubleton? Do you just reprint the two original dates and the original copyright owners, or do you copyright as a new volume?

If there is no new copyright material, only the original dates should be used and no new copyright should be taken out. If the original copyright owners still own the copyrights, their names should be given in the notice. However, if the copyrights have been assigned and the assignment has been recorded, the new owner's name may be used. The notice on the copyright page should indicate to which book each date applies.

How do you enter a copyright notice on a book whose copyright has been transferred to your company? Is the first date indicated, or the date of the transfer only?

If the copyright has been assigned and the assignment recorded, the original date of copyright and the present owners' name will suffice. If you prefer, however, you may give the original date (and original owner), and the date of assignment and the new owner. In this case, however, it must be apparent that the second date is that of an assignment, not a new copyright.

NOTICE

If a pamphlet is published without a title page or a cover, and the first page of the pamphlet is the first page of text, can the copyright notice be placed on the reverse of page 1 (that is, page 2 of the text), or must it be placed on the first page?

As a judge said in the case of a 28-page pamphlet with no title 'on the cover or elsewhere,' 'Congress in enacting the Copyright Act contemplated that each book or publication, to be protected, should have a title and should contain a page devoted, in part at least, to the title . . . I will not say that a copyright notice on the front cover or on the page following, a title page being absent, would not suffice.' From this it would seem that page 2 would suffice — but my advice is to place it on page 1.

Is it necessary to have a notice of manufacture in the United States on the copyright page?

Yes, but it has nothing to do with the validity of the copyright. It is necessary to conform with tariff regulations in case the book is ever exported. Incidentally, the United States of America must be spelled out in full, to avoid confusion with Union of South Africa, also abbreviated USA.

What is the minimum of content of a credit line, which accompanies reprint of copyright material, that will protect the owner of the copyright in the instance that he permits another to reprint his copyright material in whole or in part?

Copyright (or Copr. or ©), the year, and the name of the copyright owner. Except in cases that are really 'fair use,' the mere citing of source is not sufficient protection. Even though the publisher of the anthology disregards the instruction, the copyright owner protects himself by making the demand when granting permission.

In a printed book, the copyright notice is duly printed in the front matter. Stock is in and the publisher unavoidably must postpone until next year. Can

198

a rubber-stamped new copyright notice be stamped on, and be legal?

Yes, or even a hand-written correction. But when filing your application for registration you will save time and later correspondence by including an explanatory note to the Register of Copyrights.

Must all copyright and assignment dates appear in the notice?

The law requires only the most recent copyright date. To be absolutely safe, however, it is a good plan to include earlier copyright dates also. Assignment dates are not necessary.

If a book is published in England in 1955 and in the United States in 1956, what copyright date does it carry in the notice?

The date of its first publication: i.e. 1955.

What happens if the notice is omitted?

If it is omitted in all copies and the book is published (sold or publicly distributed) the copyright is lost. If it is omitted in only a few copies, by error, no harm is done if an effort is made to correct the error wherever possible.

PEN NAMES

My understanding of the law is that the copyright must (or should) be taken out in the 'full legal name' of the copyright owner. However, one or two literary agents with whom we do business assure us that it is perfectly safe to copyright under a fictitious name.

Nothing in the Copyright Act says that a copyright cannot be taken out under a pseudonym, nor has a case concerning the legality ever come before the courts. Formerly the Copyright Office did not favor the practice. The law seems to be that if the pseudonym is 'legal' in the state in which the book is published, it will be legal in a Federal Court. When taking out a copyright under a pseudonym, the author's real name should also be given in the copyright application to facilitate matters when the renewal of copyright is made.

PERMISSIONS

Certain publishers call themselves 'authorized publishers' of the works of well-known poets of the last century; and if one writes them about selections, they grant 'permission' to reproduce poems published over 56 years ago and ask for a footnote acknowledgment. Is there any actual obligation to obtain permission or make acknowledgment in such cases?

There is no legal obligation if you quote from an edition first published

199

over 56 years ago. Be sure, however, you do not use a later edition, which has editorial emendations or is a revised version. If a publisher has gone to the trouble to perpetuate a 'pure' text of an author, of course he wants credit. And if it is just credit he wants, it doesn't hurt to give it.

If I want to quote in my book a poem found in a periodical, should I get permission from the publisher of the periodical, or from the poet, or both?

Permission should come from the copyright owner. If there is no separate copyright notice, the publisher presumably has full responsibility from the author and you need go no farther. If there is a separate copyright in the author's name, or the copyright was assigned after magazine publication, you should go to the author — unless the publisher quotes you the author's verdict.

How many words may one quote from an excerpt without getting the permission of the copyright owner?

There is no answer to this question, for 'fair use' has never been legally defined. Many publishing houses make their own rules — anything from 50 to 200 words — but this is their own policy and has no legal basis. It is up to you to decide if your use is 'fair' — for illustration or comment, and not competing with the original publication.

Can anything definite be said regarding the use of brief quotations in copyrighted material without special permission, for purposes of critical discussion?

See preceding question. There are practically no suits on record concerning infringement through quotations in critical writing. Nevertheless, the courteous writer — and scholarly writers usually want to be courteous — likes to give credit where it is due. It is always wise to cite publisher, author, and book — and it may even sell an extra book or two if you ask permission.

A quotation of a verse from a song occurs in a story — a stanza of four lines. Should the author get permission? Would a fee be asked?

The author would prevent any possible trouble if he got the copyright owner's permission. A fee might be asked but probably would not. If the copyright owner did ask one, the quotation could not be used without payment.

POSTHUMOUS PUBLICATIONS

When copyright was taken out in the name of a person who died between the time sheets were printed and application for copyright was made, we were refused registration because the copyright was not taken out in the name of a 'living person.' What should we do?

The copyright application should be in the name of the author's executor, or if he left a will his legatee. A correction of the copyright notice may be made by rubber stamp or even written in by hand, if there is no time to tip in a new page. The circumstances should be explained to the Copyright Office in a letter accompanying the application.

PUBLIC DOMAIN

If a research worker notated a little-known folk melody and brought it out as his own composition (having changed a few notes), could he obtain a valid copyright on the tune? Also, would it be an infringement of his copyright if anyone else published the folk song in its traditional form? This question is on the supposition that the changes were so slight as to make it perfectly evident that the two songs had an identical source.

No, to both questions. To justify a new copyright, new 'creative' work must be added. Even in case he added enough to secure a copyright, the copyright holder has no exclusive ownership of the original melody. Anyone else could publish it in its traditional form or could adapt it and rework it and then copyright his new version too.

If a work is in the public domain, may a publisher by reorganization of its content and editing its moderness of language or felicity of expression, with or without altering thought content, claim a copyright in the work as a new publication?

It depends on how extensive the 'editing' is. If it is simply 'modernizing' the language — changing 'hath' to 'have,' 'should thee wish so to do' to 'should you wish to do so' — it is probable that the copyright, even if he could establish one, would do him little good, since anyone else would be free to do exactly the same thing. The validity of a copyright of new versions depends on whether the changes are valuable enough to make others adopt them rather than use the original material that is free to all. Also, since the copyright is only on the new material and anyone is free to use the old material as he will, are the changes such that another person could not do exactly the same thing, without copying?

Why is it that works by 'Samuel L. Clemens' that are in the public domain and can be reprinted without permission require permission when used under the name 'Mark Twain'? Or is this a misconception on my part? If 'Mark Twain' is registered as a trade mark, isn't the period of protection the same as for the work itself?

A trade mark cannot prolong the life of a copyright. There was long litigation and much 'bluff' on this case, but actually the works may be printed and published whether under Clemens or Mark Twain. In 1883 the court ruled that once a book is in the public domain anyone may reprint it and attribute it to the author either by his own name or pen name or both.

Suppose I wish to include a piece of old music — for example, 'My Old Kentucky Home' — in a booklet I am printing. I find it in a songbook with the ordinary harmonization and of course have the right to copy it, since it is now in the public domain. However, to save the expense of setting music type I want to have a photo-engraving made of the page from the songbook, cutting off the head and folio and such. Must I have permission from the copyright owner of the songbook to do so?

Nothing in the Copyright Act would prevent your reproducing material in the public domain by photo-engraving, but the owner of the songbook might be able to recover damages under a state law having to do with unfair competition. Also, if he had done any editing or changing of the music or words he might be able to prove that the changes were protected by his copyright on the collection.

When a book is in the public domain because its copyright has expired, can a new copyright be obtained on a new format, with new illustrations and a new introduction?

A copyright can be obtained that will cover the new illustrations and introduction. Format as such is not subject to copyright, and of course the copyright on the original material cannot be revived after its term has expired. Anyone else can publish it with other illustrations and new introduction.

RADIO AND TELEVISION

What can be done about radio use of 'books'?

Books are now protected against unauthorized use by radio and television. When permission is asked, be sure that the person granting the rights really holds them. In many publishing contracts radio and television rights are reserved by the author; in this case the publisher has no control over them, even though the book is copyrighted in the publisher's name.

At the foot of a poem that appeared in a newspaper recently was the line, 'Copyright, 1945. No part of this poem may be reprinted or read over the radio without permission.' Has this any legal significance?

The only value of such a notice is 'psychological' — certainly not legal. In the first place, the copyright owner's name is omitted, thus making the whole line ineffective. Secondly, delivery or performance rights are reserved to the copyright owners of 'books' and 'periodicals' without any special notice. If the poem is protected by the over-all copyright of the newspaper, it is legally protected against being read over the radio without permission; if it was previously registered as a monologue or drama before publication it would still be protected but the owner's name would have to appear to preserve the copyright.

I have noticed that neither on television nor radio is there much mention of copyright, even when the material has appeared in published form. Shouldn't the notice be given either orally or on the screen?

No, neither radio broadcasting nor telecasting is 'publication,' and a notice is necessary only for a 'published' film. Copyrighted material cannot be used without permission, but notice is not necessary unless such a published motion picture film is used.

RENEWALS

If a publisher inadvertently fails to renew for second period in the year due, does he forfeit protection or may he even after two years apply for renewal?

The copyright is void if the work is not renewed before the expiration of 28 years, to the day.

What is the time of grace permitted in renewing copyright? For instance, if a copyright expires in February 1956, how many days thereafter am I allowed to file copyright renewal? How far in advance may I file renewal?

If a copyright expires 14 February 1956 the application for renewal must be in the Copyright Office by midnight 13 February 1956. It may be filed there any time between 14 February 1955 and the date of expiration. Although the Copyright Office issues a renewal application form, if the deadline is upon you and no form is at hand, a letter stating the fact and enclosing the renewal fee should be sent airmail special delivery. In this case the facts are:

Name, address, and status of renewal claimant (author, widow [er], child [ren], executors, next of kin, if the author is dead and left no will) *
Complete title of the work

* If the proprietor is entitled to renewal his status is stated as:
  Proprietor of the posthumous work
  Proprietor of the composite work
  Proprietor of a work copyrighted by a corporate body otherwise than as assignee
    or licensee of the author
  Proprietor of copyright in a work made for hire

Name of each author of renewable matter
Class, number, and date of original registration
Name of the original claimant

But if the last day for renewal falls on Saturday, Sunday, or holiday observed in the District of Columbia, you may under a recent amendment to the law renew on the first business day immediately following.

The publisher is assigned copyright of an author. Author dies and copyright is about to expire. Publisher wishes to renew copyright. The understanding is that he cannot. Copyright must be renewed by author's heirs. Am I correct?

No. The publisher may renew the copyright in the name of the person entitled to renew. He cannot renew it in his own name unless he qualifies in the status as given in the footnote below.

If an author, who has been a member of a corporation (not a publishing firm), appoints as the executor of his will a certain officer of his corporation, not in that officer's personal capacity but only by virtue of his position in the corporation: and if the author's explicit intention as stated in his will and testament is that this officer's successor (or successor in office) shall on assumption of office in the corporation, ipso facto become the executor of the said will: in the case where renewal of copyright in the several works of the said author is being sought, should such officer of the corporation make application for said renewal in his own name or strictly as an officer of the corporation? In other words, should application for renewal of copyright be made in form (a) or (b)?

(a) I, John Doe, Secretary of the Hypothetic Corporation, executor of the will of the author, et cetera.
(b) I, John Doe, Erewhon Drive, Happiness, New York, executor of the will of the author, et cetera.

An author's executor ordinarily does not have renewal privilege of his works. His works may be renewed by his widow or his children. If he leaves no widow or children, his executor may renew it, but so far as the Copyright Office is concerned, the official business capacity of the executor is unimportant. In this case (b) would therefore be the proper form.

When a publisher wishes to apply for a renewal of copyright may he do so as 'proprietor of copyright in a work made for hire' if the origination of the book came about thus: The publisher hired the author to write a novel of so many words, first to be serialized by the publisher, and subsequently to be published as a book by the same publisher, in consideration for a lump

204

sum of money or several agreed-upon payments to be made at stated intervals during the author's work on the novel.

This question cannot be answered definitely by quoting the Copyright Act. However, the opinion of the Copyright Office was that a work 'made for hire' is work written by staff employees or ghost writers, or hired translators — in other words, in a situation of 'master and servant,' not of a contract. A movie script writer hired by a Hollywood producer; a composer or lyricist hired by a music publisher; a staff writer on a newspaper — these people produce work 'done for hire.'

The law says if an author is dead, the renewal must be obtained by his wife, or his heirs, or the executor named in his will. If the wife also dies, should the renewal be obtained by her executor or the executor in the author's will (presuming they are different executors, of course)?

The Copyright Act stipulates that if an author is dead the renewal may be made by

I. His widow or children. If there is no widow or child, by
II. The author's executor. If he died intestate, by
III. The author's next of kin.

Legally adopted children may qualify as I. Under III, actual blood-relatives are qualified — not a sister-in-law, uncle by marriage, et cetera.

From this it follows that the wife's executor would in no circumstances be qualified to make the renewal.

Can a publisher to whom copyright is assigned apply for renewal if the author dies during renewal year?

Not in his name, as assignee. However, if the author applied for renewal before his death and assigned the new copyright during the renewal year, the assignment would probably be binding.

TITLES

What can be said about the protection of titles of literary works?

Titles are not subject to copyright, and can only be protected through laws relating to unfair competition. A title taken from a quotation in the public domain is free to anyone. Titles of newspapers and magazines, dramas, and moving pictures are more likely to be protected by the courts than titles of short stories, poems, or novels. If a title has been used many times before, the author will have a hard time proving even unfair competition, as he will also in the case of a purely descriptive title — *Adventure, Ghost Story, Western Tales,* et cetera.

UNFAIR COMPETITION

Does a copyright holder of a book also possess the rights to the reproduc-
ibility of the type-matter in which his book is set? For example, an author
writes a series of articles for a certain magazine. Then he wishes to have
these articles appear in book form. Can he reproduce the type-matter from
the magazine by means of photography or photo-offset, without paying a fee
to the magazine whose pages he photographs? With the future developments
of offset, this may become a real problem. It has occurred in my experi-
ence once, and nobody seemed to know what the 'rights' really were.

There is no copyright on type. Probably the producer-owner of a book
would be able to protect its physical make-up through state laws relating
to unfair competition or fair trade. However, this is a matter for state courts,
not the copyright law.

UNPUBLISHED WORKS

I think one of the most frequent queries put to us is whether or not it is
possible to copyright a work before it is published; that is, authors want to
be sure that nobody kidnaps their brain children while they are still young.

If the work is a 'book' — any literary work intended for publication with
the exception of dramas, lectures, sermons, radio scripts — it cannot be
copyrighted before it is published. Publication means reproduction in copies
for public sale or distribution. Before publication it will be protected at common law. A professor who has his syllabus multigraphed and sells it in the
college co-op has published it, and let's hope he had a copyright notice on
it. If he did not, he has dedicated it to the public.

Forms

IN THE ARTICLE on Applications (see page 47) are listed the forms available at the Copyright Office. In general, the same information is requested on all forms: the name, address, and citizenship of the copyright owner(s), the author's name, address, and citizenship, the title of the work, the dates of publication and the nature of any new matter, earlier registration or publication, and the name and address of the person to whom the registration should be sent and the person sending the fee. However, there are often slight variations. For this reason, in the section that follows are reproductions of all those forms that are most frequently used by the literary author or publisher, filled in as typical registrations.

Throughout the text the reader has been advised of common pitfalls in registering material for copyright. By studying the forms themselves he will see exactly how registration should be made. It may be worth while once more to point out:

The copyright owner is not necessarily the author.
The publisher is not necessarily the copyright owner.
The translator is the author of a translation.
The citizenship of the author and copyright claimant must be known before registration can be made.
The year date of the foreign publication of an American edition must be given, as well as the American publication date.
All application forms must be filled out *in full,* even if the same name and address has to be repeated several times.

In the works selected for sample registrations, many different problems have been exemplified: the use of a *nom de plume,* co-authors, an American edition of a book on which ad interim copyright had been registered, registration (voluntary) of a book protected under UCC, and so on. While the wording of the entries as shown has in every case been accepted by the Copyright Office, it is not necessarily the only acceptable phraseology. If additional information (of special circumstances) seems to be pertinent, it should be given in an accompanying letter, not written in the margins or between the lines of the form itself.

FORM A

CLASS **A**

REGISTRATION NO.

DO NOT WRITE HERE

Application for Registration of a Claim to Copyright
in a published book manufactured in the United States of America

Instructions: Read the information provided on page 4 before completing the form. Fill in applicable items on all pages. Follow the instructions which accompany each item. The application should give the facts which existed at the date of publication. Pages 1 and 2 should be typewritten or printed with pen and ink. Pages 3 and 4 may be carbon copies. Mail all pages to the Register of Copyrights, Library of Congress, Washington 25, D. C., together with 2 copies of the best edition of the work and the registration fee of $4. Make your remittance payable to the Register of Copyrights.

1. Copyright Claimant(s) and Address(es): Give the name(s) and address(es) of the copyright owner(s). Ordinarily the name should be the same as in the notice of copyright on the copies of the work deposited.

Name .... Dash Book Company ....

Address .... 200 Blank Street, New York 3, New York ....

Name ....

Address ....

2. Title: Give the title of the work as it appears on the copies. .... Tales of Heroism, True Accounts

of the Cold Stream Guards

3. Authors: The citizenship of the author and information concerning domicile must be given. If an organization is the author and was formed under the laws of the United States or one of the States, citizenship may be stated as U. S. A. Authors may be editors, compilers, translators, illustrators, etc., as well as authors of original text. In the case of a work made for hire, the employer is the author. If the claim is based on new matter (see item 5 (a)), give information about the author of the new matter. If the author's pseudonym appears on the copies rather than his legal name, the pseudonym should be given in the application, and the legal name may be included if desired; e. g., John Doe, pseudonym of Richard Roe.

Name .... James N. Smith .... Citizenship ___Great Britain___
(Name of country)

Domiciled in U. S. A. Yes ___X___ No ___ Address ___119 Castro Blvd., Martinez, California___

Name .... Jean Duvall (illustrator) .... Citizenship ___United States___
(Name of country)

Domiciled in U. S. A. Yes ___X___ No ___ Address ___30 East 8th St., White Plains, New York___

Name .... Citizenship _____
(Name of country)

Domiciled in U. S. A. Yes ___ No ___ Address _____

4. Date and Place of Publication:

(a) Give the date (month, day, and year) when copies were first placed on sale, sold, or publicly distributed.

January 16, 1955

(b) Give the name of the country in which the work was first published.

United States

5. Previous Publication:

(a) *New matter in this version:* If any part of this work has been previously published, in the United States or elsewhere, give a brief general statement of the nature of the new matter in this version. New matter may consist of compilation, translation, abridgment, editing, and the like, as well as additional text or pictorial matter.

U.S. edition with many changes in material and style of a work

previously published in England and registered for ad interim.

(b) *United States edition of a work subject to the ad interim provisions of the law:* If the work is in the English language and all or part was previously first published outside the United States, and copyright was not secured under section 9 (c) of title 17, U. S. C., by virtue of the Universal Copyright Convention, give the year date of first publication outside the United States and state whether or not a claim to ad interim copyright was registered.

Year date of first publication outside the United States. ......1952...... Claim to ad interim copyright registered. Yes ☒ No ☐

16—68824-2 *See next page*

6. If registration fee is to be charged to an established deposit account, give name of account:

_____

7. Name and address of person to whom correspondence or refund, if any, should be sent:
Name ___Dash Book Company_____ Address ___200 Blank St., New York 3, N.Y.___

8. Send certificate to:

Name _____Dash Book Company_____

Address _____200 Blank Street_____
(Number and street)

___New York_____3_____New York___
(City)   (Zone)   (State)

9. **Affidavit:** Fill in this affidavit and sign it before an officer authorized to administer oaths within the United States, such as a notary public, who must place his signature, date of execution, and official seal upon the affidavit. The execution of this affidavit must be subsequent to the facts stated therein and must be made by an individual.

I, the undersigned, depose and say that I am the

STATE OF _____New York_____ ⎤
                                ⎟ ss:
COUNTY OF _____New York_____ ⎦

☐ Person claiming copyright in the book described in this application;

☒ The duly authorized agent of the person or organization claiming copyright in the book described in this application;

☐ The printer of the book described in this application:

that the book was published or printing completed on (give month, day, and year) ___January 16, 1955___,
that the copies deposited have been printed from type set within the limits of the United States or from plates made within the limits of the United States from type set therein or by other process performed within the limits of the United States; or if the text be produced by lithographic process, or photoengraving process, that such process was wholly performed within the limits of the United States, and that the printing of the text and binding of the said book have also been performed within the limits of the United States; and that the applicable processes described above were performed by the following establishment or establishments at the following address or addresses: (If the copies were manufactured by an individual rather than an establishment, give the name and address of the individual.)

Names _____Dutone Lithographers_____ Addresses _____Newark, New Jersey_____

_____Jansen Bindery_____ _____Pine Plains, New York_____

_____

_____

_____Arthur Jones_____
(Signature of affiant)

(Sign and notarize only on or after date of publication.)

Subscribed and sworn to / affirmed before me this ___18th___

PLACE
NOTARIAL SEAL
HERE

day of _____January_____, 19__55__

_____John Public_____
(Signature of notary)

FOR COPYRIGHT OFFICE USE ONLY	
Application and affidavit received	
Two copies received	
Fee received	
Renewal	

U. S. GOVERNMENT PRINTING OFFICE   16—63824-2

Page 2

𝔄pplication for 𝔕egistration of a 𝔔laim to 𝔄d 𝔍nterim 𝔔opyright in a book or periodical in the English language manufactured and first published outside the United States of America

CLASSES	REGISTRATION NO.
A-B	DO NOT WRITE HERE

Instructions: Read the information provided on page 4 before completing the form. Fill in applicable items on all pages. Follow the instructions which accompany each item. The application should give the facts which existed at the date of publication. Pages 1 and 2 should be typewritten or printed with pen and ink. Pages 3 and 4 may be carbon copies. Mail all pages to the Register of Copyrights, Library of Congress, Washington 25, D. C., U. S. A., together with the items specified in either Option A or B:

Option A: One copy of the work and a fee of $4. Make remittance payable to the Register of Copyrights.

Option B: Two copies of the work and a catalog card. This option is not available if the author was a United States citizen or domiciliary on the date of publication, nor if the author or proprietor is a citizen, domiciliary or resident on the date application is filed.

Registration cannot be made under either option unless all the required items are received in the Copyright Office within 6 months of the date of first publication.

1. Copyright Claimant(s) and Address(es): Give the name(s) and address(es) of the copyright owner(s). Ordinarily the name should be the same as in the notice of copyright, if any, on the copies of the work deposited. The citizenship of the claimant must be stated.

Name ..... Elisabeth Dodd ..... Citizenship ..... Great Britain .....
(Name of country)

Address ..... 2, St. John's Square, London, E.C. 2, England .....

Name ..... Citizenship .....
(Name of country)

Address .....

2. Title: *(a)* Give the title of the work as it appears on the copies. ..... Murder at Grey Abbey .....

(b) If periodical give: Vol. ..... No. ..... Date on copies. .....

3. Authors: The citizenship of the author and information concerning domicile must be given. If an organization is the author the name of the country under the laws of which the organization was formed should be given in the space for citizenship. Authors may be editors, compilers, translators, illustrators, etc., as well as authors of original text. In the case of a work made for hire the employer is the author. If the claim is based on new matter (see item 5) give information about the author of the new matter. If the author's pseudonym appears on the copies rather than his legal name, the pseudonym should be given in the application, and the legal name may be included if desired; e. g., John Doe, pseudonym of Richard Roe.

Name ..... Betsey Dean (Elisabeth Dean Dodd) ..... Citizenship ..... Great Britain .....
(Name of country)

Domiciled in U. S. A. ☐ Yes ☒ No Address ..... 2, St. John's Square, London, E.C. 2, England .....

Name ..... Citizenship .....
(Name of country)

Domiciled in U. S. A. ☐ Yes ☐ No Address .....

Name ..... Citizenship .....
(Name of country)

Domiciled in U. S. A. ☐ Yes ☐ No Address .....

4. Date and Place of Publication:

(a) Give the date (month, day, and year) when copies were first placed on sale, sold, or publicly distributed.

28 February 1956

(b) Give the name of the country in which the work was first published.

Great Britain

5. Previous Publication:

New matter in this version: If any part of this work has been previously published, give a brief general statement of the nature of the new matter in this version. New matter may consist of compilation, translation, abridgment, editing and the like as well as additional text or pictorial matter.

First eight chapters published serially in Mystery Magazine—

last fourteen chapters new material.

16—63832-2 *See next page*

6. If registration fee is to be charged to an established deposit account, give name of account:

_____

7. Name and address of person to whom correspondence or refund, if any, should be sent:
Name ___Hester James, Literary Agency___ Address ___30 West 94th St., New York, N.Y.___

8. Send certificate to:

Name _____Dash Book Company_____

Address _____200 Blank Street_____
(Number and street)

_____New York___3___New York_____
(City) (Zone) (State)

9. Certification:

I CERTIFY that the statements made by me in this application are correct to the best of my knowledge.

_____Hester James_____
(Signature of copyright claimant or duly authorized agent)

Importation of copies into the United States

Sec. 16 of Title 17 of the United States Code, the Copyright Law, permits the importation of 1,500 copies of works in which claims to ad interim copyright have been registered. The Copyright Office will issue an import statement at the time of registration to be presented to the customs officer at the port of entry. The statement, indicating the number of copies imported, will be returned to the Copyright Office by the customs officer. If less than 1,500 copies are imported the Copyright Office will issue an import statement for the balance.

If the import statement is to be sent to a person other than the one named in item 8 give the name and address here.

Name _____ Address _____

Application Forms

Copies of the following forms will be supplied by the Copyright Office without charge upon request.

Class A Form A—Published book manufactured in the United States of America.
Class A { Form A-B Foreign—Book or periodical manufactured and first published outside the United States of America
or B { (except works subject to the ad interim provisions of the copyright law of the United States of America).
 { Form A-B Ad Interim—Book or periodical in the English language manufactured and first published outside the
 { United States of America and subject to the ad interim provisions of the copyright law of the United States of
 { America.
Class B { Form B—Periodical manufactured in the United States of America.
 { Form BB—Contribution to a periodical manufactured in the United States of America.
Class C Form C—Lecture, sermon, address, prepared for oral delivery.
Class D Form D—Dramatic or dramatico-musical composition.
Class E { Form E—Musical composition by an author who is a citizen or domiciliary of the United States of America or
 { which is first published in the United States of America.
 { Form E Foreign—Musical composition by an author who is not a citizen or domiciliary of the United States of
 { America and which is not first published in the United States of America.
Class F Form F—Map.
Class G Form G—Work of art; model or design for work of art.
Class H Form H—Reproduction of a work of art.
Class I Form I—Drawing or plastic work of a scientific or technical character.
Class J Form J—Photograph.
Class K { Form K—Print or pictorial illustration.
 { Form KK—Print or label used for article of merchandise.
Class L { Form L-M—Motion Picture.
or M {
 Form R—Renewal copyright.
 Form U—Notice of use of musical composition on mechanical instruments.

FOR COPYRIGHT OFFICE USE ONLY	
Application received	
One copy received	
Two copies received	
Catalog card received	
Fee received	
Renewal	

Page 2

FORM A-B FOREIGN

CLASSES   REGISTRATION NO.

A-B

DO NOT WRITE HERE

Application for Registration of a Claim to Copyright

in a book or periodical manufactured and first published outside the United States of America (except works subject to the ad interim provisions of the copyright law of the United States of America)

Instructions: Read the information provided on page 4 before completing the form. Fill in applicable items on all pages. Follow the instructions which accompany each item. The application should give the facts which existed at the date of publication. Pages 1 and 2 should be typewritten or printed with pen and ink. Pages 3 and 4 may be carbon copies. Mail all pages to the Register of Copyrights, Library of Congress, Washington 25, D. C., U. S. A., together with the items specified in either Option A or B:

Option A: One copy of the work and a fee of $4. Make remittance payable to the Register of Copyrights.

Option B: Two copies of the work and a catalog card. This option is available only if a properly completed application, copies and catalog card are received in the Copyright Office within 6 months of the date of first publication. This option is not available if the author or proprietor is a citizen, domiciliary or resident of the United States of America on the date application is filed.

1. Copyright Claimant(s) and Address(es): Give the name(s) and address(es) of the copyright owner(s). Ordinarily the name should be the same as in the notice of copyright on the copies of the work deposited.

Name ...... José Benitez

Address ...... University of San Tomas, Manila, Philippines

Name ......

Address ......

2. Title: (*a*) Give the title of the work as it appears on the copies. ..Life of José Rizal, with an

Introduction by Professor Edward Stern

(*b*) If periodical give: Vol. ...... No. ...... Date on copies. ......

3. Authors: The citizenship of the author and information concerning domicile must be given. If an organization is the author the name of the country under the laws of which the organization was formed should be given in the space for citizenship. Authors may be editors, compilers, translators, illustrators, etc., as well as authors of original text. In the case of a work made for hire the employer is the author. If the claim is based on new matter (see item 5) give information about the author of the new matter. If the author's pseudonym appears on the copies rather than his legal name, the pseudonym should be given in the application, and the legal name may be included if desired; e. g., John Doe, pseudonym of Richard Roe.

Name ...... José Juan Benitez   Citizenship Philippine Republic
(Name of country)

Domiciled in U. S. A. Yes ☐ No ☒ Address University of San Tomas, Manila, Philippines

Name ...... Edward Stern   Citizenship Great Britain
(Name of country)

Domiciled in U. S. A. Yes ☐ No ☒ Address University of San Tomas, Manila, Philippines

Name ......   Citizenship ......
(Name of country)

Domiciled in U. S. A. Yes ☐ No ☐ Address ......

4. Date and Place of Publication:

(*a*) Give the date (month, day, and year) when copies were first placed on sale, sold, or publicly distributed.

15 March 1956

(*b*) Give the name of the country in which the work was first published.

Philippine Republic

5. Previous Publication:

New matter in this version: If any part of this work has been previously published, give a brief general statement of the nature of the new matter in this version. New matter may consist of compilation, translation, abridgment, editing, and the like, as well as additional text or pictorial matter.

16—63831-2   *See next page*

1. A catalog card supplied by a library in the country of publication will be accepted.

2. SAMPLE CATALOG CARD.—The card immediately below illustrates the necessary elements of information in the order in which they should appear on the card.

Full name of author of original work and year of birth	Dumas, Alexandre, père, 1802-1870
Title and description from title page; paging	La jeunesse de Monte-Cristo. Adaptation de Madeleine Chavanon; illustrations de Jacques Galan. 237 p.
Copyright claimant	Maison Mame
Place (city) and year of publication	Tours 1954
Full name of other authors, editors, etc., and year of birth	Chavanon, Madeleine, 1900– Galan, Jacques, 1925–

3. FORM.—Fill in the card below in the same style as the sample card above. To facilitate use of the form in the Copyright Office, use a typewriter or print with pen and ink. If the form is not used, the size of the card should preferably be 3 x 5 inches or 7½ x 12½ cm. The Register of Copyrights reserves the right to accept catalog cards not complying with the above requirements.

| Name | Benitez | José | Juan | 1912 | Full name of author of original work and year of birth |
| | (Last) | (First) | (Middle) | Year of birth | |

Title and description: Life of José Rizal, with an Introduction — Title and description from title page

by Edward Stern

196pp. — Paging

José Benitez — Copyright claimant
Copyright claimant

Manila — Place of publication (City)   1956 — Year of publication — Place (city) and year of publication

REGISTRATION NO.

DO NOT WRITE HERE

Name	Stern	Edward	L.	1901	Full name of other authors, editors, etc., and year of birth
	(Last)	(First)	(Middle)	Year of birth	
Name	(Last)	(First)	(Middle)	Year of birth	
Name	(Last)	(First)	(Middle)	Year of birth	

CLASS	REGISTRATION NO.
B	DO NOT WRITE HERE

Application for Registration of a Claim to Copyright
in a periodical manufactured in the United States of America

Instructions: Read the information provided on page 4 before completing the form. Fill in applicable items on all pages. Follow the instructions which accompany each item. The application should give the facts which existed at the date of publication. Pages 1 and 2 should be typewritten or printed with pen and ink. Pages 3 and 4 may be carbon copies. Mail all pages to the Register of Copyrights, Library of Congress, Washington 25, D. C., together with two copies of the best edition of the work and the registration fee of $4. Make your remittance payable to the Register of Copyrights.

1. Copyright Claimant(s) and Address(es): Give the name(s) and address(es) of the copyright owner(s). Ordinarily the name should be the same as in the notice of copyright on the copies of the work deposited.

Name ___ Blank Publications, Inc. ___

Address ___ 90 Westover Square, Philadelphia, Pennsylvania ___

Name ___

Address ___

2. Title: Give the title of the periodical as it appears on the copies. ___ The Naturalist's Weekly ___

Vol. ___ XX ___ No. ___ 1 ___ Date on copies. ___ January 3, 1956 ___

3. Citizenship of Author: The law requires a statement of the citizenship of the author. In the case of a work made for hire the employer is the author. Ordinarily the publisher of a periodical is the author of the periodical. If the author is an organization which was formed under the laws of the United States or one of the States the citizenship may be stated as U. S. A.

Citizenship ___ United States ___
(Name of country)

4. Date and Place of Publication:

(a) Give the date (month, day, and year) when copies were first placed on sale, sold, or publicly distributed.

___ December 29, 1955 ___

(b) Give the name of the country in which the work was first published.

___ United States ___

5. Manufacture: If any part of the printing, typesetting, platemaking, lithographing, photoengraving or other process in the manufacture of the copies deposited was performed outside the United States describe the part and process and give the place of manufacture.

___

___

16—63825-2

See next page

Application for Registration of a Claim to Copyright

in a contribution to a periodical manufactured in the
United States of America

FORM BB

CLASS **B**

REGISTRATION NO.

DO NOT WRITE HERE

Instructions: Read the information provided on page 4 before completing the form. Fill in applicable items on all pages. Follow the instructions which accompany each item. The application should give the facts which existed at the date of publication. Pages 1 and 2 should be typewritten or printed with pen and ink. Pages 3 and 4 may be carbon copies. Mail all pages to the Register of Copyrights, Library of Congress, Washington 25, D. C., together with one complete copy of the issue of the periodical containing the contribution and the registration fee of $4. Make your remittance payable to the Register of Copyrights.

1. Copyright Claimant(s) and Address(es): Give the name(s) and address(es) of the copyright owner(s). Ordinarily the name should be the same as in the notice of copyright on the copy of the contribution deposited.

Name Robert B. Gross

Address 200 Grassy Place, Greenport, Minnesota

Name

Address

2. Title: Give the title of the contribution as it appears on the copies. Mystery Killer,

Part III: The Hidden Knife

3. Authors: The citizenship of the author and information concerning domicile must be given. If an organization is the author and was formed under the laws of the United States or one of the States, citizenship may be stated as U. S. A. Authors may be editors, compilers, translators, illustrators, etc., as well as authors of original text. In the case of a work made for hire the employer is the author. If the claim is based on new matter (see item 5 (a)) give information about the author of the new matter. If the author's pseudonym appears on the copies rather than his legal name, the pseudonym should be given in the application, and the legal name may be included if desired; e. g., John Doe, pseudonym of Richard Roe.

Name Robert B. Gross   Citizenship U.S.A.
(Name of country)

Domiciled in U. S. A. Yes ☒ No ☐   Address 200 Grassy Place, Greenport, Minnesota

Name Herbert Mann (maps and charts)   Citizenship U.S.A.
(Name of country)

Domiciled in U. S. A. Yes ☒ No ☐   Address 4279 Avenue B., Chicago 19, Illinois

4. Date and Place of Publication:

(a) Give the date (month, day, and year) when copies were first placed on sale, sold, or publicly distributed.
February 20, 1956

(b) Give the name of the country in which the work was first published.
United States

(c) Published in True Thrillers
(Title of periodical)

Vol. III   No. 3   Date on copies March 1956   Page 15-18

5. Previous Publication:

(a) *New matter in this version:* If any part of this work has been previously published, in the United States or elsewhere, give a brief general statement of the nature of the new matter in this version. New matter may consist of compilation, translation, abridgment, editing, and the like, as well as additional text or pictorial matter.

Diagram map of "Old Lewis" previously published in

"Tales of Old Lewis"--all the rest new matter.

(b) *United States edition of a work subject to the ad interim provisions of the law:* If the work is in the English language and all or part was previously first published outside the United States, and copyright was not secured under Section 9 (c) of Title 17, U. S. C., by virtue of the Universal Copyright Convention, give the year date of first publication outside the United States and state whether or not a claim to ad interim copyright was registered.

Year date of first publication outside the United States. ....   Claim to ad interim copyright registered. Yes ☐ No ☐

16—63820-2

See next page

CLASS	REGISTRATION NO.
C	DO NOT WRITE HERE

Application for Registration of a Claim to Copyright
in a lecture or similar production prepared for oral delivery

Instructions: Read the information provided on page 4 before completing the form. Fill in applicable items on all pages. Follow the instructions which accompany each item. Pages 1 and 2 should be typewritten or printed with pen and ink. Pages 3 and 4 may be carbon copies. Mail all pages to the Register of Copyrights, Library of Congress, Washington 25, D. C., together with one copy of the work and the registration fee of $4. Make your remittance payable to the Register of Copyrights.

1. Copyright Claimant(s) and Address(es): Give the name(s) and address(es) of the copyright owner(s).

Name ___Frances Hodge___

Address ___293 East High Street, Baltimore, Maryland___

Name ___Lewis D. Hodge___

Address ___293 East High Street, Baltimore, Maryland___

2. Title: Give the title of the work as it appears on the copies. ___Auntie Fran's Fun School:___

___Series C--How to Give a Party (radio-TV script)___

3. Authors: The citizenship of the author and information concerning domicile must be given. If an organization is the author and was formed under the laws of the United States or one of the States, citizenship may be stated as U. S. A. In the case of a work made for hire the employer is the author. If the claim is based on new matter (see item 4) give information about the author of the new matter. If the author's pseudonym appears on the copies rather than his legal name, the pseudonym should be given in the application, and the legal name may be included if desired; e. g., John Doe, pseudonym of Richard Roe.

Name ___Fran Francis (Frances Hodge)___ Citizenship ___U.S.A.___
(Name of country)

Domiciled in U. S. A. Yes ☒ No ☐ Address ___293 East High Street, Baltimore, Maryland___

Name ___(Lewis D. Hodge--does not appear on script)___ Citizenship ___U.S.A.___
(Name of country)

Domiciled in U. S. A. Yes ☒ No ☐ Address ___293 East High Street, Baltimore, Maryland___

Name _____ Citizenship _____
(Name of country)

Domiciled in U. S. A. Yes ☐ No ☐ Address _____

4. Previous Registration or Publication:

If a claim to copyright in any part of the work was previously registered, or if part of the work was previously published, check the appropriate space (check both if applicable):

☒ previous registration
☐ previous publication

and give a brief general statement of the nature of the new matter in this version:

___All new except three minute introduction, previously registered.___

See next page

FORM D

REGISTRATION NO.

DO NOT WRITE HERE

Application for Registration of a Claim to Copyright
in a dramatic or dramatico-musical composition

Instructions: Read the information provided on page 4 before completing the form. Fill in applicable items on all pages. Follow the instructions which accompany each item. In the case of published works the application should give the facts which existed at the date of publication. Pages 1 and 2 should be typewritten or printed with pen and ink. Pages 3 and 4 may be carbon copies. Mail all pages to the Register of Copy-

rights, Library of Congress, Washington 25, D. C., together with:
  (*a*) If unpublished, one copy of the composition and the registration fee of $4.
  (*b*) If published, two copies of the composition and the registration fee of $4.
  Make your remittance payable to the Register of Copyrights.

1. Copyright Claimant(s) and Address(es): Give the name(s) and address(es) of the copyright owner(s). In the case of published works the name should ordinarily be the same as in the notice of copyright on the copies of the work deposited.

Name ___Peter Smith___

Address ___20 East 9th Street, New York 3, New York___

Name ___Mary E. Gray___

Address ___Westover Arms, Nyack, New York___

2. Title: Give the title of the dramatic or dramatico-musical composition as it appears on the copies. ___

The Last Waltz

3. Authors: The citizenship of the author and information concerning domicile must be given. If an organization is the author and was formed under the laws of the United States or one of the States, citizenship may be stated as U. S. A. In the case of a work made for hire the employer is the author. If the work consists partly of music indicate which author is the

author of the music. If the claim is based on new matter (see item 5) give information about the author of the new matter. If the author's pseudonym appears on the copies rather than his legal name, the pseudonym should be given in the application, and the legal name may be included if desired; e. g., John Doe, pseudonym of Richard Roe.

Name ___Peter Smith___ Citizenship ___U.S.A.___
(Name of country)

Domiciled in U. S. A. Yes ☒ No ☐ Address___20 East 9th Street, New York 3, New York___

Name ___Betty Gray (Mary E. Gray)___ Citizenship ___Canada___
(Name of country)

Domiciled in U. S. A. Yes ☒ No ☐ Address___Westover Arms, Nyack, New York___

Name ___ Citizenship ___
(Name of country)

Domiciled in U. S. A. Yes ☐ No ☐ Address___

4. Date and Place of Publication (for published works only):
  (*a*) Give the date (month, day, and year) when copies were first placed on sale, sold, or publicly distributed.

August 2, 1956

  (*b*) Give the name of the country in which the work was first published.

Canada

5. Previous Registration or Publication:
  If a claim to copyright in any part of the work was previously registered, or if part of the work was previously published, check the appropriate space (check both if applicable):
  ☒ Previous registration
  ☐ Previous publication
and give a brief general statement of the nature of the new matter in this version:

___Two acts reworked; Act III new (earlier registration of Acts I and II___

___as "unpublished" under the title "The Curtain Falls").___

16—63835-2

See next page

Page 2 is the same on all forms except Form A on which the affidavit is given.

Form E APPLICATION FOR REGISTRATION

A musical composition the author of which is a citizen or domiciliary of the United States or which was first published in the United States

Exactly like E Foreign.

Form GG APPLICATION FOR REGISTRATION

A published three-dimensional work of art

No new forms yet issued (1955).

Form I APPLICATION FOR REGISTRATION

A drawing or plastic work of a scientific or technical character

No new forms yet issued (1955).

Form K APPLICATION FOR REGISTRATION

A print or pictorial illustration

No new forms yet issued (1955). See Form H for general style.

Form U

Notice of use of music on mechanical instruments

Calls for name and address of copyright owner and title, composers, authors, and copyright registration number (if known) of each musical composition included in this notice, which the copyright owner named above has used, or licensed the use of, for the manufacture of parts of instruments serving to reproduce mechanically the musical work.

FORM E FOREIGN

CLASS   REGISTRATION NO.

E

DO NOT WRITE HERE

Application for Registration of a Claim to Copyright

In a musical composition the author of which is not a citizen or domiciliary of the United States of America and which was not first published in the United States of America

Instructions: Read the information provided on page 4 before completing the form. Fill in applicable items on all pages. Follow the instructions which accompany each item. In the case of published works the application should give the facts which existed at the date of publication. Pages 1 and 2 should be typewritten or printed with pen and ink. Pages 3 and 4 may be carbon copies. Mail all pages to the Register of Copyrights, Library of Congress, Washington 25, D. C., U. S. A., together with the items specified in either Option A or B:

Option A: One copy of the musical composition and a fee of $4. Make remittance payable to the Register of Copyrights.

Option B: Two copies of the musical composition and a catalog card. This option is not available for unpublished works, nor if the author or proprietor is a citizen, domiciliary or resident of the United States of America at the date application is filed, and is available only if the copies, a properly completed application, and catalog card are received in the Copyright Office within six months of the date of first publication.

1. Copyright Claimant(s) and Address(es): Give the name(s) and address(es) of the copyright owner(s). In the case of published works the name should ordinarily be the same as in the notice of copyright on the copies of the work deposited.

Name ..... Henri Castille et Cie

Address ..... 2, Rue de la Paix, Paris, France

Name .....

Address .....

2. Title: Give the title of the musical composition as it appears on the copies. ..... Chanson d'Amour

3. Authors: The citizenship of the author and information concerning domicile must be given. If an organization is the author the name of the country under the laws of which the organization was formed should be given in the space for citizenship. The term authors includes authors of music, words, arrangement, and any other copyrightable part of the work. In the case of a work made for hire the employer is the author. If the claim is based on new matter (see item 5) give information about the author of the new matter. If the author's pseudonym appears on the copies rather than his legal name, the pseudonym should be given in the application, and the legal name may be included if desired; e. g., John Doe, pseudonym of Richard Roe.

Name ..... Jean Gallant   Citizenship ..... France
(Name of country)

Domiciled in U. S. A.   Yes ☐   No ☒   Address ..... Saint-Malo, France ..... Author of ..... music
(State which: words, music, arrangement, etc.)

Name ..... Blaise Gautier   Citizenship ..... France
(Name of country)

Domiciled in U. S. A.   Yes ☐   No ☒   Address ..... c/o Henri Castille, Paris, France ..... Author of ..... words
(State which: words, music, arrangement, etc.)

Name .....   Citizenship .....
(Name of country)

Domiciled in U. S. A.   Yes ☐   No ☐   Address ..... Author of .....
(State which: words, music, arrangement, etc.)

4. Date and Place of Publication (for published works only):
(*a*) Give the date (month, day, and year) when copies were first placed on sale, sold, or publicly distributed.

February 14, 1956

(*b*) Give the name of the country in which the work was first published.

France

5. Previous Registration or Publication:
If a claim to copyright in any part of the work was previously registered, or if part of the work was previously published, check the appropriate space (check both if applicable):

☒ previous registration

☒ previous publication

and give a brief general statement of the nature of the new matter in this version:

Words new; music is piano arrangement (with changes) of same

composer's "Chansonette (pour violon)"

16—63833-3   *See next page*

Application for Registration of a Claim to Copyright
in a map

CLASS

F

REGISTRATION NO.

DO NOT WRITE HERE

Instructions: Read the information provided on page 4 before completing the form. Fill in applicable items on all pages. Follow the instructions which accompany each item. The application should give the facts which existed at the date of publication. Pages 1 and 2 should be typewritten or printed with pen and ink. Pages 3 and 4 may be carbon copies. Mail all pages to the Register of Copyrights, Library of Congress, Washington 25, D. C., together with two copies of the best edition of the work and the registration fee of $4. Make your remittance payable to the Register of Copyrights.

1. Copyright Claimant(s) and Address(es): Give the name(s) and address(es) of the copyright owner(s). Ordinarily the name should be the same as in the notice of copyright on the copies or, if initials are used in the notice, the name should be the same as appears elsewhere on the copies of the work deposited.

Name ___ Dash Book Company ___

Address ___ 200 Blank Street, New York 3, New York ___

Name ___

Address ___

2. Title: Give the title of the map as it appears on the copies. ___ Literary Map of Old New York ___

3. Authors: The citizenship of the author and information concerning domicile must be given. If an organization is the author and was formed under the laws of the United States, or one of the States, citizenship may be stated as U. S. A. In the case of a work made for hire the employer is the author. If the claim is based on new matter (see item 5) give information about the author of the new matter.

Name ___ Dash Book Company (staff artists) ___ Citizenship ___ U.S.A. ___
(Name of country)

Domiciled in U. S. A. Yes ☒ No ☐ Address ___ 200 Blank Street, New York 3, New York ___

Name ___ Citizenship ___
(Name of country)

Domiciled in U. S. A. Yes ☐ No ☐ Address ___

4. Date and Place of Publication and Place of Manufacture:

(a) Give the date (month, day, and year) when copies were first placed on sale, sold, or publicly distributed.
July 3, 1956

(b) Give the name of the country in which the work was first published.

U.S.A.

(c) If manufactured outside the United States by lithographic or photoengraving process (see Section 16 of Title 17 of the United States Code on page 2) state where. ___
(Name of country)

5. Previous Publication:
New matter in this version: If any part of this work has been previously published, in the United States or elsewhere, give a brief general statement of the nature of the new matter in this version.

___ All new except skeleton outline taken from "Geography of the ___

___ New World," published 1832. ___

16—63902-2

See next page

APPLICATION FOR REGISTRATION
OF A CLAIM TO COPYRIGHT IN A WORK OF ART,
OR A MODEL OR DESIGN FOR WORK OF ART

INSTRUCTIONS.—Fill in the applicable items on pages 1 and 1a. Page 1 should be an original copy either printed with pen and ink or typewritten. Page 1a will be returned to you as your Certificate of Registration and therefore should be filled in with care to agree with page 1. Carbon paper may be used for page 1a, but as most carbons will smudge, the Certificate will look neater if typed separately. Mail all pages to the Register of Copyrights, Library of Congress, Washington 25, D. C., and:

    (a) IF UNPUBLISHED, a photograph or other identifying reproduction of the work and the registration fee of $4.

    (b) IF PUBLISHED, two copies and the registration fee of $4. In case the work is by a foreign author and published in a foreign country, one copy is sufficient.

    Make your remittance payable to the Register of Copyrights. See page 2a for full instructions.

1. COPYRIGHT CLAIMANT OR CLAIMANTS (Full NAMES and ADDRESSES)·

    David L. Miller

    Hillsdale, New York

2. TITLE OF WORK_____ The Red Mill

3. State whether the work is a painting, drawing, sculpture, model or design for a work of art.

    Painting (oils)

4. AUTHOR (i. e., Painter, Sculptor, or other artist. The word "author" also includes an employer in the case of works made for hire). Full name, and pseudonym, if any, are requested for cataloging purposes. Citizenship *must* be given.

Name ____ David _____ L. _____ Miller ____ Citizenship ____ United States ____
        (First)   (Middle)   (Last)   (Give name of country)

Domicile _____ Hillsdale, New York _____
                   (Address)

5. FOR PUBLISHED WORKS ONLY:

    (a) Published by _____ at _____
                  (Name)   (Place)

    (b) Date first placed on sale, sold, or publicly distributed _____
                                  (Month, day, and year)

6. IF PRODUCED OUTSIDE OF THE UNITED STATES by lithographic or photoengraving process (see

    Section 16 of Title 17 of the United States Code) state where _____
                                        (Country)

7. SEND CERTIFICATE TO: (If refund or other communications are to be sent to another person, give his name in space 8.)

Name ___ Country Artists, Association ___

Address _____
                (Number and street)

    Great Barrington, Massachusetts
       (City)   (Zone)   (State)

8. Name _____ Address _____

APPLICATION FOR REGISTRATION
OF A CLAIM TO COPYRIGHT IN A REPRODUCTION
OF A WORK OF ART

REGISTRATION NO.

DO NOT WRITE HERE

CLASS

H

FORM H

INSTRUCTIONS.—Fill in the applicable items on pages 1 and 1a. Page 1 should be an original copy either printed with pen and ink or typewritten. Page 1a will be returned to you as your Certificate of Registration and therefore should be filled in with care to agree with page 1. Carbon paper may be used for page 1a, but as most carbons will smudge, the Certificate will look neater if typed separately. Mail all pages to the Register of Copyrights, Library of Congress, Washington 25, D. C., together with two copies and the registration fee of $4. In case the work is by a foreign author and published in a foreign country, one copy is sufficient. Make your remittance payable to the Register of Copyrights. See page 2a for full instructions.

1. COPYRIGHT CLAIMANT OR CLAIMANTS (Full NAMES and ADDRESSES):

Norene Brown

29 West Street, Otisville, North Carolina

2. TITLE OF WORK Vroe's 'Spring' (in Tempera)

3. AUTHORS (The word "author" includes an employer in the case of works made for hire). Full name and pseudonym, if any, are requested for cataloging purposes. Citizenship *must* be given.

(*a*) Author of the reproduction:

Name __Norene__ __Brown__ Citizenship __United States__
    (First)   (Middle)   (Last)   (Give name of country)

Domicile __29 West Street, Otisville, North Carolina__
    (Address)

(*b*) Author of original work which has been reproduced:

Name __Antoine__ __D.__ __Vroe__
    (First)   (Middle)   (Last)

4. PUBLISHER AND DATE:

(*a*) Published by __Southern Art Galleries, Inc.__ at __Charleston, N.C.__
    (Name)   (Place)

(*b*) Date first placed on sale, sold, or publicly distributed __March 2, 1956__
    (Month, day, and year)

5. IF PRODUCED OUTSIDE OF THE UNITED STATES by lithographic or photoengraving process

(see Section 16 of Title 17 of the United States Code)

state where ....
    (Country)

6. SEND CERTIFICATE TO: (If refund or other communications are to be sent to another person, give his name in space 7.)

Name __Southern Art Galleries, Inc.__

Address __Salmon Road__
    (Number and street)
__Charleston, N.C.__
    (City)   (Zone)   (State)

7. Name .... Address ....

FOR COPYRIGHT OFFICE USE ONLY
APPLICATION RECEIVED
ONE COPY RECEIVED
TWO COPIES RECEIVED
FEE RECEIVED

16—63905-1

𝕬pplication for 𝕽egistration of a 𝕮laim to 𝕮opyright
in a photograph

FORM J

CLASS **J**

REGISTRATION NO.

DO NOT WRITE HERE.

Instructions: Read the information provided on page 4 before completing the form. Fill in applicable items on all pages. Follow the instructions which accompany each item. In the case of published works the application should give the facts which existed at the date of publication. Pages 1 and 2 should be typewritten or printed with pen and ink. Pages 3 and 4 may be carbon copies. Mail all pages to the Register of Copyrights,

Library of Congress, Washington 25, D. C., together with:

(*a*) If unpublished, one copy of the photograph and the registration fee of $4.

(*b*) If published, two copies of the photograph and the registration fee of $4.

Make your remittance payable to the Register of Copyrights.

1. Copyright Claimant(s) and Address(es): Give the name(s) and address(es) of the copyright owner(s). In the case of published works the name should ordinarily be the same as in the notice of copyright on the copies or, if initials are used in the notice, the name should be the same as appears elsewhere on the copies of the work deposited.

Name ____ Junior Camera Club _____

Address ____ Westfield, New Jersey _____

Name _____

Address _____

2. Title: Give the title of the photograph as it appears on the copies. For purposes of identification each copy deposited should bear a title.

_____ Tourists at Stratford _____

3. Author: The citizenship of the author and information concerning domicile must be given. If an organization is the author and was formed under the laws of the United States, or one of the States, citizenship may be stated as U. S. A. In the case of a work made for hire the employer is the author. If the claim is based on new matter (see item 5) give information about the author of the new matter.

Name ____ James Martin _____ Citizenship Great Britain ____
(Name of country)

Domiciled in U. S. A. Yes ☐ No ☒ Address ____ Chester House, Avon, England _____

4. Date and Place of Publication (for published works only):

(*a*) Give the date (month, day, and year) when copies were first placed on sale, sold, or publicly distributed,

_____

(*b*) Give the name of the country in which the work was first published.

_____

5. Previous Registration or Publication:

If a claim to copyright in any portion of the work was previously registered, or if part of the work was previously published, check the appropriate space (check both if applicable):

☐ Previous registration

☐ Previous publication

and give a brief general statement of the nature of the new matter in this version:

_____

_____

_____

16—63827-3

See next page

223

APPLICATION FOR REGISTRATION
OF A CLAIM TO COPYRIGHT IN A PRINT OR LABEL
USED FOR ARTICLE OF MERCHANDISE

REGISTRATION NO.

DO NOT WRITE HERE

CLASS **K**

FORM KK

INSTRUCTIONS.—Fill in the applicable items on pages 1 and 1a. Page 1 should be an original copy either printed with pen and ink or typewritten. Page 1a will be returned to you as your Certificate of Registration and therefore should be filled in with care to agree with page 1. Carbon paper may be used for page 1a, but as most carbons will smudge, the Certificate will look neater if typed separately. Mail all pages to the Register of Copyrights, Library of Congress, Washington 25, D. C., together with two copies of the work and the registration fee of $6. Make your remittance payable to the Register of Copyrights. See page 2a for full instructions.

1. COPYRIGHT CLAIMANT OR CLAIMANTS (Full NAMES and ADDRESSES):

   Motor Cars Corp.

   Motor Building Annex, Chicago, Illinois

2. TITLE OF ☒ PRINT OR ☐ LABEL   SPEED AHEAD
   (Check which)

3. AUTHOR (The word "author" includes an employer in the case of works made for hire):

   Motor Cars Corp. _____ Citizenship United States
   (Give name in full)   (Give name of country)

   Domicile   Motor Building Annex, Chicago, Illinois
                              (Address)

4. TYPE OF MERCHANDISE FOR WHICH PRINT OR LABEL IS USED Automobile

5. PUBLISHED ON THE ____Fifth____ DAY OF ____June____, 1956
                    (Give date on which print or label was first placed on sale, sold, or publicly distributed)

6. IF PRODUCED OUTSIDE THE UNITED STATES by lithographic or photoengraving process (see Section 16 of Title 17 of the United States Code) state where _____
                                                                                (Country)

7. FILL IN THE FOLLOWING SPACES ONLY IF THE PRINT IS A CONTRIBUTION TO A PERIODICAL:

   Published in ____Speed Magazine____
                         (Give title of periodical)

   Vol. __vii__ No. __6__ Issue ____June____ On Page back cover

8. SEND CERTIFICATE TO: (If refund or other communications are to be sent to another person, give his name in space 9.)

   Name _____Motor Cars Corp._____

   Address _____Motor Building Annex_____
                       (Number and street)

   _____Chicago 11, Illinois_____
   (City)   (Zone)   (State)

9. Name _____ Address _____

FOR COPYRIGHT OFFICE USE ONLY
APPLICATION RECEIVED
TWO COPIES RECEIVED
FEE RECEIVED

16—63829-1

FORM L-M

CLASSES	REGISTRATION NO.
L-M	DO NOT WRITE HERE

Application for Registration of a Claim to Copyright
in a motion picture

Instructions: Read the information provided on page 4 before completing the form. Fill in applicable items on all pages. Follow the instructions which accompany each item. In the case of published works the application should give the facts which existed at the date of publication. Pages 1 and 2 should be typewritten or printed with pen and ink. Pages 3 and 4 may be carbon copies. Mail all pages to the Register of Copyrights, Library of Congress, Washington 25, D. C., together with:

(*a*) If unpublished, title and description, prints as described on page 4, and the registration fee of $4.

(*b*) If published, two complete copies, description, and the registration fee of $4.

Make your remittance payable to the Register of Copyrights.

1. Copyright Claimant(s) and Address(es): Give the name(s) and address(es) of the copyright owner(s). In the case of published works the name should ordinarily be the same as in the notice of copyright on the copies of the work deposited.

Name .... Educational Films, Inc.

Address .... 29 K Street, Boston, Massachusetts

Name ....

Address ....

2. (a) Title of ☐ Photoplay or ☒ Motion Picture Other Than a Photoplay: Give the title of the motion picture as it
(Check appropriate space)
appears on the copies. .... A Trip to Concord

(*b*) Running time, footage, or number of reels. .... 30 minutes

(*c*) Number of prints deposited (for unpublished works only). 4

3. Author: The citizenship of the author and information concerning domicile must be given. If an organization is the author and was formed under the laws of the United States, or one of the States, citizenship may be stated as U. S. A. In the case of a work made for hire the employer is the author. If the claim is based on new matter (see item 5) give information about the author of the new matter.

Name .... Educational Films, Inc. .... Citizenship .... U.S.A.
(Name of country)

Domiciled in U. S. A. Yes ☒ No ☐ Address....... 29 K Street, Boston, Massachusetts

4. Date and Place of Publication (for published works only):

(*a*) Give the date (month, day, and year) when copies were first placed on sale, sold, or publicly distributed.

(*b*) Give the name of the country in which the work was first published.

5. Previous Registration or Publication:

If a claim to copyright in any part of the work was previously registered, or if part of the work was previously published, check the appropriate space (check both if applicable):

☐ Previous registration
☐ Previous publication

and give a brief general statement of the nature of the new matter in this version:

16—63908-2

See next page

225

APPLICATION FOR REGISTRATION
OF A CLAIM TO THE RENEWAL OF A COPYRIGHT

REGISTRATION NO.

DO NOT WRITE HERE

FORM
R

INSTRUCTIONS.—Fill in the applicable items on pages 1 and 1a. Page 1 should be an original copy either printed with pen and ink or typewritten. Page 1a will be returned to you as your Certificate of Registration and therefore should be filled in with care to agree with page 1. Carbon paper may be used for page 1a, but as most carbons will smudge, the Certificate will look neater if typed separately. Mail all pages to the Register of Copyrights, Library of Congress, Washington 25, D. C., together with the registration fee of $2. Make your remittance payable to the Register of Copyrights. See page 2a for full instructions.

1. NAME OF CLAIMANT OR CLAIMANTS OF THE RENEWAL COPYRIGHT:

    (a)   Janet Lewis King   Four Corners, Connecticut
                  (Name)   (Address)

       claiming as   child of deceased author
                              (See instructions on page 2a)

    (b) _____
                  (Name)   (Address)

       claiming as _____

    (c) _____
                  (Name)   (Address)

       claiming as _____

2. COMPLETE TITLE OF WORK   Handyman's Work Book, 2nd edition.
                               (Including specific instrumentation in the case of music)
            (1st edition entitled "Jim Lewis's Work Book")

3. NAMES OF ALL AUTHORS OF RENEWABLE MATTER:
            James Z. Lewis ("Jim Lewis")

            Arthur Bailey (illustrator)

4. FACTS OF ORIGINAL REGISTRATION:

       Original registration number. CLASS   A 1   xxc. No.   A 984251

       If registered as published   January 16, 1928
                              (Give date of publication)

       If registered as unpublished _____
                                    (Give date)

       Original copyright claimant   Dash Book Company
                              (Name of claimant in original registration)

5. SEND CERTIFICATE TO: (If refund or other communications are to be sent to another person, give his name in space 6.)

Name   Dash Book Company

Address   200 Blank Street
                 (Number and street)

       New York   3   New York
       (City)   (Zone)   (State)

6. Name _____ Address _____

FOR COPYRIGHT OFFICE USE ONLY

APPLICATION RECEIVED

FEE RECEIVED

16—63330-1

226

Appendix

COPYRIGHT LAW OF THE UNITED STATES OF AMERICA

United States Code   Title 17 — Copyrights
[As amended to take effect 16 September 1955]

CHAPTER	SECTION
1. Registration of copyright	1
2. Infringement proceedings	101
3. Copyright Office	201

Chapter 1 – Registration of Copyrights

§ 1. Exclusive rights as to copyrighted works.

§ 2. Rights of author or proprietor of unpublished work.

§ 3. Protection of component parts of work copyrighted; composite works or periodicals.

§ 4. All writings of author included.

§ 5. Classification of works for registration.

§ 6. Registration of prints and labels.

§ 7. Copyright on compilations of works in public domain or of copyrighted works; subsisting copyrights not affected.

§ 8. Copyright not to subsist in works in public domain, or published prior to July 1, 1909, and not already copyrighted, or Government publications; publication by Government of copyrighted material.

§ 9. Authors or proprietors, entitled; aliens.

§ 10. Publication of work with notice.

§ 11. Registration of claim and issuance of certificate.

§ 12. Works not reproduced for sale.

§ 13. Deposit of copies after publication; action or proceeding for infringement.

§ 14. Same; failure to deposit; demand; penalty.

§ 15. Same; postmaster's receipt; transmission by mail without cost.

§ 16. Mechanical work to be done in United States.

§ 17. Affidavit to accompany copies.

§ 18. Making false affidavit.

§ 19. Notice; form.

§ 20. Same; place of application of; one notice in each volume or number of newspaper or periodical.

§ 21. Same; effect of accidental omission from copy or copies.

§ 22. Ad interim protection of book or periodical published abroad.

§ 23. Same; extension to full term.

§ 24. Duration; renewal and extension.

§ 25. Renewal of copyrights registered in Patent Office under repealed law.

§ 26. Terms defined.

§ 27. Copyright distinct from property in object copyrighted; effect of sale of object, and of assignment of copyright.

§ 28. Assignments and bequests.
§ 29. Same; executed in foreign country; acknowledgment and certificate.
§ 30. Same; record.
§ 31. Same; certificate of record.
§ 32. Same; use of name of assignee in notice.

---

§ 1. EXCLUSIVE RIGHTS AS TO COPY-RIGHTED WORKS. — Any person entitled thereto, upon complying with the provisions of this title, shall have the exclusive right:

(a) To print, reprint, publish, copy, and vend the copyrighted work;

(b) To translate the copyrighted work into other languages or dialects, or make any other version thereof, if it be a literary work; to dramatize it if it be a nondramatic work; to convert it into a novel or other nondramatic work if it be a drama; to arrange or adapt it if it be a musical work; to complete, execute, and finish it if it be a model or design for a work of art;

(c) To deliver, authorize the delivery of, read, or present the copyrighted work in public for profit if it be a lecture, sermon, address or similar production, or other nondramatic literary work; to make or procure the making of any transcription or record thereof by or from which, in whole or in part, it may in any manner or by any method be exhibited, delivered, presented, produced, or reproduced; and to play or perform it in public for profit, and to exhibit, represent, produce, or reproduce it in any manner or by any method whatsoever. The damages for the infringement by broadcast of any work referred to in this subsection shall not exceed the sum of $100 where the infringing broadcaster shows that he was not aware that he was infringing and that such infringement could not have been reasonably foreseen;

(d) To perform or represent the copyrighted work publicly if it be a drama or, if it be a dramatic work and not reproduced in copies for sale, to vend any manuscript or any record whatsoever thereof; to make or to procure the making of any transcription or record thereof by or from which, in whole or in part, it may in any manner or by any method be exhibited, performed, represented, produced, or reproduced; and to exhibit, perform, represent, produce, or reproduce it in any manner or by any method whatsoever; and

(e) To perform the copyrighted work publicly for profit if it be a musical composition; and for the purpose of public performance for profit, and for the purposes set forth in subsection (a) hereof, to make any arrangement or setting of it or of the melody of it in any system of notation or any form of record in which the thought of an author may be recorded and from which it may be read or reproduced: *Provided,* That the provisions of this title, so far as they secure copyright controlling the parts of instruments serving to reproduce mechanically the musical work, shall include only compositions published and copyrighted after July 1, 1909, and shall not include the works of a foreign author or composer unless the foreign state or nation of which such author or composer is a citizen or subject grants, either by treaty, convention, agreement, or law, to citizens of the United States similar rights. And as a condition of extending the copyright control to such mechanical reproductions, that whenever the owner of a musical copyright has used or permitted or knowingly acquiesced in the use of the copyrighted work upon the parts of instruments serving to reproduce mechanically the musical work, any other person may make similar use of the copyrighted work upon the payment to the copyright proprietor of a royalty of 2 cents on each such part manufactured, to be paid by the manufacturer thereof; and the copyright proprietor may require, and if so the manufacturer shall furnish, a report under oath on the 20th day of each month on the number of parts of instruments manufactured during the previous month serving to reproduce mechanically said musical work, and royalties shall be due on the parts manufactured during any month upon the 20th of the next succeeding month. The payment of the royalty provided for by this section shall free the articles or devices for which such royalty has been paid from further contribution to the copyright except in case of public performance for profit. It shall be the duty of the copyright owner, if he uses

228

the musical composition himself for the manufacture of parts of instruments serving to reproduce mechanically the musical work, or licenses others to do so, to file notice thereof, accompanied by a recording fee, in the copyright office, and any failure to file such notice shall be a complete defense to any suit, action, or proceeding for any infringement of such copyright.

In case of failure of such manufacturer to pay to the copyright proprietor within thirty days after demand in writing the full sum of royalties due at said rate at the date of such demand, the court may award taxable costs to the plaintiff and a reasonable counsel fee, and the court may, in its discretion, enter judgment therein for any sum in addition over the amount found to be due as royalty in accordance with the terms of this title, not exceeding three times such amount.

The reproduction or rendition of a musical composition by or upon coin-operated machines shall not be deemed a public performance for profit unless a fee is charged for admission to the place where such reproduction or rendition occurs.

§ 2. RIGHTS OF AUTHOR OR PROPRIETOR OF UNPUBLISHED WORK. — Nothing in this title shall be construed to annul or limit the right of the author or proprietor of an unpublished work, at common law or in equity, to prevent the copying, publication, or use of such unpublished work without his consent, and to obtain damages therefor.

§ 3. PROTECTION OF COMPONENT PARTS OF WORK COPYRIGHTED; COMPOSITE WORKS OR PERIODICALS. — The copyright provided by this title shall protect all the copyrightable component parts of the work copyrighted, and all matter therein in which copyright is already subsisting, but without extending the duration or scope of such copyright. The copyright upon composite works or periodicals shall give to the proprietor thereof all the rights in respect thereto which he would have if each part were individually copyrighted under this title.

§ 4. ALL WRITINGS OF AUTHOR INCLUDED. — The works for which copyright may be secured under this title shall include all the writings of an author.

§ 5. CLASSIFICATION OF WORKS FOR REGISTRATION. — The application for registration shall specify to which of the following classes the work in which copyright is claimed belongs:

(a) Books, including composite and cyclopedic works, directories, gazetteers, and other compilations.

(b) Periodicals, including newspapers.

(c) Lectures, sermons, addresses (prepared for oral delivery).

(d) Dramatic or dramatico-musical compositions.

(e) Musical compositions.

(f) Maps.

(g) Works of art; models or designs for works of art.

(h) Reproductions of a work of art.

(i) Drawings or plastic works of a scientific or technical character.

(j) Photographs.

(k) Prints and pictorial illustrations including prints or labels used for articles of merchandise.

(l) Motion-picture photoplays.

(m) Motion pictures other than photoplays.

The above specifications shall not be held to limit the subject matter of copyright as defined in section 4 of this title, nor shall any error in classification invalidate or impair the copyright protection secured under this title.

§ 6. REGISTRATION OF PRINTS AND LABELS. — Commencing July 1, 1940, the Register of Copyrights is charged with the registration of claims to copyright properly presented, in all prints and labels published in connection with the sale or advertisement of articles of merchandise, including all claims to copyright in prints and labels pending in the Patent Office and uncleared at the close of business June 30, 1940. There shall be paid for registering a claim of copyright in any such print or label not a trade-mark $6, which sum shall cover the expense of furnishing a certificate of such registration, under the seal of the Copyright Office, to the claimant of copyright.

§ 7. COPYRIGHT ON COMPILATIONS OF WORKS IN PUBLIC DOMAIN OR OF COPYRIGHTED WORKS; SUBSISTING COPYRIGHTS NOT AFFECTED. — Compilations or abridgments, adaptations, arrangements, dramatizations, translations, or other versions of works in the public domain or of copyrighted works when produced with the consent of the proprietor of the copyright in such works, or works republished with new matter, shall be regarded as new works subject to copyright under the provisions of this title; but the publication of any such new works shall not affect the force or validity of any subsisting copyright upon the matter employed or any part thereof, or be construed to imply an exclusive right to such use of the original works, or to secure or extend copyright in such original works.

§ 8. COPYRIGHT NOT TO SUBSIST IN WORKS IN PUBLIC DOMAIN, OR PUBLISHED PRIOR TO JULY 1, 1909, AND NOT ALREADY COPYRIGHTED, OR GOVERNMENT PUBLICATIONS; PUBLICATION BY GOVERNMENT OF COPYRIGHTED MATERIAL. — No copyright shall subsist in the original text of any work which is in the public domain, or in any work which was published in this country or any foreign country prior to July 1, 1909, and has not been already copyrighted in the United States, or in any publication of the United States Government, or any reprint, in whole or in part, thereof: *Provided,* That copyright may be secured by the Postmaster General on behalf of the United States in the whole or any part of the publications authorized by section 1 of the Act of January 27, 1938 (39 U. S. C. 371).

The publication or republication by the Government, either separately or in a public document, of any material in which copyright is subsisting shall not be taken to cause any abridgment or annulment of the copyright or to authorize any use or appropriation of such copyright material without the consent of the copyright proprietor.

§ 9. AUTHORS OR PROPRIETORS, ENTITLED; ALIENS. — The author or proprietor of any work made the subject of copyright by this title, or his executors, administrators, or assigns, shall have copyright for such work under the conditions and for the terms specified in this title: *Provided, however,* That the copyright secured by this title shall extend to the work of an author or proprietor who is a citizen or subject of a foreign state or nation only under the conditions described in subsections (a), (b), or (c) below:

(a) When an alien author or proprietor shall be domiciled within the United States at the time of the first publication of his work; or

(b) When the foreign state or nation of which such author or proprietor is a citizen or subject grants, either by treaty, convention, agreement, or law, to citizens of the United States the benefit of copyright on substantially the same basis as to its own citizens, or copyright protection, substantially equal to the protection secured to such foreign author under this title or by treaty; or when such foreign state or nation is a party to an international agreement which provides for reciprocity in the granting of copyright, by the terms of which agreement the United States may, at its pleasure, become a party thereto.

The existence of the reciprocal conditions aforesaid shall be determined by the President of the United States, by proclamation made from time to time, as the purposes of this title may require: *Provided,* That whenever the President shall find that the authors, copyright owners, or proprietors of works first produced or published abroad and subject to copyright or to renewal of copyright under the laws of the United States, including works subject to ad interim copyright, are or may have been temporarily unable to comply with the conditions and formalities prescribed with respect to such works by the copyright laws of the United States, because of the disruption or suspension of facilities essential for such compliance, he may by proclamation grant such extension of time as he may deem appropriate for the fulfillment of such conditions or formalities by authors, copyright owners, or proprietors who are citizens of the United States or who are nationals of countries which accord substantially equal treatment in this respect to authors, copyright owners, or proprietors who are citizens of the United States: *Provided further,* That no liability shall attach under this title for lawful uses made or acts done prior to the effective date of such proclamation in connection with such works, or in respect to the continuance for one year subsequent to such date of any business undertaking or enterprise lawfully undertaken prior to such date involving expenditure or contractual obligation in connection with the exploitation, production, reproduction, circulation, or performance of any such work.

The President may at any time terminate any proclamation authorized herein or any part thereof or suspend or extend its operation for such period or periods of time as in his judgment the interests of the United States may require.

(c) When the Universal Copyright Convention, signed at Geneva on September 6, 1952, shall be in force between the United States of America and the foreign state or nation of which such author is a citizen or subject, or in which the work was first published. Any work to which copyright is extended pursuant to this subsection shall be exempt from the following provisions of this title: (1) The requirement in section 1 (e) that a foreign state or nation must grant to United States citizens mechanical reproduction rights similar to those specified therein; (2) the obligatory deposit requirements of the first sentence of section 13; (3) the provisions of sections 14, 16, 17, and 18; (4) the import prohibitions of section 107, to the extent that they are related to the manufacturing requirements of section 16; and (5) the requirements of sections 19 and 20: *Provided, however,* That such exemptions shall apply only if from the time of first publication all the copies of the work published with the authority of the author or other copyright proprietor shall bear the symbol © accompanied by the name of the copyright proprietor and the year of first publication placed in such manner and location as to give reasonable notice of claim of copyright.

Upon the coming into force of the Universal Copyright Convention in a foreign state or nation as hereinbefore provided, every book or periodical of a citizen or subject thereof in which ad interim copyright was subsisting on the effective date of said coming into force shall have copyright for twenty-eight years from the date of first publication abroad without the necessity of complying with the further formalities specified in section 23 of this title.

The provisions of this subsection shall not be extended to works of an author who is a citizen of, or domiciled in the United States of America regardless of place of first publication, or to works first published in the United States.

§ 10. PUBLICATION OF WORK WITH NOTICE. — Any person entitled thereto by this title may secure copyright for his work by publication thereof with the notice of copyright required by this title; and such notice shall be affixed to each copy thereof published or offered for sale in the United States by authority of the copyright proprietor, except in the case of

books seeking ad interim protection under section 22 of this title.

§ 11. REGISTRATION OF CLAIM AND ISSUANCE OF CERTIFICATE. — Such person may obtain registration of his claim to copyright by complying with the provisions of this title, including the deposit of copies, and upon such compliance the Register of Copyrights shall issue to him the certificates provided for in section 209 of this title.

§ 12. WORKS NOT REPRODUCED FOR SALE. — Copyright may also be had of the works of an author, of which copies are not reproduced for sale, by the deposit, with claim of copyright, of one complete copy of such work if it be a lecture or similar production or a dramatic, musical, or dramatico-musical composition; of a title and description, with one print taken from each scene or act, if the work be a motion-picture photoplay; of a photographic print if the work be a photograph; of a title and description, with not less than two prints taken from different sections of a complete motion picture, if the work be a motion picture other than a photoplay; or of a photograph or other identifying reproduction thereof, if it be a work of art or a plastic work or drawing. But the privilege of registration of copyright secured hereunder shall not exempt the copyright proprietor from the deposit of copies, under sections 13 and 14 of this title, where the work is later reproduced in copies for sale.

§ 13. DEPOSIT OF COPIES AFTER PUBLICATION; ACTION OR PROCEEDING FOR INFRINGEMENT. — After copyright has been secured by publication of the work with the notice of copyright as provided in section 10 of this title, there shall be promptly deposited in the copyright office or in the mail addressed to the Register of Copyrights, Washington, District of Columbia, two complete copies of the best edition thereof then published, or if the work is by an author who is a citizen or subject of a foreign state or nation and has been published in a foreign country, one complete copy of the best edition then published in such foreign country, which copies or copy, if the work be a book or periodical, shall have been produced in accordance with the manufacturing provisions specified in section 16 of this title; or if such work be a contribution to a periodical, for which contribution special registration is requested, one copy of the issue or issues containing such contribution; or if the work is not reproduced in copies for sale there shall be deposited the copy, print, photograph, or other identifying reproduction provided by section 12 of this title, such copies or copy, print, photograph, or other reproduction to be accompanied in each case by a claim of copyright. No action or proceeding shall be maintained for infringement of copyright in any work until the provisions of this title with respect to the deposit of copies and registration of such work shall have been complied with.

§ 14. SAME; FAILURE TO DEPOSIT; DEMAND; PENALTY. — Should the copies called for by section 13 of this title not be promptly deposited as provided in this title, the Register of Copyrights may at any time after the publication of the work, upon actual notice, require the proprietor of the copyright to deposit them, and after the said demand shall have been made, in default of the deposit of copies of the work within three months from any part of the United States, except an outlying territorial possession of the United States, or within six months from any outlying territorial possession of the United States, or from any foreign country, the proprietor of the copyright shall be liable to a fine of $100 and to pay to the Library of Congress twice the amount of the retail price of the best edition of the work, and the copyright shall become void.

§ 15. SAME; POSTMASTER'S RECEIPT; TRANSMISSION BY MAIL WITHOUT COST. — The postmaster to whom are delivered the articles deposited as provided in sections 12 and 13 of this title shall, if requested, give a receipt therefor and shall mail them to their destination without cost to the copyright claimant.

§ 16. MECHANICAL WORK TO BE DONE IN UNITED STATES. — Of the printed book or periodical specified in section 5, subsections (a) and (b), of this title, except the original text of a book or periodical of foreign origin in a language or languages other than English, the text of all copies accorded protection under this title, except as below provided, shall be printed from type set within the limits of the United States, either by hand or by the aid of any kind of typesetting machine, or from plates made within the limits of the United States from type set therein,

or, if the text be produced by lithographic process, or photoengraving process, then by a process wholly performed within the limits of the United States, and the printing of the text and binding of the said book shall be performed within the limits of the United States; which requirements shall extend also to the illustrations within a book consisting of printed text and illustrations produced by lithographic process, or photoengraving process, and also to separate lithographs or photoengravings, except where in either case the subjects represented are located in a foreign country and illustrate a scientific work or reproduce a work of art: Provided, however, That said requirements shall not apply to works in raised characters for the use of the blind, or to books or periodicals of foreign origin in a language or languages other than English, or to works printed or produced in the United States by any other process than those above specified in this section, or to copies of books or periodicals, first published abroad in the English language, imported into the United States within five years after first publication in a foreign state or nation up to the number of fifteen hundred copies of each such book or periodical if said copies shall contain notice of copyright in accordance with sections 10, 19, and 20 of this title and if ad interim copyright in said work shall have been obtained pursuant to section 22 of this title prior to the importation into the United States of any copy except those permitted by the provisions of section 107 of this title: Provided further, That the provisions of this section shall not affect the right of importation under the provisions of section 107 of this title.

§ 17. AFFIDAVIT TO ACCOMPANY COPIES. — In the case of the book the copies so deposited shall be accompanied by an affidavit under the official seal of any officer authorized to administer oaths within the United States, duly made by the person claiming copyright or by his duly authorized agent or representative residing in the United States, or by the printer who has printed the book, setting forth that the copies deposited have been printed from type set within the limits of the United States or from plates made within the limits of the United States from type set therein; or, if the text be produced by lithographic process, or photoengraving process, that such process was wholly performed within the limits of the United States and that the printing of the text and binding of the said book have also been performed within the limits of the United States. Such affidavit shall state also the place where and the establishment or establishments in which such type was set or plates were made or lithographic process, or photoengraving process or printing and binding were performed and the date of the completion of the printing of the book or the date of publication.

§ 18. MAKING FALSE AFFIDAVIT. — Any person who, for the purpose of obtaining registration of a claim to copyright, shall knowingly make a false affidavit as to his having complied with the above conditions shall be deemed guilty of a misdemeanor, and upon conviction thereof shall be punished by a fine of not more than $1,000, and all of his rights and privileges under said copyright shall thereafter be forfeited.

§ 19. NOTICE; FORM. — The notice of copyright required by section 10 of this title shall consist either of the word 'Copyright,' the abbreviation 'Copr.,' or the symbol ©, accompanied by the name of the copyright proprietor, and if the work be a printed literary, musical, or dramatic work, the notice shall include also the year in which the copyright was secured by publication. In the case, however, of copies of works specified in subsections (f) to (k), inclusive, of section 5 of this title, the notice may consist of the letter C enclosed within a circle, thus ©, accompanied by the initials, monogram, mark, or symbol of the copyright proprietor: *Provided,* That on some accessible portion of such copies or of the margin, back, permanent base, or pedestal, or of the substance on which such copies shall be mounted, his name shall appear. But in the case of works in which copyright was subsisting on July 1, 1909, the notice of copyright may be either in one of the forms prescribed herein or may consist of the following words: 'Entered according to Act of Congress, in the year   , by A. B., in the office of the Librarian of Congress, at Washington, D. C.,' or, at his option, the word 'Copyright,' together with the year the copyright was entered and the name of the party by whom it was taken out; thus, 'Copyright, 19—, by A. B.'

§ 20. SAME; PLACE OF APPLICATION OF; ONE NOTICE IN EACH VOLUME OR NUMBER OF NEWSPAPER OR PERIODICAL. — The notice of copyright shall be applied, in the case of a book or other printed publication, upon its title page or the page immediately following, or if a periodical either upon the title page or upon the first page of text of each separate number or under the title heading, or if a musical work either upon its title page or the first page of music. One notice of copyright in each volume or in each number of a newspaper or periodical published shall suffice.

§ 21. SAME; EFFECT OF ACCIDENTAL OMISSION FROM COPY OR COPIES. — Where the copyright proprietor has sought to comply with the provisions of this title with respect to notice, the omission by accident or mistake of the prescribed notice from a particular copy or copies shall not invalidate the copyright or prevent recovery for infringement against any person who, after actual notice of the copyright, begins an undertaking to infringe it, but shall prevent the recovery of damages against an innocent infringer who has been misled by the omission of the notice; and in a suit for infringement no permanent injunction shall be had unless the copyright proprietor shall reimburse to the innocent infringer his reasonable outlay innocently incurred if the court, in its discretion, shall so direct.

§ 22. AD INTERIM PROTECTION OF BOOK OR PERIODICAL PUBLISHED ABROAD. — In the case of a book or periodical first published abroad in the English language, the deposit in the Copyright Office, not later than six months after its publication abroad, of one complete copy of the foreign edition, with a request for the reservation of the copyright and a statement of the name and nationality of the author and of the copyright proprietor and of the date of publication of the said book or periodical, shall secure to the author or proprietor an ad interim copyright therein, which shall have all the force and effect given to copyright by this title, and shall endure until the expiration of five years after the date of first publication abroad.

§ 23. SAME; EXTENSION TO FULL TERM. — Whenever within the period of such ad interim protection an authorized edition of such books or periodicals shall be published within the United States, in accordance with the manufacturing provisions specified in section 16 of this title, and whenever the provisions of this title as to deposit of copies, registration, filing of affidavits, and the printing of the copyright notice shall have been duly complied with, the copyright shall be extended to endure in such book or periodical for the term provided in this title.

§ 24. DURATION; RENEWAL AND EXTENSION. — The copyright secured by this title shall endure for twenty-eight years from the date of first publication, whether the copyrighted work bears the author's true name or is published anonymously or under an assumed name: *Provided,* That in the case of any posthumous work or of any periodical, cyclopedic, or other composite work upon which the copyright was originally secured by the proprietor thereof, or of any work copyrighted by a corporate body (otherwise than as assignee or licensee of the individual author) or by an employer for whom such work is made for hire, the proprietor of such copyright shall be entitled to a renewal and extension of the copyright in such work for the further term of twenty-eight years when application for such renewal and extension shall have been made to the copyright office and duly registered therein within one year prior to the expiration of the original term of copyright: *And provided further,* That in the case of any other copyrighted work, including a contribution by an individual author to a periodical or to a cyclopedic or other composite work, the author of such work, if still living, or the widow, widower, or children of the author, if the author be not living, or if such author, widow, widower, or children, be not living, then the author's executors, or in the absence of a will, his next of kin shall be entitled to a renewal and extension of the copyright in such work for a further term of twenty-eight years when application for such renewal and extension shall have been made to the copyright office and duly registered therein within one year prior to the expiration of the original term of copyright: *And provided further,* That in default of the registration of such application for renewal and extension, the copyright in any work shall determine at the expiration of twenty-eight years from first publication.

§ 25. RENEWAL OF COPYRIGHTS REGISTERED IN PATENT OFFICE UNDER REPEALED LAW. — Subsisting copyrights originally registered in the Patent Office prior to July 1, 1940, under section 3 of the act of June 18, 1874, shall be subject to renewal in behalf of the proprietor upon application made to the Register of Copyrights within one year prior to the expiration of the original term of twenty-eight years.

§ 26. TERMS DEFINED. — In the interpretation and construction of this title "the date of publication" shall in the case of a work of which copies are reproduced for sale or distribution be held to be the earliest date when copies of the first authorized edition were placed on sale, sold, or publicly distributed by the proprietor of the copyright or under his authority, and the word "author" shall include an employer in the case of works made for hire.

§ 27. COPYRIGHT DISTINCT FROM PROPERTY IN OBJECT COPYRIGHTED; EFFECT OF SALE OF OBJECT, AND OF ASSIGNMENT OF COPYRIGHT. — The copyright is distinct from the property in the material object copyrighted, and the sale or conveyance, by gift or otherwise, of the material object shall not of itself constitute a transfer of the copyright, nor shall the assignment of the copyright constitute a transfer of the title to the material object; but nothing in this title shall be deemed to forbid, prevent, or restrict the transfer of any copy of a copyrighted work the possession of which has been lawfully obtained.

§ 28. ASSIGNMENTS AND BEQUESTS. — Copyright secured under this title or previous copyright laws of the United States may be assigned, granted, or mortgaged by an instrument in writing signed by the proprietor of the copyright, or may be bequeathed by will.

§ 29. SAME; EXECUTED IN FOREIGN COUNTRY; . ACKNOWLEDGMENT AND CERTIFICATE. — Every assignment of copyright executed in a foreign country shall be acknowledged by the assignor before a consular officer or secretary of legation of the United States authorized by law to administer oaths or perform notarial acts. The certificate of such acknowledgment under the hand and official seal of such consular officer or secretary of legation shall be prima facie evidence of the execution of the instrument.

§ 30. SAME; RECORD. — Every assignment of copyright shall be recorded in the copyright office within three calendar months after its execution in the United States or within six calendar months after its execution without the limits of the United States, in default of which it shall be void as against any subsequent purchaser or mortgagee for a valuable consideration, without notice, whose assignment has been duly recorded.

§ 31. SAME; CERTIFICATE OF RECORD. — The Register of Copyrights shall, upon payment of the prescribed fee, record such assignment, and shall return it to the sender with a certificate of record attached under seal of the copyright office, and upon the payment of the fee prescribed by this title he shall furnish to any person requesting the same a certified copy thereof under the said seal.

§ 32. SAME; USE OF NAME OF ASSIGNEE IN NOTICE. — When an assignment of the copyright in a specified book or other work has been recorded the assignee may substitute his name for that of the assignor in the statutory notice of copyright prescribed by this title.

Chapter 2 – Infringement Proceedings

§ 101. Infringement:
    (a) Injunction.
    (b) Damages and profits; amounts; other remedies.
    (c) Impounding during action.
    (d) Destruction of infringing copies and plates.
    (e) Royalties for use of mechanical reproduction of musical works.
§ 104. Willful infringement for profit.
§ 105. Fraudulent notice of copyright, or removal or alteration of notice.
§ 106. Importation of article bearing false notice or piratical copies of copyrighted work.
§ 107. Importation, during existence of copyright, of piratical copies, or of copies not produced in accordance with section 16 of this title.
§ 108. Forfeiture and destruction of articles prohibited importation.
§ 109. Importation of prohibited articles; regulations; proof of deposit of copies by complainants.
§ 112. Injunctions; service and enforcement.
§ 113. Transmission of certified copies of papers for enforcement of injunction by other court.
§ 114. Review of orders, judgments, or decrees.
§ 115. Limitation of criminal proceedings.
§ 116. Costs; attorney's fees.

---

§ 101. INFRINGEMENT. — If any person shall infringe the copyright in any work protected under the copyright laws of the United States such person shall be liable:

(a) INJUNCTION. — To an injunction restraining such infringement;

(b) DAMAGES AND PROFITS; AMOUNT; OTHER REMEDIES. — To pay to the copyright proprietor such damages as the copyright proprietor may have suffered due to the infringement, as well as all the profits which the infringer shall have made from such infringement, and in proving profits the plaintiff shall be required to prove sales only, and the defendant shall be required to prove every element of cost which he claims, or in lieu of actual damages and profits, such damages as to the court shall appear to be just, and in assessing such damages the court may, in its discretion, allow the amounts as hereinafter stated, but in case of a newspaper reproduction of a copyrighted photograph, such damages shall not exceed the sum of $200 nor be less than the sum of $50, and in the case of the infringement of an undramatized or nondramatic work by means of motion pictures, where the infringer shall show that he was not aware that he was infringing, and that such infringement could not have been reasonably foreseen, such damages shall not exceed the sum of $100; and in the case of an infringement of a copyrighted dramatic or dramatico-musical work by a maker of motion pictures and his agencies for distribution thereof to exhibitors, where such infringer shows that he was not aware that he was infringing a copyrighted work, and that such infringements could not reasonably have been foreseen, the entire sum of such damages recoverable by the copyright proprietor from such infringing maker and his agencies for the distribution to exhibitors of such infringing motion picture shall not exceed the sum of $5,000 nor be less than $250, and such damages shall in no other case exceed the sum of $5,000 nor be less than the sum of $250, and shall not be regarded as a penalty. But the foregoing exceptions shall not deprive the copyright proprietor of any other remedy given him under this law, nor shall the limitation as to the amount of recovery apply to infringements occurring after the actual notice to a defendant, either by service of process in a suit or other written notice served upon him.

First. In the case of a painting, statue, or sculpture, $10 for every infringing copy made or sold by or found in the possession of the infringer or his agents or employees;

Second. In the case of any work enumerated in section 5 of this title, except a painting, statue, or sculpture, $1 for every infringing copy made or sold by or found in the possession of the infringer or his agents or employees;

Third. In the case of a lecture, sermon, or address, $50 for every infringing delivery;

Fourth. In the case of a dramatic or dramatico-musical or a choral or orchestral composition, $100 for the first and $50 for every subsequent infringing performance; in the case of other musical compositions $10 for every infringing performance;

(c) IMPOUNDING DURING ACTION. — To deliver upon oath, to be impounded during the pendency of the action, upon such terms and conditions as the court may prescribe, all articles alleged to infringe a copyright;

(d) DESTRUCTION OF INFRINGING COPIES AND PLATES. — To deliver up on oath for destruction all the infringing copies or devices, as well as all plates, molds, matrices, or other means for making such infringing copies as the court may order.

(e) ROYALTIES FOR USE OF MECHANICAL REPRODUCTION OF MUSICAL WORKS.

— Whenever the owner of a musical copyright has used or permitted the use of the copyrighted work upon the parts of musical instruments serving to reproduce mechanically the musical work, then in case of infringement of such copyright by the unauthorized manufacture, use, or sale of interchangeable parts, such as disks, rolls, bands, or cylinders for use in mechanical music-producing machines adapted to reproduce the copyrighted music, no criminal action shall be brought, but in a civil action an injunction may be granted upon such terms as the court may impose, and the plaintiff shall be entitled to recover in lieu of profits and damages a royalty as provided in section 1, subsection (e), of this title: *Provided also,* That whenever any person, in the absence of a license agreement, intends to use a copyrighted musical composition upon the parts of instruments serving to reproduce mechanically the musical work, relying upon the compulsory license provision of this title, he shall serve notice of such intention, by registered mail, upon the copyright proprietor at his last address disclosed by the records of the copyright office, sending to the copyright office a duplicate of such notice; and in case of his failure so to do the court may, in its discretion, in addition to sums hereinabove mentioned, award the complainant a further sum, not to exceed three times the amount provided by section 1, subsection (e), of this title, by way of damages, and not as a penalty, and also a temporary injunction until the full award is paid.

§ 104. WILLFUL INFRINGEMENT FOR PROFIT. — Any person who willfully and for profit shall infringe any copyright secured by this title, or who shall knowingly and willfully aid or abet such infringement, shall be deemed guilty of a misdemeanor, and upon conviction thereof shall be punished by imprisonment for not exceeding one year or by a fine of not less than $100 nor more than $1,000, or both, in the discretion of the court: *Provided, however,* That nothing in this title shall be so construed as to prevent the performance of religious or secular works such as oratorios, cantatas, masses, or octavo choruses by public schools, church choirs, or vocal societies, rented, borrowed, or obtained from some public library, public school, church choir, school choir, or vocal society, provided the performance is given for charitable or educational purposes and not for profit.

§ 105. FRAUDULENT NOTICE OF COPYRIGHT, OR REMOVAL OR ALTERATION OF NOTICE. — Any person who, with fraudulent intent, shall insert or impress any notice of copyright required by this title, or words of the same purport, in or upon any uncopyrighted article, or with fraudulent intent shall remove or alter the copyright notice upon any article duly copyrighted shall be guilty of a misdemeanor, punishable by a fine of not less than $100 and not more than $1,000. Any person who shall knowingly issue or sell any article bearing a notice of United States copyright which has not been copyrighted in this country, or who shall knowingly import any article bearing such notice or words of the same purport, which has not been copyrighted in this country, shall be liable to a fine of $100.

§ 106. IMPORTATION OF ARTICLE BEARING FALSE NOTICE OR PIRATICAL COPIES OF COPYRIGHTED WORK. — The importation into the United States of any article bearing a false notice of copyright when there is no existing copyright thereon in the United States, or of any piratical copies of any work copyrighted in the United States, is prohibited.

§ 107. IMPORTATION, DURING EXISTENCE OF COPYRIGHT, OF PIRATICAL COPIES, OR OF COPIES NOT PRODUCED IN ACCORDANCE WITH SECTION 16 OF THIS TITLE. — During the existence of the American copyright in any book the importation into the United States of any piratical copies thereof or of any copies thereof (although authorized by the author or proprietor) which have not been produced in accordance with the manufacturing provisions specified in section 16 of this title, or any plates of the same not made from type set within the limits of the United States, or any copies thereof produced by lithographic or photoengraving process not performed within the limits of the United States, in accordance with the provisions of section 16 of this title, is prohibited: *Provided, however,* That, except as regards piratical copies, such prohibition shall not apply:

(a) To works in raised characters for the use of the blind.

(b) To a foreign newspaper or magazine, although containing matter copyrighted in the United States printed or reprinted by authority of the copyright proprietor, unless such newspaper or magazine contains also copyright matter printed or reprinted without such authorization.

(c) To the authorized edition of a book in a foreign language or languages of which only a translation into English has been copyrighted in this country.

(d) To any book published abroad with the authorization of the author or copyright proprietor when imported under the circumstances stated in one of the four subdivisions following, that is to say:

First. When imported, not more than one copy at one time, for individual use and not for sale; but such privilege of importation shall not extend to a foreign reprint of a book by an American author copyrighted in the United States.

Second. When imported by the authority or for the use of the United States.

Third. When imported, for use and not for sale, not more than one copy of any such book in any one invoice, in good faith by or for any society or institution incorporated for educational, literary, philosophical, scientific, or religious purposes, or for the encouragement of the fine arts, or for any college, academy, school, or seminary of learning, or for any State, school, college, university, or free public library in the United States.

Fourth. When such books form parts of libraries or collections purchased en bloc for the use of societies, institutions, or libraries designated in the foregoing paragraph, or form parts of the libraries or personal baggage belonging to persons or families arriving from foreign countries and are not intended for sale: *Provided,* That copies imported as above may not lawfully be used in any way to violate the rights of the proprietor of the American copyright or annul or limit the copyright protection secured by this title, and such unlawful use shall be deemed an infringement of copyright.

§ 108. FORFEITURE AND DESTRUCTION OF ARTICLES PROHIBITED IMPORTATION. — Any and all articles prohibited importation by this title which are brought into the United States from any foreign country (except in the mails) shall be seized and forfeited by like proceedings as those provided by law for the seizure and condemnation of property imported into the

United States in violation of the customs revenue laws. Such articles when forfeited shall be destroyed in such manner as the Secretary of the Treasury or the court, as the case may be, shall direct: *Provided, however,* That all copies of authorized editions of copyright books imported in the mails or otherwise in violation of the provisions of this title may be exported and returned to the country of export whenever it is shown to the satisfaction of the Secretary of the Treasury, in a written application, that such importation does not involve willful negligence or fraud.

§ 109. IMPORTATION OF PROHIBITED ARTICLES; REGULATIONS; PROOF OF DEPOSIT OF COPIES BY COMPLAINANTS. — The Secretary of the Treasury and the Postmaster General are hereby empowered and required to make and enforce individually or jointly such rules and regulations as shall prevent the importation into the United States of articles prohibited importation by this title, and may require, as conditions precedent to exclusion of any work in which copyright is claimed, the copyright proprietor or any person claiming actual or potential injury by reason of actual or contemplated importations of copies of such work to file with the Post Office Department or the Treasury Department a certificate of the Register of Copyrights that the provisions of section 13 of this title have been fully complied with, and to give notice of such compliance to postmasters or to customs officers at the ports of entry in the United States in such form and accompanied by such exhibits as may be deemed necessary for the practical and efficient administration and enforcement of the provisions of sections 106 and 107 of this title.

§ 112. INJUNCTIONS; SERVICE AND ENFORCEMENT. — Any court mentioned in section 1338 of Title 28 or judge thereof shall have power, upon complaint filed by any party aggrieved, to grant injunctions to prevent and restrain the violation of any right secured by this title, according to the course and principles of courts of equity, on such terms as said court or judge may deem reasonable. Any injunction that may be granted restraining and enjoining the doing of anything forbidden by this title may be served on the parties against whom such injunction may be granted anywhere in the United States, and shall be operative throughout the United States and be enforceable by proceedings in contempt or otherwise by any other court or judge possessing jurisdiction of the defendants.

§ 113. TRANSMISSION OF CERTIFIED COPIES OF PAPERS FOR ENFORCEMENT OF INJUNCTION BY OTHER COURT. — The clerk of the court, or judge granting the injunction, shall, when required so to do by the court hearing the application to enforce said injunction, transmit without delay to said court a certified copy of all the papers in said cause that are on file in his office.

§ 114. REVIEW OF ORDERS, JUDGMENTS, OR DECREES. — The orders, judgments, or decrees of any court mentioned in section 1338 of Title 28 arising under the copyright laws of the United States may be reviewed on appeal in the manner and to the extent now provided by law for the review of cases determined in said courts, respectively.

§ 115. LIMITATIONS OF CRIMINAL PROCEEDINGS. — No criminal proceeding shall be maintained under the provisions of this title unless the same is commenced within three years after the cause of action arose.

§ 116. COSTS; ATTORNEY'S FEES. — In all actions, suits, or proceedings under this title, except when brought by or against the United States or any officer thereof, full costs shall be allowed, and the court may award to the prevailing party a reasonable attorney's fee as part of the costs.

Chapter 3 – *Copyright Office*

§ 201. Copyright office; preservation of records.
§ 202. Register, assistant register, and subordinates.
§ 203. Same; deposit of moneys received; reports.
§ 204. Same; bond.
§ 205. Same; annual report.
§ 206. Seal of copyright office.

§ 207. Rules for registration of claims.
§ 208. Record books in copyright office.
§ 209. Certificates of registration; effect as evidence; receipt for copies deposited.
§ 210. Catalogs of copyright entries; effect as evidence.
§ 211. Same; distribution and sale; disposal of proceeds.
§ 212. Records and works deposited in copyright offices open to public inspection; taking copies of entries.
§ 213. Disposition of articles deposited in office.
§ 214. Destruction of articles deposited in office remaining undisposed of; removal of by author or proprietor; manuscripts of unpublished works.
§ 215. Fees.
§ 216. When the day for taking action falls on Saturday, Sunday, or a holiday.

§ 201. COPYRIGHT OFFICE; PRESERVATION OF RECORDS. — All records and other things relating to copyrights required by law to be preserved shall be kept and preserved in the copyright office, Library of Congress, District of Columbia, and shall be under the control of the register of copyrights, who shall, under the direction and supervision of the Librarian of Congress, perform all the duties relating to the registration of copyrights.

§ 202. REGISTER, ASSISTANT REGISTER, AND SUBORDINATES. — There shall be appointed by the Librarian of Congress a Register of Copyrights, and one Assistant Register of Copyrights, who shall have authority during the absence of the Register of Copyrights to attach the copyright office seal to all papers issued from the said office and to sign such certificates and other papers as may be necessary. There shall also be appointed by the Librarian such subordinate assistants to the register as may from time to time be authorized by law.

§ 203. SAME; DEPOSIT OF MONEYS RECEIVED; REPORTS. — The Register of Copyrights shall make daily deposits in some bank in the District of Columbia, designated for this purpose by the Secretary of the Treasury as a national depository, of all moneys received to be applied as copyright fees, and shall make weekly deposits with the Secretary of the Treasury, in such manner as the latter shall direct, of all copyright fees actually applied under the provisions of this title, and annual deposits of sums received which it has not been possible to apply as copyright fees or to return to the remitters, and shall also make monthly reports to the Secretary of the Treasury and to the Librarian of Congress of the applied copyright fees for each calendar month, together with a statement of all remittances received, trust funds on hand, moneys refunded, and unapplied balances.

§ 204. SAME; BOND. — The Register of Copyrights shall give bond to the United States in the sum of $20,000, in form to be approved by the General Counsel for the Department of the Treasury and with sureties satisfactory to the Secretary of the Treasury, for the faithful discharge of his duties.

§ 205. SAME; ANNUAL REPORT. — The Register of Copyrights shall make an annual report to the Librarian of Congress, to be printed in the annual report on the Library of Congress, of all copyright business for the previous fiscal year, including the number and kind of works which have been deposited in the copyright office during the fiscal year, under the provisions of this title.

§ 206. SEAL OF COPYRIGHT OFFICE. — The seal used in the copyright office on July 1, 1909, shall be the seal of the copyright office, and by it all papers issued from the copyright office requiring authentication shall be authenticated.

§ 207. RULES FOR REGISTRATION OF CLAIMS. — Subject to the approval of the Librarian of Congress, the Register of Copyrights shall be authorized to make rules and regulations for the registration of claims to copyright as provided by this title.

§ 208. RECORD BOOKS IN COPYRIGHT OFFICE. — The Register of Copyrights shall provide and keep such record books in the copyright office as are required to carry out the provisions of this title, and whenever deposit has been made in the copyright office of a copy of any work under the provisions of this title he shall make entry thereof.

§ 209. CERTIFICATE OF REGISTRATION; EFFECT AS EVIDENCE; RECEIPT FOR COPIES DEPOSITED. — In the case of each entry the person recorded as the claimant of the copyright shall be entitled to a certificate of registration under seal of the copyright office, to contain the name and address of said claimant, the name of the country of which the author of the work is a citizen or subject, and when an alien author domiciled in the United States at the time of said registration, then a statement of that fact, including his place of domicile, the name of the author (when the records of the copyright office shall show the same), the title of the work which is registered for which copyright is claimed, the date of the deposit of the copies of such work, the date of publication if the work has been reproduced in copies for sale, or publicly distributed, and such marks as to class designation and entry number as shall fully identify the entry. In the case of a book, the certificate shall also state the receipt of the affidavit, as provided by section 17 of this title, and the date of the completion of the printing, or the date of the publication of the book, as stated in the said affidavit. The Register of Copyrights shall prepare a printed form for the said certificate, to be filled out in each case as above provided for in the case of all registrations made after July 1, 1909, and in the case of all previous registrations so far as the copyright office record books shall show such facts, which certificate, sealed with the seal of the copyright office, shall, upon payment of the prescribed fee, be given to any person making application for the same. Said certificate shall be admitted in any court as prima facie evidence of the facts stated therein. In addition to such certificate the Register of Copyrights shall furnish, upon request, without additional fee, a receipt for the copies of the work deposited to complete the registration.

§ 210. CATALOG OF COPYRIGHT ENTRIES; EFFECT AS EVIDENCE. — The Register of Copyrights shall fully index all copyright registrations and assignments and shall print at periodic intervals a catalog of the titles of articles deposited and registered for copyright, together with suitable indexes, and at stated intervals shall print complete and indexed catalog for each class of copyright entries, and may thereupon, if expedient, destroy the original manuscript catalog cards containing the titles included in such printed volumes and representing the entries made

during such intervals. The current catalog of copyright entries and the index volumes herein provided for shall be admitted in any court as prima facie evidence of the facts stated therein as regards any copyright registration.

§ 211. SAME; DISTRIBUTION AND SALE; DISPOSAL OF PROCEEDS. — The said printed current catalogs as they are issued shall be promptly distributed by the Superintendent of Documents to the collectors of customs of the United States and to the postmasters of all exchange offices of receipt of foreign mails, in accordance with revised list of such collectors of customs and postmasters prepared by the Secretary of the Treasury and the Postmaster General, and they shall also be furnished in whole or in part to all parties desiring them at a price to be determined by the Register of Copyrights for each part of the catalog not exceeding $25 for the complete yearly catalog of copyright entries. The consolidated catalogs and indexes shall also be supplied to all persons ordering them at such prices as may be fixed by the Register of Copyrights, and all subscriptions for the catalogs shall be received by the Superintendent of Documents, who shall forward the said publications; and the moneys thus received shall be paid into the Treasury of the United States and accounted for under such laws and Treasury regulations as shall be in force at the time.

§ 212. RECORDS AND WORKS DEPOSITED IN COPYRIGHT OFFICE OPEN TO PUBLIC INSPECTION; TAKING COPIES OF ENTRIES. — The record books of the copyright office, together with the indexes to such record books, and all works deposited and retained in the copyright office, shall be open to public inspection; and copies may be taken of the copyright entries actually made in such record books, subject to such safeguards and regulations as shall be prescribed by the Register of Copyrights and approved by the Librarian of Congress.

§ 213. DISPOSITION OF ARTICLES DEPOSITED IN OFFICE. — Of the articles deposited in the copyright office under the provisions of the copyright laws of the United States, the Librarian of Congress shall determine what books and other articles shall be transferred to the permanent collections of the Library of Congress, including the law library, and what other books or articles shall be placed in the reserve collections of the Library of Congress for sale or exchange, or be transferred to other governmental libraries in the District of Columbia for use therein.

§ 214. DESTRUCTION OF ARTICLES DEPOSITED IN OFFICE REMAINING UNDISPOSED OF; REMOVAL OF BY AUTHOR OR PROPRIETOR; MANUSCRIPTS OF UNPUBLISHED WORKS. — Of any articles undisposed of as above provided, together with all titles and correspondence relating thereto, the Librarian of Congress and the Register of Copyrights jointly shall, at suitable intervals, determine what of these received during any period of years it is desirable or useful to preserve in the permanent files of the copyright office, and, after due notice as hereinafter provided, may within their discretion cause the remaining articles and other things to be destroyed: *Provided,* That there shall be printed in the Catalog of Copyright Entries from February to November, inclusive, a statement of the years of receipt of such articles and a notice to permit any author, copyright proprietor, or other lawful claimant to claim and remove before the expiration of the month of December of that year anything found which relates to any of his productions deposited or registered for copyright within the period of years stated, not reserved or disposed of as provided for in this title. No manuscript of an unpublished work shall be destroyed during its term of copyright without specific notice to the copyright proprietor of record, permitting him to claim and remove it.

§ 215. FEES. — The Register of Copyrights shall receive, and the persons to whom the services designated are rendered shall pay, the following fees:

For the registration of a claim to copyright in any work, except a print or label used for articles of merchandise, $4; for the registration of a claim to copyright in a print or label used for articles of merchandise, $6; which fees shall include a certificate of registration under seal for each work registered: *Provided,* That only one registration fee shall be required in the case of several volumes of the same book published and deposited at the same time: *And provided further,* That with respect to works of foreign origin, in lieu of payment of the copyright fee of $4 together with one copy of the work and application, the foreign author or proprietor may at any time within six months from the date of first publication abroad deposit in the Copyright Office an application for registration and two copies of the work which shall be accompanied by a catalog card in form and content satisfactory to the Register of Copyrights.

For recording the renewal of copyright and issuance of certificate therefor, $2.

For every additional certificate of registration, $1.

For certifying a copy of an application for registration of copyright, and for all other certifications, $2.

For recording every assignment, agreement, power of attorney, or other paper not exceeding six pages, $3; for each additional page or less, 50 cents; for each title over one in the paper recorded, 50 cents additional.

For recording a notice of use, $2, for each notice of not more than five titles; and 50 cents for each additional title.

For any requested search of Copyright Office records, or works deposited, or services rendered in connection therewith, $3 for each hour of time consumed.

§ 216. WHEN THE DAY FOR TAKING ACTION FALLS ON SATURDAY, SUNDAY, OR A HOLIDAY.

When the last day for making any deposit or application, or for paying any fee, or for delivering any other material to the copyright office falls on Saturday, Sunday, or a holiday within the District of Columbia, such action may be taken on the next succeeding business day.

UNIVERSAL COPYRIGHT CONVENTION

The Contracting States,

Moved by the desire to assure in all countries copyright protection of literary, scientific and artistic works,

Convinced that a system of copyright protection appropriate to all nations of the world and expressed in a universal convention, additional to, and without impairing international systems already in force, will ensure respect for the rights of the individual and encourage the development of literature, the sciences and the arts,

Persuaded that such a universal copyright system will facilitate a wider dissemination of works of the human mind and increase international understanding,

Have agreed as follows:

ARTICLE I

Each Contracting State undertakes to provide for the adequate and effective protection of the rights of authors and other copyright proprietors in literary, scientific and artistic works, including writings, musical, dramatic and cinematographic works, and paintings, engravings and sculpture.

ARTICLE II

1. Published works of nationals of any Contracting State and works first published in that State shall enjoy in each other Contracting State the same protection as that other State accords to works of its nationals first published in its own territory.

2. Unpublished works of nationals of each Contracting State shall enjoy in each other Contracting State the same protection as that other State accords to unpublished works of its own nationals.

3. For the purpose of this Convention any Contracting State may, by domestic legislation, assimilate to its own nationals any person domiciled in that State.

ARTICLE III

1. Any Contracting State which, under its domestic law, requires as a condition of copyright, compliance with formalities such as deposit, registration, notice, notarial certificates, payment of fees or manufacture or publication in that Contracting State, shall regard these requirements as satisfied with respect to all works protected in accordance with this Convention and first published outside its territory and the author of which is not one of its nationals, if from the time of the first publication all the copies of the work published with the authority of the author or other copyright proprietor bear the symbol © accompanied by the name of the copyright proprietor and the year of first publication placed in such manner and location as to give reasonable notice of claim of copyright.

2. The provisions of paragraph 1 of this article shall not preclude any Contracting State from requiring formalities or other conditions for the acquisition and enjoyment of copyright in respect of works first published in its territory or works of its nationals wherever published.

3. The provisions of paragraph 1 of this article shall not preclude any Contracting State from providing that a person seeking judicial relief must, in bringing the action, comply with procedural requirements, such as that the complainant must appear through domestic counsel or that the complainant must deposit with the court or an administrative office, or both, a copy of the work involved in the litigation; provided that failure to comply with such requirements shall not affect the validity of the copyright, nor shall any such requirement be imposed upon a national of another Contracting State if such requirement is not imposed on nationals of the State in which protection is claimed.

4. In each Contracting State there shall be legal means of protecting without formalities the unpublished works of nationals of other Contracting States.

5. If a Contracting State grants protection for more than one term of copyright and the first term is for a period longer than one of the minimum periods prescribed in article IV, such State shall not be required to comply with the pro-

visions of paragraph 1 of this article III in respect of the second or any subsequent term of copyright.

ARTICLE IV

1. The duration of protection of a work shall be governed, in accordance with the provisions of article II and this article, by the law of the Contracting State in which protection is claimed.

2. The term of protection for works protected under this Convention shall not be less than the life of the author and 25 years after his death.

However, any Contracting State which, on the effective date of this Convention in that State, has limited this term for certain classes of works to a period computed from the first publication of the work, shall be entitled to maintain these exceptions and to extend them to other classes of works. For all these classes the term of protection shall not be less than 25 years from the date of first publication.

Any Contracting State which, upon the effective date of this Convention in that State, does not compute the term of protection upon the basis of the life of the author, shall be entitled to compute the term of protection from the date of the first publication of the work or from its registration prior to publication, as the case may be, provided the term of protection shall not be less than 25 years from the date of first publication or from its registration prior to publication, as the case may be.

If the legislation of a Contracting State grants two or more successive terms of protection, the duration of the first term shall not be less than one of the minimum periods specified above.

3. The provisions of paragraph 2 of this article shall not apply to photographic works or to works of applied art; provided, however, that the term of protection in those Contracting States which protect photographic works, or works of applied art in so far as they are protected as artistic works, shall not be less than ten years for each of said classes of works.

4. No Contracting State shall be obliged to grant protection to a work for a period longer than that fixed for the class of works to which the work in question belongs, in the case of unpublished works by the law of the Contracting State of which the author is a national, and in the case of published works by the law of the Contracting State in which the work has been first published.

For the purposes of the application of the preceding provision, if the law of any Contracting State grants two or more successive terms of protection, the period of protection of that State shall be considered to be the aggregate of those terms. However, if a specified work is not protected by such State during the second or any subsequent term for any reason, the other Contracting States shall not be obliged to protect it during the second or any subsequent term.

5. For the purposes of the application of paragraph 4 of this article, the work of a national of a Contracting State, first published in a non-Contracting State, shall be treated as though first published in the Contracting State of which the author is a national.

6. For the purposes of the application of paragraph 4 of this article, in case of simultaneous publication in two or more Contracting States, the work shall be treated as though first published in the State which affords the shortest term; any work published in two or more Contracting States within thirty days of its first publication shall be considered as having been published simultaneously in said Contracting States.

ARTICLE V

1. Copyright shall include the exclusive right of the author to make, publish, and authorize the making and publication of translations of works protected under this Convention.

2. However, any Contracting State may, by its domestic legislation, restrict the right of translation of writings, but only subject to the following provisions:

If, after the expiration of a period of seven years from the date of the first publication of a writing, a translation of such writing has not been published in the national language or languages, as the case may be, of the Contracting State, by the owner of the right of translation or with his authorization, any national of such Contracting State may obtain a non-exclusive license from the competent authority thereof to translate the work and publish the work so translated in any of the national languages in which it has not

243

been published; provided that such national, in accordance with the procedure of the State concerned, establishes either that he has requested, and been denied, authorization by the proprietor of the right to make and publish the translation, or that, after due diligence on his part, he was unable to find the owner of the right. A license may also be granted on the same conditions if all previous editions of a translation in such language are out of print.

If the owner of the right of translation cannot be found, then the applicant for a license shall send copies of his application to the publisher whose name appears on the work and, if the nationality of the owner of the right of translation is known, to the diplomatic or consular representative of the State of which such owner is a national, or to the organization which may have been designated by the government of that State. The license shall not be granted before the expiration of a period of two months from the date of the dispatch of the copies of the application.

Due provision shall be made by domestic legislation to assure to the owner of the right of translation a compensation which is just and conforms to international standards, to assure payment and transmittal of such compensation, and to assure a correct translation of the work.

The original title and the name of the author of the work shall be printed on all copies of the published translation. The license shall be valid only for publication of the translation in the territory of the Contracting State where it has been applied for. Copies so published may be imported and sold in another Contracting State if one of the national languages of such other State is the same language as that into which the work has been so translated, and if the domestic law in such other State makes provision for such licenses and does not prohibit such importation and sale. Where the foregoing conditions do not exist, the importation and sale of such copies in a Contracting State shall be governed by its domestic law and its agreements. The license shall not be transferred by the licensee.

The license shall not be granted when the author has withdrawn from circulation all copies of the work.

ARTICLE VI

'Publication,' as used in this Convention, means the reproduction in tangible form and the general distribution to the public of copies of a work from which it can be read or otherwise visually perceived.

ARTICLE VII

This Convention shall not apply to works or rights in works which, at the effective date of the Convention in a Contracting State where protection is claimed, are permanently in the public domain in the said Contracting State.

ARTICLE VIII

1. This Convention, which shall bear the date of September 6, 1952, shall be deposited with the Director-General of the United Nations Educational, Scientific and Cultural Organization and shall remain open for signature by all States for a period of 120 days after that date. It shall be subject to ratification or acceptance by the signatory States.

2. Any State which has not signed this Convention may accede thereto.

3. Ratification, acceptance or accession shall be effected by the deposit of an instrument to that effect with the Director-General of the United Nations Educational, Scientific and Cultural Organization.

ARTICLE IX

1. This Convention shall come into force three months after the deposit of twelve instruments of ratification, acceptance or accession, among which there shall be those of four States which are not members of the International Union for the Protection of Literary and Artistic Works.

2. Subsequently, this Convention shall come into force in respect of each State three months after that State has deposited its instrument of ratification, acceptance or accession.

ARTICLE X

1. Each State party to this Convention undertakes to adopt, in accordance with its Constitution, such measures as are necessary to ensure the application of this Convention.

2. It is understood, however, that at the

time an instrument of ratification, acceptance or accession is deposited on behalf of any State, such State must be in a position under its domestic law to give effect to the terms of this Convention.

ARTICLE XI

1. An Intergovernmental Committee is hereby established with the following duties:

    a) to study the problems concerning the application and operation of this Convention;

    b) to make preparation for periodic revisions of this Convention;

    c) to study any other problems concerning the international protection of copyright, in co-operation with the various interested international organizations, such as the United Nations Educational, Scientific and Cultural Organization, the International Union for the Protection of Literary and Artistic Works and the Organization of American States;

    d) to inform the Contracting States as to its activities.

2. The Committee shall consist of the representatives of twelve Contracting States to be selected with due consideration to fair geographical representation and in conformity with the Resolution relating to this article, annexed to this Convention.

The Director-General of the United Nations Educational, Scientific and Cultural Organization, the Director of the Bureau of the International Union for the Protection of Literary and Artistic Works and the Secretary-General of the Organization of American States, or their representatives, may attend meetings of the Committee in an advisory capacity.

ARTICLE XII

The Intergovernmental Committee shall convene a conference for revision of this Convention whenever it deems necessary, or at the request of at least ten Contracting States, or of a majority of the Contracting States if there are less than twenty Contracting States.

ARTICLE XIII

Any Contracting State may, at the time of deposit of its instrument of ratification, acceptance or accession, or at any time thereafter, declare by notification addressed to the Director-General of the United Nations Educational, Scientific and Cultural Organization that this Convention shall apply to all or any of the countries or territories for the international relations of which it is responsible and this Convention shall thereupon apply to the countries or territories named in such notification after the expiration of the term of three months provided for in article IX. In the absence of such notification, this Convention shall not apply to any such country or territory.

ARTICLE XIV

1. Any Contracting State may denounce this Convention in its own name or on behalf of all or any of the countries or territories as to which a notification has been given under article XIII. The denunciation shall be made by notification addressed to the Director-General of the United Nations Educational, Scientific and Cultural Organization.

2. Such denunciation shall operate only in respect of the State or of the country or territory on whose behalf it was made and shall not take effect until twelve months after the date of receipt of the notification.

ARTICLE XV

A dispute between two or more Contracting States concerning the interpretation or application of this Convention, not settled by negotiation, shall, unless the States concerned agree on some other method of settlement, be brought before the International Court of Justice for determination by it.

ARTICLE XVI

1. This Convention shall be established in English, French and Spanish. The three texts shall be signed and shall be equally authoritative.

2. Official texts of this Convention shall be established in German, Italian and Portuguese.

Any Contracting State or group of Contracting States shall be entitled to have established by the Director-General of the United Nations Educational, Scientific and Cultural Organization other texts in the language of its choice by arrangement with the Director-General.

245

APPENDIX

All such texts shall be annexed to the signed texts of this Convention.

ARTICLE XVII

1. This Convention shall not in any way affect the provisions of the Berne Convention for the Protection of Literary and Artistic Works or membership in the Union created by that Convention.

2. In application of the foregoing paragraph, a Declaration has been annexed to the present article. This Declaration is an integral part of this Convention for the States bound by the Berne Convention on January 1, 1951, or which have or may become bound to it at a later date. The signature of this Convention by such States shall also constitute signature of the said Declaration, and ratification, acceptance or accession by such States shall include the Declaration as well as the Convention.

ARTICLE XVIII

This Convention shall not abrogate multilateral or bilateral copyright conventions or arrangements that are or may be in effect exclusively between two or more American Republics. In the event of any difference either between the provisions of such existing conventions or arrangements and the provisions of this Convention, or between the provisions of this Convention and those of any new convention or arrangement which may be formulated between two or more American Republics after this Convention comes into force, the convention or arrangement most recently formulated shall prevail between the parties thereto. Rights in works acquired in any Contracting State under existing conventions or arrangements before the date this Convention comes into force in such State shall not be affected.

ARTICLE XIX

This Convention shall not abrogate multilateral or bilateral conventions or arrangements in effect between two or more Contracting States. In the event of any difference between the provisions of such existing conventions or arrangements and the provisions of this Convention, the provisions of this Convention shall prevail. Rights in works acquired in any Contracting State under existing conventions or arrangements before the date on which this Convention comes into force in such State shall not be affected. Nothing in this article shall affect the provisions of articles XVII and XVIII of this Convention.

ARTICLE XX

Reservations to this Convention shall not be permitted.

ARTICLE XXI

The Director-General of the United Nations Educational, Scientific and Cultural Organization shall send duly certified copies of this Convention to the States interested, to the Swiss Federal Council and to the Secretary-General of the United Nations for registration by him.

He shall also inform all interested States of the ratifications, acceptances and accessions which have been deposited, the date on which this Convention comes into force, the notifications under article XIII of this Convention, and denunciations under article XIV.

APPENDIX DECLARATION RELATING TO ARTICLE XVII

The States which are members of the International Union for the Protection of Literary and Artistic Works, and which are signatories to the Universal Copyright Convention,

Desiring to reinforce their mutual relations on the basis of the said Union and to avoid any conflict which might result from the co-existence of the Convention of Berne and the Universal Convention,

Have, by common agreement, accepted the terms of the following declaration:

a) Works which, according to the Berne Convention, have as their country of origin a country which has withdrawn from the International Union created by the said Convention, after January 1, 1951, shall not be protected by the Universal Copyright Convention in the countries of the Berne Union;

b) The Universal Copyright Convention shall not be applicable to the relationships among countries of the Berne Union insofar as it relates to the protection of works having as their country of origin, within the meaning of the Berne Convention, a country of the International Union created by the said Convention.

246

RESOLUTION CONCERNING ARTICLE XI

The Intergovernmental Copyright Conference

Having considered the problems relating to the Intergovernmental Committee provided for in article XI of the Universal Copyright Convention

resolves

1. The first members of the Committee shall be representatives of the following twelve States, each of those States designating one representative and an alternate: Argentine, Brazil, France, Germany, India, Italy, Japan, Mexico, Spain, Switzerland, United Kingdom, and United States of America.

2. The Committee shall be constituted as soon as the Convention comes into force in accordance with article XI of this Convention;

3. The Committee shall elect its Chairman and one Vice-Chairman. It shall establish its rules of procedure having regard to the following principles:

a) the normal duration of the term of office of the representatives shall be six years; with one-third retiring every two years;

b) before the expiration of the term of office of any members, the Committee shall decide which States shall cease to be represented on it and which States shall be called upon to designate representatives; the representatives of those States which have not ratified, accepted or acceded shall be the first to retire;

c) the different parts of the world shall be fairly represented;

and expresses the wish

that the United Nations Educational, Scientific, and Cultural Organization provide its Secretariat.

THE BERNE CONVENTION *

For the Protection of Literary and Artistic Works Signed on the 9th September 1886, completed at Paris on the 4th May 1896, revised at Berlin on the 13th November 1908, completed at Berne on the 20th March 1914, revised at Rome on the 2nd June 1928, and REVISED at Brussels on the 26th June 1948.

ARTICLE 1

The Countries to which this Convention applies constitute a Union for the protection of the rights of authors over their literary and artistic works.

ARTICLE 2

(1) The term 'literary and artistic works' shall include every production in the literary, scientific, and artistic domain, whatever may be the mode or form of its expression, such as books, pamphlets, and other writings; lectures, addresses, sermons, and other works of the same nature; dramatic or dramatico-musical works; choreographic works and entertainments in dumb show, the acting form of which is fixed in writing or otherwise; musical compositions with or without words; cinematographic works and works produced by a process analogous to cinematography; works of drawing, painting, architecture, sculpture, engraving, and lithography; photographic works and works produced by a process analogous to photography; works of applied art; illustrations, geographical charts, plans, sketches, and plastic works relative to geography, topography, architecture, or science.

(2) Translations, adaptations, arrangements of music, and other alterations of a literary or artistic work shall be protected as original works without prejudice to the rights of the author of the original work. It shall, however, be a matter for legislation in Countries of the Union to determine the protection to be granted to translations of official texts of a legislative, administrative, and legal nature.

(3) Collections of literary or artistic works such as encyclopaedias and anthologies which by reason of the selection and arrangement of their contents constitute intellectual creations shall be protected as such without prejudice to the rights of the authors in respect of each of the works forming part of such collections.

(4) The works mentioned in this Article shall enjoy protection in all Countries of the Union. This protection shall operate for the benefit of the author and his legal representatives and assignees.

(5) It shall be a matter for legislation in the Countries of the Union to determine the extent of the application of their laws to works of applied art and industrial designs and models, as well as the conditions under which such works, designs, and models shall be protected.

Works protected in the Country of origin solely as designs and models shall be entitled in other Countries of the Union only to such protection as shall be accorded to designs and models in such Countries.

ARTICLE 2bis

(1) It shall be a matter for legislation in Countries of the Union to exclude wholly or in part from the protection afforded by the preceding Article political speeches and speeches delivered in the course of legal proceedings.

(2) It shall also be a matter for legislation in Countries of the Union to determine the conditions under which lectures, addresses, sermons, and other works of the same nature may be reproduced by the press.

(3) Nevertheless, the author alone shall have the right of making a collections of his works mentioned in the above paragraphs.

* Several Articles having to do with procedures, etc., have been omitted.

ARTICLE 3 (omitted)

ARTICLE 4

(1) Authors who are nationals of any of the Countries of the Union shall enjoy in Countries other than the Country of origin of the work, for their works, whether unpublished or first published in a Country of the Union, the rights which their respective laws do now or may hereafter grant to their nationals, as well as the rights specially granted by this Convention.

(2) The enjoyment and the exercise of these rights shall not be subject to any formality; such enjoyment and such exercise shall be independent of the existence of protection in the Country of origin of the work. Consequently, apart from the provisions of this Convention, the extent of protection, as well as the means of redress afforded to the author to protect his rights, shall be governed exclusively by the laws of the Country where protection is claimed.

(3) The Country of origin shall be considered to be, in the case of published works, the Country of first publication, even in the case of works published simultaneously in several Countries of the Union which grant the same term of protection; in the case of works published simultaneously in several Countries of the Union which grant different terms of protection, the Country of which the legislation grants the shortest term of protection. In the case of works published simultaneously in a Country outside the Union and in a Country of the Union, the latter Country shall be considered exclusively as the Country of origin.

A work shall be considered as having been published simultaneously in several Countries which has been published in two or more Countries within thirty days of its first publication.

(4) For the purposes of Articles 4, 5, and 6, 'published works' shall be understood to be works copies of which have been issued and made available in sufficient quantities to the public, whatever may be the means of manufacture of the copies. The presentation of a dramatic, dramatico-musical, or cinematographic work, the performance of a musical work, the public recitation of a literary work, the transmission or the radio-diffusion of literary or artistic works, the exhibition of a work of art and the construction of a work of architecture shall not constitute publication.

(5) The Country of origin shall be considered to be, in the case of unpublished works, the Country to which the author belongs. However, in the case of works of architecture or of graphic and plastic works forming part of a building, the Country of the Union where these works have been built or incorporated in a building shall be considered as the Country of origin.

ARTICLE 5

Authors who are nationals of one of the Countries of the Union, and who first publish their works in another Country of the Union, shall have in the latter Country the same rights as native authors.

ARTICLE 6

(1) Authors who are not nationals of one of the Countries of the Union, and who first publish their works in one of those Countries, shall enjoy in that Country the same rights as native authors, and in the other Countries of the Union the rights granted by the present Convention.

(2) Nevertheless, where any Country outside the Union fails to protect in an adequate manner the works of authors who are nationals of one of the Countries of the Union, the latter Country may restrict the protection given to the works of authors who are, at the date of the first publication thereof, nationals of the other Country and are not effectively domiciled in one of the Countries of the Union. If the Country of first publication avails itself of this right, the other Countries of the Union shall not be required to grant to works thus subjected to special treatment a wider protection than that granted to them in the Country of first publication.

(3) No restrictions introduced by virtue of the preceding paragraph shall affect the rights which an author may have acquired in respect of a work published in a Country of the Union before such restrictions were put into force.

(4) The Countries of the Union which restrict the grant of copyright in accordance with this Article shall give notice thereof to the Government of the Swiss

249

Confederation by a written declaration specifying the Countries in regard to which protection is restricted, and the restrictions to which rights of authors who are nationals of those Countries are subjected. The Government of the Swiss Confederation shall immediately communicate this declaration to all the Countries of the Union.

ARTICLE 6*bis*

(1) Independently of the author's copyright, and even after the transfer of the said copyright, the author shall have the right, during his lifetime, to claim authorship of the work and to object to any distortion, mutilation, or other alteration thereof, or any other action in relation to the said work, which would be prejudicial to his honor or reputation.

(2) In so far as the legislation of the Countries of the Union permits, the rights granted to the author in accordance with the preceding paragraph shall, after his death, be maintained, at least until the expiry of the copyright, and shall be exercisable by the persons or institutions authorized by the said legislation.

The determination of the conditions under which the rights mentioned in this paragraph shall be exercised shall be governed by the legislation of the Countries of the Union.

(3) The means of redress for safeguarding the rights granted by this Article shall be governed by the legislation of the Country where protection is claimed.

ARTICLE 7

(1) The term of protection granted by this Convention shall be the life of the author and fifty years after his death.

(2) However, where one or more Countries of the Union grant a term of protection in excess of that provided by paragraph 1, the term shall be governed by the law of the Country where protection is claimed, but shall not exceed the term fixed in the Country of origin of the work.

(3) In the case of cinematographic works, as well as works produced by a process analogous to cinematography or photography and of works of applied art, the term of protection shall be governed by the law of the Country where protection is claimed, but shall not exceed the term fixed in the Country of origin of the work.

(4) In the case of anonymous and pseudonymous works, the term of protection shall be fixed at fifty years from the date of their publication. However, when the pseudonym adopted by the author leaves no doubt as to his identity, the term of protection shall be that provided in paragraph 1. If the author of an anonymous or pseudonymous work discloses his identity during the abovementioned period, the term of protection applicable shall be that provided in paragraph 1.

(5) In the case of posthumous works which do not fall within the categories of works included in paragraphs 3 and 4 the term of the protection afforded to the heirs and the legal representatives and assignees of the author shall end at the expiry of fifty years after the death of the author.

(6) The term of protection subsequent to the death of the author and the terms provided by paragraphs 3, 4, and 5 shall run from the date of his death or of publication, but such terms shall always be deemed to begin on the first of January of the year following the event which gives rise to them.

ARTICLE 7*bis*

In the case of a work of joint authorship, the term of protection shall be calculated from the date of the death of the last surviving author.

ARTICLE 8

Authors of literary and artistic works protected by this Convention shall have the exclusive right of making and of authorizing the translation of their works throughout the term of protection of their rights in the original works.

ARTICLE 9

(1) Serial novels, short stories, and all other works, whether literary, scientific, or artistic, whatever their purpose, and which are published in the newspapers or periodicals of one of the Countries of the Union shall not be reproduced in the other Countries without the consent of the authors.

(2) Articles on current economic, political, or religious topics may be reproduced by the press unless the reproduction

thereof is expressly reserved; nevertheless, the source must always be clearly indicated. The legal consequences of the breach of this obligation shall be determined by the laws of the Country where protection is claimed.

(3) The protection of this Convention shall not apply to news of the day nor to miscellaneous information having the character of mere items of news.

ARTICLE 10

(1) It shall be permissible in all Countries of the Union to make short quotations from newspaper articles and periodicals, as well as to include them in press summaries.

(2) The right to include excerpts of literary or artistic works in educational or scientific publications, or in chrestomathies, in so far as this inclusion is justified by its purpose, shall be a matter for legislation in the Countries of the Union, and for special arrangements existing or to be concluded between them.

(3) Quotations and excerpts shall be accompanied by an acknowledgment of the source and by the name of the author, if his name appears thereon.

ARTICLE 10bis

It shall be a matter for legislation in Countries of the Union to determine the conditions under which recording, reproduction, and public communication of short extracts from literary and artistic works may be made for the purpose of reporting current events by means of photography, cinematography, or by radiodiffusion.

ARTICLE 11

(1) The authors of dramatic, dramatico-musical, or musical works shall enjoy the exclusive right of authorizing: 1° the public presentation and public performance of their works; 2° the public distribution by any means of the presentation and performance of their works.

The application of the provisions of Articles 11bis and 13 is always reserved.

(2) Authors of dramatic or dramatico-musical works, during the full term of their rights over the original works, shall enjoy the same right with respect to translations thereof.

(3) In order to enjoy the protection of this Article, authors shall not be bound, when publishing their works, to forbid the public presentation of performance thereof.

ARTICLE 11bis

(1) Authors of literary and artistic works shall have the exclusive right of authorizing: 1° the radio-diffusion of their works or the communication thereof to the public by any other means of wireless diffusion of signs, sounds, or images; 2° any communication to the public, whether over wires or not, of the radio-diffusion of the work, when this communication is made by a body other than the original one; 3° the communication to the public by loudspeaker or any other similar instrument transmitting, by signs, sounds, or images, the radio-diffusion of the work.

(2) It shall be a matter for legislation in the Countries of the Union to determine the conditions under which the rights mentioned in the preceding paragraph may be exercised, but these conditions shall apply only in the Countries where they have been prescribed. They shall not in any circumstances be prejudicial to the moral right of the author, nor to his right to obtain just remuneration which, in the absence of agreement, shall be fixed by competent authority.

(3) Except where otherwise provided, permission granted in accordance with the first paragraph of this Article shall not imply permission to record the work radio-diffused by means of instruments recording sounds or images.

It shall, however, be a matter for legislation in the Countries of the Union to determine the regulations for ephemeral recordings made by a broadcasting body by means of its own facilities and used for its own emissions. The preservation of these recordings in official archives may, on the ground of their exceptional documentary character, be authorized by legislation.

ARTICLE 11ter

Authors of literary works shall enjoy the exclusive right of authorizing the public recitation of their works.

ARTICLE 12

Authors of literary, scientific, or artistic works shall enjoy the exclusive right of authorizing adaptations, arrangements, and other alterations of their works.

ARTICLE 13

(1) Authors of musical works shall have the exclusive right of authorizing: 1° the recording of such works by instruments capable of reproducing them mechanically; 2° the public performance of works thus recorded by means of such instruments.

(2) Reservations and conditions relating to the application of the rights mentioned in the preceding paragraph may be determined by legislation in each Country of the Union, in so far as it may be concerned; but all such reservations and conditions shall apply only in the Countries which have prescribed them and shall not, in any circumstances, be prejudicial to the author's right to obtain just remuneration which, in the absence of agreement, shall be fixed by competent authority.

(3) The provisions of the first paragraph of this Article shall not be retroactive and consequently shall not be applicable in a Country of the Union to works which, in that Country, may have been lawfully adapted to mechanical instruments before the coming into force of the Convention signed in Berlin on the 13th November 1908, and, in the case of a Country having acceded to the Convention since that date or acceding to it in the future, before the date of its accession.

(4) Recordings made in accordance with paragraphs 2 and 3 of this Article and imported without permission from the parties concerned into a Country where they are not lawfully allowed, shall be liable to seizure.

ARTICLE 14

(1) Authors of literary, scientific, or artistic works shall have the exclusive right of authorizing: 1° the cinematographic adaptation and reproduction of these works, and the distribution of the works thus adapted or reproduced; 2° the public presentation and performance of the works thus adapted or reproduced.

(2) Without prejudice to the rights of the author of the work adapted or reproduced, a cinematographic work shall be protected as an original work.

(3) The adaptation under any other artistic form of cinematographic productions derived from literary, scientific, or artistic works shall, without prejudice to the authorization of their authors, remain subject to the authorization of the author of the original work.

(4) Cinematographic adaptations of literary, scientific, or artistic works shall not be subject to the reservations and conditions contained in Article 13, paragraph 2.

(5) The provisions of this Article shall apply to reproduction or production effected by any other process analogous to cinematography.

ARTICLE 14*bis*

(1) The author or, after his death, the persons or institutions authorized by national legislation shall, in respect of original works of art and original manuscripts of writers and composers, enjoy the inalienable right to an interest in any sale of the work subsequent to the first disposal of the work by the author.

(2) The protection provided by the preceding paragraph may be claimed in a Country of the Union only if legislation in the Country to which the author belongs so permits, and to the degree permitted by the Country where this protection is claimed.

(3) The procedure for collection and the amounts shall be matters for determination by national legislation.

ARTICLE 15

(1) In order that the author of a literary or artistic work protected by this Convention shall, in the absence of proof to the contrary, be regarded as such, and consequently be entitled to institute infringement proceedings in Countries of the Union, it shall be sufficient for his name to appear on the work in the usual manner. This paragraph shall be applicable even if this name is a pseudonym, where the pseudonym adopted by the author leaves no doubt as to his identity.

(2) In the case of anonymous and pseudonymous works, other than those referred to in the preceding paragraph, the publisher whose name appears on the work shall, in the absence of proof to the contrary, be regarded as representing the author, and in this capacity he shall be entitled to protect and enforce the author's rights. The provisions of this paragraph shall cease to apply if the author reveals his identity and establishes his claim to authorship of the work.

ARTICLE 16

(1) Works infringing copyright may be seized by the competent authorities of any Country of the Union where the original work enjoys legal protection.

(2) In such a Country the seizures may also apply to reproductions imported from a Country where the work is not protected, or has ceased to be protected.

(3) The seizure shall take place in accordance with the legislation of each country.

ARTICLE 17

The provisions of this Convention cannot in any way affect the right of the Government of each Country of the Union to permit, to control, or to prohibit by legislation or regulation, the circulation, presentation, or exhibition of any work or production in regard to which the competent authority may find it necessary to exercise that right.

ARTICLE 18

(1) This Convention shall apply to all works which at the moment of its coming into force have not yet fallen into the public domain in the Country of origin through the expiry of the term of protection.

(2) If, however, through the expiry of the term of protection which was previously granted, a work has fallen into the public domain of the Country where protection is claimed, that work shall not be protected anew.

(3) The application of this principle shall be in accordance with the provisions contained in special Conventions to that effect existing or to be concluded between Countries of the Union. In the absence of such provisions, the respective Countries shall determine, each in so far as it is concerned, the manner in which the said principle is to be applied.

(4) The above provisions shall apply equally in the case of new accessions to the Union, and in the event of protection being extended by the application of Article 7 or by abandonment of reservations.

ARTICLE 19

The provisions of this Convention shall not preclude the making of a claim to the benefit of any wider provisions which may be afforded by legislation in a Country of the Union.

ARTICLE 20

The Governments of the Countries of the Union reserve to themselves the right to enter into special arrangements between each other, in so far as such arrangements shall confer upon authors more extended rights than those granted by the Convention, or embody other provisions not contrary to this Convention. The provisions of existing arrangements which satisfy these conditions shall remain applicable.

ARTICLE 21

(1) The International Office established under the name of the 'Office of the International Union for the Protection of Literary and Artistic Works' shall be maintained.

(2) That Office shall be placed under the high authority of the Government of the Swiss Confederation, which shall regulate its organization and supervise its working.

(3) The official language of the Office shall be the French language.

ARTICLE 22

(1) The International Office shall collect information of every kind relating to the protection of the rights of authors over their literary and artistic works. It shall co-ordinate and publish such information. It shall undertake the study of questions of general interest to the Union, and, by the aid of documents placed at its disposal by the different Administrations, it shall edit a periodical publication in the French language on the questions which concern the purpose of the Union. The Government of the Countries of the Union reserve to themselves the power to authorize by agreement the publication by the Office of an edition in one or more other languages, if by experience, this should be shown to be necessary.

(2) The International Office shall always place itself at the disposal of members of the Union in order to provide them with any special information which they may require relating to the protection of literary and artistic works.

(3) The Director of the International Office shall make an annual report on his

administration, which shall be communicated to all the members of the Union.

[Articles 23 and 24 have to do with expenses and revisions.]

ARTICLE 25

(1) Countries outside the Union which make provision for the legal protection of the rights forming the object of the present Convention may accede thereto upon request.

(2) Such accession shall be notified in writing to the Government of the Swiss Confederation, who shall communicate it to all the other Countries of the Union.

(3) Such accession shall imply full acceptance of all the clauses and admission to all the advantages provided by this Convention, and shall take effect one month after the date of the notification made by the Government of the Swiss Confederation to the other Countries of the Union, unless some later date has been indicated by the acceding Country. It may, nevertheless, contain an indication that the adhering Country wishes to substitute, provisionally at least, for Article 8, which relates to translations, the provisions of Article 5 of the Convention of 1886 revised at Paris in 1896, on the understanding that those provisions shall apply only to translations into the language or languages of that Country.

[Article 26 relates to the application of the Convention to territories and possessions of member Countries.]

ARTICLE 27

(1) This Convention shall replace, in relations between the Countries of the Union, the Convention of Berne of the 9th September 1886, and the subsequent revisions thereof. The instruments previously in force shall continue to be applicable in relations with Countries which do not ratify this Convention.

(2) The Countries on whose behalf this Convention is signed may retain the benefit of the reservations which they have previously formulated, on condition that they make declaration to that effect at the time of the deposit of their ratifications.

(3) Countries which are at present members of the Union, but on whose behalf this Convention is not signed, may accede to it at any time in the form provided for in Article 25. In that event they may enjoy the benefit of the provisions of the preceding paragraph.

[Articles 27*bis* to 31 concern disputes on interpretation, means of ratification, means of withdrawal, reservations, and provide for the official text of the Convention.]

Selected Bibliography

Although the literature on copyright law is voluminous, most writing on the subject is directed to the reader with legal training. The books listed below have been chosen as being most valuable and comprehensible to the average layman.

Amdur, Leon H., *Copyright Law and Practice*, New York, 1936

Bowker, Richard R., *Copyright, Its History and Its Law*, Boston, 1912

Bulletins of the Copyright Society of the U.S.A., New York, 1953 to date

Canyes, Manuel, et al., *Copyright Protection in the Americas*, Washington, D.C., 1950

Copinger, W. A., *The Law of Copyright*, London, 1936

DeWolf, Richard C., *An Outline of Copyright Law*, Boston, 1925

Howell, Herbert A., *The Copyright Law*, Washington, D.C., 1952

Ladas, Stephen P., *The International Protection of Literary and Artistic Property*, New York, 1938

Robertson, G. S., *The Law of Copyright*, Oxford, 1912

Solberg, Thorvald, *Copyright Miscellany*, Boston, 1939

Spring, Samuel, *Risks and Rights in Publishing, Television, Radio, Motion Pictures, Advertising, and the Theater*, New York, 1952

UNESCO Copyright Bulletins, Paris, 1948 to date

U.S. Library of Congress, Copyright Office, *The Copyright Law of the United States of America*, Washington, D.C.

———— *The Copyright Office of the United States of America*, Washington, D.C., 1952

———— *Decisions of the United States Courts involving Copyright*, Washington, D.C., 1909 to date

Wincor, Richard, *How to Secure Copyright*, New York, 1950

Weil, Arthur W., *American Copyright Law*, Chicago, 1917

Wittenberg, Philip, *The Protection and Marketing of Literary Property*, New York, 1937

Cases Cited

The subject of the account in the text to which each case refers is indicated in brackets unless the reference is obvious. The year date is given in parentheses. The final figures in each case refer to the page of the text reference in this book. Most cases will be found in *Decisions of the United States Courts involving Copyright,* Copyright Office Bulletins 17 to 29. See also General Index.

Adventures in Good Eating, Inc. v. *Best Places to Eat* (1942), 98

Advertisers Exchange, Inc. v. *Thomas Drug Store* (1938) [*Successful Drug-store* . . .], 41

Andrews v. *Guenther Publishing Company* (1932) [Government map], 123

Atlas Mfg. Co. v. *Street and Smith* (1913) [*Nick Carter*], 168

Avon Periodicals, Inc. v. *Ziff-Davis Pub. Co.* (1952) ['secondary meaning'], 168

Ballentine v. *DeSylva* (1955) [illegitimate son], 162

B & I Publishing Co., Inc. v. *Ace Magazines, Inc.* (1950) [*Adventures into the Unknown*], 169

Alfred Bell & Co. Ltd. v. *Catalda Fine Arts, Inc.* (1947, 1951) [mezzotints; 'original'], 55, 61

Black v. *Ehrich* (quoted in *Atlas Mfg. Co.* . . . above [trade marks], 168

Blanc v. *Lantz* (1949) ['publication' of motion pictures], 127

Bleistein v. *Donaldson Lithographing Co.* (1903) [Justice Holmes], 42, 54

Brady v. *Reliance Motion Picture Corp.* (1916) [dramatization of novel], 99

Broadway Music Corp. v. *F-R Publishing Corp.* (1940) [*Poor Pauline*], 91

Brondfield v. *Paramount Pictures Corp.* (1951) ['palming off'], 170

James M. Cain v. *Universal Pictures Co., Inc.* (1942) [*Serenade*], 64

Charlie Chaplin v. *Amador* (1928), 169

Clemens v. *Belford* (1883) [Mark Twain], 168

Collins v. *Metro-Goldwyn Pictures Corp.* (1939) [*Test Pilot*], 167

Crimi v. *Rutgers Presbyterian Church in the City of New York* (1949) [mural], 36, 125

Curwood v. *Affiliated Distributors, Inc.* (1922), 124

De Costa v. *Brown* (1944) [Clara Barton], 100

Dreiser v. *Paramount Publix Co.* (1931) [*American Tragedy*], 124

Eggers v. *Sun Sales Corp.* (1920) [Gen. Pershing's report], 148

Eliot v. *Geare Marston, Inc.* (1939) [Nina Wilcox Putnam], 117

Eliot v. *Jones;* v. *Circle Publishing Co.* (1910) [*Dr. Eliot's Five Foot Shelf*], 169

Fisher v. *Star Co.* (1921) [*Mutt and Jeff*], 169

Fleischer Studios, Inc. v. *Ralph A. Freundlich, Inc.* (1934) [doll infringes book], 98

Gordon v. *Weir* (1953) [contest infringed], 98

Gross v. *Seligman* (1914) [photograph], 142

Haas v. *Leo Feist, Inc.* (1916) [innocent infringers; illegal name], 98, 146

Hemingway v. *Film Alliance of the U.S. Inc.* (1940) [*Fifth Column*], 165, 167

Hill v. *Whalen and Martell, Inc.* (1914) [*Mutt and Jeff*], 92

Hirsh v. *Paramount Pictures* (1937) [Strauss], 148

Karll v. *The Curtis Publishing Co.* (1941) [Green Bay Packers], 187

Leon v. *Pacific Telephone and Telegraph Co.* (1937) [phone book], 98–9

Macdonald v. *DuMaurier* (1944) [*Rebecca*], 100

Macmillan v. *King* (1914) [mimeographed sheets], 36

Madison Square Garden Corp. v. *Universal Pictures, Inc.* (quoted in *Metropolitan Opera. . .* below), 169

Edwin B. Marks Music Corp. v. *Borst Music Publishing Co., Inc.* (1953) [widow remarries], 162

Cliff May and Christian E. Choate v. *William M. Bray* (1955) [ranch houses], 52–3

Mazer v. *Stein* (1954) [Balinese dancers], 54

McConnor v. *Kaufman* (1943) [Woollcott], 100

In re McCormick et al. (1952) [soldier's letter to children], 116

Meccano Ltd. v. *Wagner* (1916) [affidavit], 44

Metro-Goldwyn-Mayer Distributing Corp. v. *Bijou Theatre Co.* (1932) ['copying' of motion picture], 127

Metropolitan Opera Association, Inc. v. *Wagner-Nichols Recorder Corp.* (1950), 169

Morton v. *Raphael* (1948) ['publication' of picture], 55

Mutual Broadcasting System v. *Muzak Corp.* (quoted in *Metropolitan Opera . . .* above) [world series], 169

National Comics Publications v. *Fawcett Publications, Inc.* (1951) [*Superman;* 'proprietor'], 118, 145

National Geographic Society v. *Classified Geographic, Inc.* (1939), 99

O'Rourke v. *RKO Radio Pictures, Inc.* (1942) [women's reformatory], 100

Paramore v. *Mack Sennett, Inc.* (1925) [*Yukon Jake*], 127

Patten v. *Superior Talking Pictures* (1934) [*Frank Merriwell*], 165

Photo-Drama Motion Picture Co., Inc. v. *Social Uplift Film Corp.* (1915) [assignment], 60

Pittsburgh Athletic Co. v. *KQV Broadcasting Co.* (quoted in *Metropolitan Opera . . .* above) [baseball], 160

Prouty v. *National Broadcasting Company, Inc.* (1939) [*Stella Dallas*], 124, 170

J. A. Richards, Inc. v. *New York Post, Inc.* (1938) [notice], 198

G. Ricordi and Co. v. *Mason* (1912, 1913) [opera plots], 35, 92

G. Ricordi and Co. v. *Paramount Pictures* (1950) [*Madame Butterfly*], 128

Rudolph Mayer Pictures, Inc. v. *Pathe News, Inc.* (quoted in *Metropolitan Opera. . .* above) [Sharkey-Walker], 169

Sayers v. *Sigmund Spaeth* (1932), 93, 154, 157, 187

Sebring Pottery Co. v. *Steubenville Pottery Co.* (1934) [affidavit; quotation], 44, 69

Shapiro, Bernstein and Co., Inc. v. *P. F. Collier and Son Co. and Joseph P. Mc-Evoy* (1934) ['You Can't Stop Me from Lovin' You'], 91, 93, 187

Stanley v. *Columbia Broadcasting System* (1950), 152

Stein v. *Expert Lamp Company* (1951) [Balinese dancer; see also *Mazer* v. *Stein,* above], 54

Todamerica Musica Ltd. v. *RCA* (1948) [recordings], 106

Toksvig v. *Bruce Publishing Co.* (1950) [Hans Christian Andersen], 99

Twentieth Century Sporting Club, Inc. v. *Transradio Press Service, Inc.* (quoted in *Metropolitan Opera. . .* above) [boxing matches], 169

Walt Disney Productions, Inc. v. *Souvaine Selective Pictures, Inc.* (1951) [*Alice in Wonderland*], 148

259

CASES CITED

Warner Bros. Pictures, Inc. v. *Majestic Pictures Corp.* (1934) [*Gold Diggers*], 127, 167

Washingtonian Publishing Co. v. *Pearson* (1939) [Drew Pearson, deposit], 86

White v. *Kimmell et al.* (1952), 152

Wright v. *Eisle* (1903) [architectural plans], 54

Index

Figures in brackets refer to sections of the Copyright Act, given in full, pages 227–41, and in outline, pages 19–24. Preceding the general index is an alphabetical list of cases cited in the text.

A

Abie's Irish Rose, 98
Abraham Lincoln, 166, 167
Abridgments, 19, 20, 35–6, 92, 133, 135, 148 [1b, 7]
Access, in infringement, 98, 99
Acknowledgment of source material, 83, 187, 199–200; *see also* Credit
Act of 8 Anne, 3–4, 5
Acting versions, 76, 88, 151, 184
Actors' rights, 159, 169
Ad interim copyright, 20, 21, 22, 37–9, 179–80 [9c, 16, 22, 23]
Adaptations, 19, 20, 35–6 [1b, 7]
  of maps, 123
  of music, 130
  of works in public domain, 35–6, 62, 76, 88, 148
  American edition of, 102, 138, 151, 168, 180, 195
  and importation, 7–8, 179–80
  notice in, 17, 137, 151, 179
  periodicals, 134
  and U.S. citizens, 8, 180
  vitiation of, 147, 179
Administrator, as copyright proprietor, 16, 20 [9]
Adventures in Good Eating, 98
Adventures into the Unknown, 169
Advertisements, 20, 40–42 [6]
  catalogues, 14, 95
  classification, 14, 77–8
  may appear before title page, 138
  quotations in, 156
  use of letters in, 115–16; of photographs, 142
  see also Prints and Labels
Affidavit, 17, 21, 23, 43–4, 122, 134, 180 [17, 18, 209]
Alice in Wonderland, 148
'All rights reserved,' 102, 105, 140

American edition of foreign works, 22, 37–8, 102, 168 [23]
  see also Ad interim copyright; Foreign works
American Tragedy, An, 124
Anatomical models, 49
Andersen, Hans, 99
Anonymous works, 17, 66, 103, 112, 113
Anthologies, 82–3, 180–81
  material in, 118, 131, 138, 156
  see also Compilations
Applications, 17, 19, 22, 30, 47–51 [5, 22, 24]
  for Canadian registration, 104
  with deposit copy, 85
  false information in, 64
  and notice, 139
  statement of new matter in, 132
Applied art, in Berne Convention, 111
  in UCC, 171
Architecture, 20, 21, 49, 52–3, 76, 110, 111, 142, 151 [5g, i, 12e, 19]
'Are you Listening?' 91, 93, 187
Art and designs for works of art, 54–6
  see also Artistic works
Artistic works, 20, 21, 54–6 [5g, i, 12e, 19]
  classification of, 14, 76
  commercial, *see* Advertisements; Prints and Labels
  in early copyright law, 6, 7
  notice, 137
  in periodicals and books, 95, 118
  publication of, 150
  radio and television use, 159
  unpublished, 174
  see also Illustrations
Assignee, as copyright claimant, 22, 46, 59, 115, 146 [32]
  in notice, 135, 182
  acquires all rights, 59, 117
Assignment, 22, 59–60, 181–3 [28–32]
  of contributions, 65, 119–20, 135, 138

261

Assignment (*continued*)
fee for recording, 57–8, 94
in foreign countries, 46, 58, 112, 118
of illustrations, 95
not license, 114
and moral rights, 125
of music, 131
and notice, 133, 138, 140, 145, 199
of posthumous works, 139
reasons for making, 65
recording of, 6, 9
of renewals, 162
of serials, 181
Author, 19, 20, 22, 61–8 [1, 2, 9, 10, 24c]
and abridgments, 35
in the Act of Anne, 3
co-author, 65, 130, 156
common-law rights of, 66, 80–81
of contributions, 119–20
and copyright notice, 64–5, 66, 118; *see also* Notice
deceased, 139, 196–7, 200
employer as, 61–2, 66, 145
foreign, 17, 45–6, 101; *see also under* Foreign works
ghost writers, 61
and illustrators, 66, 96
and infringement, 97
and International Copyright Union, 113
moral rights of, 124–5
and permissions, 62, 156
pseudonyms, *see* Pen Names
and publication, 174
of radio and television material, 158
renewal rights of, 18, 160–63
responsibilities of, 62–4
rights granted to, 66, 97
translators, 61
'Authorized agent,' 43
Autobiography of Mr. Tutt, 63

B

Background use, 91, 100, 130
Balinese dancer lamp base, 54
'Ballad of Yukon Jake,' 127
Ballets, 48, 73, 184
Bankruptcy, 59, 64, 66
Barton, Clara, 100
Berne Convention, *see* International Copyright Union
Biography, infringed, 100
Blind, works for, 21, 23, 121 [16, 107a]
Bodleian Library, 86
Bolivia, 105

Books, 16–18, 19–23, 28–31, 69–72 [1, 5a, 7, 16–17, 19–23, 26, 107–9]
and Berne Convention, 110–11, 113
'best edition,' 37, 84
classification of, 13–14, 47–8, 74–5
covers, 95
of foreign origin, *see* Foreign works
manufacture of, 121–2
new editions of, 132, 183–4, 195–8
notice in, 137–8
photographs and illustrations in, 55–6, 95, 141
published before registration, 69, 71, 75, 150, 174
and radio and television, 159, 202
see also Ad interim; Contributions; Deposit
Bookseller, culpable in infringement, 97
British Museum, 86, 103
Brussels Convention, *see* International Copyright Union
Buenos Aires Convention, 90, 105–6, 107–9, 140, 189
Bulletins, classification of, 14, 75
Business names, 15, 139, 145–6
Byron, George Gordon, 64

C

C in a circle (©), 8, 20, 21, 25, 72, 123, 137, 140, 172–3 [9c, 19]
Cain, James, 64
Cain, 64
Cambridge University Library, 86
Canada, 90, 104, 105, 111
registration form, 104
Carols, book of, 69
Cartoons, 56, 74, 75, 136, 169
Catalog of Copyright Entries, 12, 23, 164, 165 [210, 211]
Catalogue card with foreign deposits, 37, 85, 130, 188, 213
Catalogues, 40–42, 47
see also Advertisements
Caxton, William, 3
Certificate of registration, 17, 20, 23, 24 [10, 209, 215]
Chace Act, 7
Characters, 170
Charlie Chaplin, 169
Charts, 14, 77
Check books, 62
Check list for copyrighting literary works, 28–31
Children of authors, renewal rights, 22, 160–62 [24]
Choreographic works, 73, 111
Circulars, *see* Advertisements

Circus acts, 76, 87
Citation of sources, 91, 99; *see also* Credit
Classification, 13-15, 17, 19, 74-8, 183-4 [5]
  of architectural designs, 52
  of books, 19
  common errors in, 50
  of motion pictures, 126
  of works for oral delivery, 114
  of periodicals, 134
  of photographs, 141-2
  of radio and television material, 158, 183
  of typical copyright material, 13-15, 77-8
Clay, Henry, 6
Clemens, Samuel, 168, 201
Co-authors, *see* Author
'Coastal Route to Florida,' 117
Cohens and the Kellys, 98
Collaborations, 60; *see also* Authors
Collective works, *see* Compilations
Colliers, 91
Comic books, 71
Comic operas, 76; *see also* Dramas; Musical works
Comic strips, 74
Commercial art, 40-42, 77; *see also* Advertisements
Common errors
  on affidavits, 43-4
  on application forms, 50-51
  of fees, 94
  of notice, 139-40
Common source material, not infringement, 98
Common-law rights, 3, 17, 19, 66, 79-81 [2]
  of alien authors, 45
  assignment of, 58
  after author's death, 144
  cessation of, 80-81
  defined, 80
  of dramatists, 88
  on letters, 116
  of maps, 76, 123
  and moral rights, 124
  and radio and television, 158-9
  and unpublished works, 114, 115 126, 174-5, 206
Compilations, 13, 14, 20, 22, 47, 74, 82-3, 92, 118, 155, 185 [7, 24]
  notice in, 138
  of work in the public domain, 148
  see also Composite works
Composer, may renew, 161
Composite works, 19, 22, 47 [3, 5a, 24]
  contributions to, 84-5

renewal of, 18, 146, 162
  see also Compilations
Condensations, 124, 135
Constitution of the United States, basis of copyright law, 3, 5, 61, 93
Construction, of architecture, 52, 110, 112
Containers, 40-41
Contest, infringed, 98
Contracts, 61
  determine position of proprietor, 87, 117, 144, 145
  essential information of, 118, 128
  and moral rights, 124
  and renewal rights, 163
  and unfair competition, 170
Contributions to periodicals, 21, 22, 97, 119-20, 182 [13, 24]
  ad interim copyright on, 47
  advertisements, 15, 40, 135
  application form, 47-8, 210
  architectural plans, 53
  assignment of, 60, 65, 135
  classification of, 75
  deposit, 84
  enlarged into books, 132, 138, 183, 196
  to foreign periodicals, 47, 75
  illustrations, 56, 95
  and license, 117-18
  and notice, 135
  photographs, 77, 135, 141
  renewal of, 146, 162
  special registration for, 119-20
'Copying,' 92, 97
Copyright
  abandonment of, 39, 148
  of art work, 95
  common law *v.* statutory, 79-80
  of contributions, 119
  depends on first publication, 67, 150, 151-2
  depends on notice, 147
  early history of, 3-8
  expiration of, 147
  flaw in invites infringement, 128
  indivisibility of, 59, 119
  material not subject to, 15, 38, 41, 62
  of periodical protects contents, 135
  prolongation of, 132, 148
  renewal of, 160-61
  of whole protects parts, 9, 135
Copyright Act, 222-41
  and ad interim copyright, 38
  administration of, 9
  and affidavit, 43
  on copyright material, 13
  on fair use, 154
  moral rights not mentioned in, 124

Copyright Act (*continued*)
  outline of, 19–24
  on pen names, 139
  'publication with notice,' 137
  and radio and television, 158, 159
  Sunday, holiday provision, 150, 160
Copyright Office, 9–12, 23–4 [201–15]
  calls attention to errors, 44
  can refuse to register, 132
  circulars issued by, 106n.
  on fair use, 154
  furnishes forms, 47
  under Library of Congress, 7
  makes searches, 164
  may demand deposit, 83–6
  registers prints and labels, 40
  and renewals, 160–64
Copyright owner, 16, 20 [9]
  in application forms, 43, 70
  of art work, 95–6
  assumed to be author, 103
  in Berne Convention, 113
  not responsible for unauthorized acts,
    152
  of photographs, 142
  and radio, 158
  of reproductions, 76
  see also Author; Proprietor
Copyright symbol, *see* C in a circle
Corporations, as author, 22, 43, 145–6
  [24]
Courtesy fees, *see* Fees
Cover, as title page, 138, 198
Credit (lines), 82, 156–7, 189–90, 198
Criticism, as fair use, 91–2, 131, 154, 200
Curll, Edmund, 115
Curwood, Oliver, 124
Cyclopedic works, 19, 22, 74, 146, 161
  [5a, 24]
  British, 103

D

Damages, 42, 80, 99 [2, 101b]
Dances, 73, 75, 76
Dates, 21, 22 [17, 19, 26]
  of ad interim copyright, 38, 138
  of affidavit, 43–4
  of completion of printing, 43
  in notice, 55, 123, 137–9, 141, 171
  of publication, 43, 137, 199
Deception of the public, 63–4, 124, 136,
  169–70
  see also Unfair competition
*Decisions of the U.S. Courts involving
  Copyrights*, 10, 225
Dedication to the public, 66, 80, 149

Definitions, 74–7
  art, 54
  author entitled to copyright, 20 [9]
  books, 13–14, 16n., 69
  copyright claimant, 16
  date of publication, 150
  domiciled, 16n., 45
  dramas, 87
  fair use, 93
  labels, 40
  limited publication, 151–2
  periodicals, 134
  'print, publish, and vend,' 97
  prints, 40
  property rights, 169
  publication, 150–51
  trade mark, 41
  unfair competition, 170
Deposit accounts, 94
Deposit and deposit copies, 17, 20–21,
    22, 23, 84–6, 184–5 [11–15, 22–3,
    213–14]
  of ad interim books, 37, 84–5, 137
  of art, 55
  of books, 72
  in British law, 86, 103
  in Canada, 105
  of contributions to periodicals, 84,
    119
  of dramas, 87
  in early law, 4, 6, 7, 9
  of foreign works, 37, 84–5, 137
  of illustrations, 75
  no action for infringement before, 21
    [13], 25 (III.3), 86
  justification for, 86
  of lectures and addresses, 114
  mailing of, 85
  of maps, 123
  of motion pictures, 126
  of music, 129; and music dramas, 87
  of newspapers and periodicals, 134
  penalties for failure to, 85–6
  of photographs, 141
  of published works, 17–18
  renewals do not require, 161
  sheets not acceptable, 185
  of unpublished works, 85, 151, 175
Designs for works of art, 6, 7, 19, 21,
    54–6 [5g, 13, 19]
  architects, 52–3, 54
  stage designs, 54
DeWolf, Richard, 69, 93, 105
Diaries, 79
Dictionaries, 14, 74
  used in comparing, 92
Digests, 35–6
  and moral rights, 124

of textbooks, 36
written permission for, 155, 156
Directories, 47
Disney, Walt, 148
'Dr. Eliot's Five Foot Shelf,' 169
Doll, infringed, 98
Domicile, 45
Dramatic works, 19, 20, 21, 87–8 [1, 5d, 7, 12, 19]
  acting versions of, 76, 88, 151
  application forms, 48, 75, 217
  in Berne Convention, 113
  not books, 16, 69, 87
  in collections, 14, 180
  importation allowed, 87
  U.S. manufacture not required, 87, 121
  may be reviewed, 136
  notice in, 88, 137
  performance not publication, 88, 151
  radio and television scripts, 87, 158–9
  rights of authors, 67, 88, 124
  titles of, 88, 165
  unpublished, 17, 88, 174
  in UCC, 171, 185
Dramatico-musical works, 14, 15, 19, 48, 73, 75, 87–8, 127, 130, 159, 174 [5d]
Dramatizations, 13, 19, 97, 127 [1, 7]
  fair use in, 91
  license of, 117
  of news, 88
  on radio and television, 124, 136, 159
Drawings and plastic works, 12, 15, 19, 21, 49, 76, 174 [5i, 13, 19]
  architect's plans, 52
  relief maps, 76 (F and I), 123
  see also Artistic works; Designs
Dreiser, Theodore, 124
Drinkwater, John, 166, 167
Dumas, Alexandre, 92
Du Maurier, Daphne, 100
Duration of copyright, 18, 22, 89–90, 150, 185 [24–5]
  of ad interim books, 38
  of antedated copyrights, 89, 138
  in Berne Convention, 112
  British, 90, 103–4
  Buenos Aires Convention, 90, 105
  of contributions, 119
  of dramas, unpublished, 88
  foreign, 66, 89–90, 103–4, 191
  of lectures, 114
  licenses, 117
  of posthumous works, 144
  not affected by suspended publication, 90, 185; or by trade mark, 168
  starts with first publication, 150
  in UCC, 171–2

E

Edinburgh University, Library of, 86
Editing and editorial equipment, 13, 35, 82, 132, 148
  comment, 91, 136
Employers of work done for hire, 18, 22, 61–2, 66, 145, 204–5 [24]
  in British law, 103
  of illustrations, 95–6
  of photographs, 141–2
  may renew, 146, 161
Encyclopedias, 14, 18
Engineering designs, 76
Engravings, 6, 7, 55, 76; see also Photo-engravings
Errors, 20, 21 [5, 21]
  in affidavits, 43–4
  in applications, 50–51
  in classification not fatal, 74
  evidence of copying, 99
  in fees, 94
  in forms, 50–51
  in quotations, 98
Essays, see Books; Contributions
Etchings, 6, 49, 76
Eurythmics, 73
Executors, 16, 18, 20, 22, 161–2, 204–5 [9, 24]
Exhibition, of art, 55–6, 112, 151
  of films, 127, 151

F

Facts not copyrightable, 15, 135, 148
Fair trade laws, see Unfair competition
Fair use, 91–3, 98, 154, 185–7
  background use, 91, 100, 130
  checking for comparison, 92
  comment, 91
  in common law, 79
  for critical or scholarly purposes, 91–2, 154–5
  to determine, 92, 187
  length of quotation, 92–3, 155, 186–7, 200
  of music, 130, 186
  plot résumés, 35, 92, 155
  see also Infringement; Quotations
Federal courts, 80
Federal Trade Commission, 35, 38, 133
Fees, 24, 94 [215]
  for ad interim registration, 37
  for advertisements, 40
  for books and other registered works, 18, 24, 72
  courtesy fees, 102, 155, 192

Fees (*continued*)
  for permission to quote, 157, 180, 187–8
  for recording assignments, 57–8
  for renewals, 161
  for search, 164
Fictional biography, infringed, 100
Field and Stream, 168
Fifth Column, The, 165, 167
Filmstrips, 49
Fines, *see* Penalties
Firebird case, 157
Fledermaus, Die, 148
Foreign countries, 21, 101–9, 110–13, 118n. [16]
  assignments in, 58
  copyright term in, 89–90, 103–5
  moral rights in, 124
  performers' rights in, 169
  photographs in, 142
Foreign language books, 23, 121–2 [107]
Foreign rights, 118
Foreign works, 17, 20, 21, 22, 23, 173, 189–95 [9b and c, 13, 22, 107]
  authors of, 45–6, 101
  copyright status, 155
  deposit copies of, 84–6
  duration of copyright of, 66, 90, 151, 191
  in English, 45–6, 121–2
  importation of, 121
  music, 129–30
  should carry a notice, 46, 137n., 140
  periodicals, 134
  permission to quote from, 155–6
  posthumous, 144
  registration of, 37, 47–8, 75
  unprotected, 46, 147
Forest and Stream, 168
Formalities, 16–17, 20–22 [10–25]
  under British law, 56, 103, 191
  in International Copyright Union, 86, 112
  under UCC, 46, 101, 171
  see also Deposit; Manufacturing clause; Notice; Registration
Forms, 47–51, 207–26
  ad interim, 37–8, 47, 210
  affidavit, 43, 209
  book published in U.S., 47, 70, 208
  commercial print or label, 40, 50, 224
  contribution to a periodical, 48, 119, 215
  design for art, 49, 54, 221
  drama and music drama, 48, 87, 217
  foreign books, 47–8, 212

  lectures and works for oral delivery, 48, 114, 216
  maps, 49, 123, 220
  motion pictures, 50, 126, 225
  music, 48–9, 129, 219
  periodicals, 48, 134, 214
  photographs, 49, 141, 223
  prints and pictorial illustrations, 50, 95, 224
  renewals, 50, 160, 226
  U.S. edition of ad interim, 38, 47, 208
'Frank Merriwell,' 165
Fraud, 165, 167, 169, 170
Fraudulent notice, *see* Notice
Fraudulent writings, 63–4, 124

G

Gags, 15
Games, 14, 15, 54, 72
Gazetteers, 19, 74
General Pershing's Report, 148
Ghost writers, 61
Glassware, 49, 76
Globes, 49, 76
Gold Diggers, The, 127, 167
Good will, 97, 169, 170
Government, publications of, 20, 116, 123, 147–8 [8]
Graphic arts, *see* Architecture; Designs; Drawings; Maps; Photographs
Great Britain, 101–4, 189–94
  advertising protected in, 42
  author as copyright owner, 103
  compulsory license in, 103
  deposit in, 86, 103
  duration of copyright in, 90, 103–4, 163, 185
  early laws on copyright in, 3, 4, 5
  and International Copyright Union, 103
  simultaneous publication in, 110
Greeting cards, 50, 72, 77
Guide books, 92

H

Haas and Cahalin, 146
Halftones, classification of, 141
Havana Conference, 105
Hemingway, Ernest, 165, 167
Hoax, 63
Holland, 111
Holmes, Justice, 42, 54
Hopwood, Avery, 127
House organs, 61
How to copyright literary works, 16–18
Hymnals, 130

I

Ideas, plans, systems, 14, 15, 79, 88, 98, 158, 169, 182–3
Illustrations, 21, 75–6 [16]
  in advertising, 40
  application form for, 50, 224
  in books, 56, 121, 132, 188
  in magazines, 56, 77
  and manufacturing clause, 21, 121
  of material in public domain, 147
  musical, 130–31
  permission to use, 156
  photographs, 142
  renewal of, 146, 162
  see also Artistic works
Illustrators, 66
  may renew, 161–2
Immoral works, 15, 64
Importation, 16, 21, 22, 23, 38–9, 121–2, 151, 192 [16, 22, 107–8]
  in Canadian law, 103
Incidents, not copyrightable, 88
Indexes, 132
Industrial art, 54
Information Please, 168
Infringement, 21, 22–3, 44, 97–100, 145 [21, 101–5]
  abridgment may be, 35–6
  of alien's rights, 45, 102
  acknowledgment does not excuse, 99
  of architectural design, 53–4
  of books, 98, 99, 124, 159
  in Buenos Aires Convention, 105
  competition a factor in, 154
  of compilations, 83
  before deposit, 86
  of derivative works, 148
  digests of textbooks, 36
  of dramas, 88
  of engravings, 55
  innocent, 38, 59, 60, 62, 99
  of lamp base, 54
  of lecture, 114
  and licensee, 117
  of maps, 99, 123
  of motion pictures, 127–8
  of music, 130, 146, 148, 158
  of newspaper, 135–6
  of photographs, 42, 93, 142–3
  of unpublished works, 79
  by not verifying sources, 92
  see also Fair use; Unfair competition
Inge, W. R., 98
Initials in notice, 40
Innocents, The, 163

International Copyright relations, 45–6, 101–9, 171–3, 189–95
  table of, 107–9
International Copyright Union, 4, 5, 7, 101, 103, 110–13, 189
  advertising and commercial work, 42
  deposit, 86
  duration of copyright, 89–90, 112
  member countries, 107–9
  moral rights, 113, 124, 157
  obstacles to U.S. joining, 111
  posthumous works, 112, 144
  publication, 112, 153
  to secure copyright in, 103, 111–12
Invalidation of copyright, 44, 60, 144, 146, 151, 160

J

Jackets, dust, 42, 167, 188
James, Henry, 163
Jewelry, 49, 76
Journals, 14, 16, 134
Juke boxes, 130
Jurisdiction of courts, 6, 9

K

Keys, to maps, etc., 76, 123
Kilmer, Joyce, 91
Kipling, Rudyard, 193

L

Labels, see Prints and Labels
Ladas, Stephen, 92
Lanham Trade-Mark Act, 41
Latin American countries, see Buenos Aires Convention
Law digests, 92
Leaflets, 14, 40, 47, 74
Lectures, 14, 19, 20, 76, 114 [1, 5c, 12]
  application form, 216
  copyrightable unpublished, 174
  and radio, 158
  reading of not publication, 151
  may be reported, 136
Letters, 42, 79, 115–16
Liability, 97
Libel, 63
Librarian of Congress, 7, 10, 23–4, 86 [213, 214]
Libraries, British, 86, 103, 191
Libretti, 15, 130
License, 117–18
  for abridgments and adaptations, 36
  from aliens, 46

License (*continued*)
  vs. assignment, 58, 59, 65, 138, 182
  of contributions, 119
  granted by, 67
  and moral rights, 124
  to reprint in Canada, 104, 111; in England, 103
  rights controlled by, 64
  see also Contracts
Licensee, proprietor as, 145
Literary merit, not essential to copyright, 13, 75
Literary property, check list for copyrighting, 28–31
  how to copyright, 16–18
  rights granted to owners of, 67, 97
  see also Books
Lithographs, and lithography, 21, 49, 77, 96, 121 [16]
Luther's catechism, 4
Lyricist, may renew for composer, 161
Lyrics, 14, 74, 129–30
  see also Songs

M

McEvoy, J. P., 91, 93
Madame Butterfly, 178
Magazines, 14, 48, 134–6
  digest, 35
  illustrations, 95
  manufacture of, 121
  publication of, 150
  renewal of, 18, 146, 162
  titles, 165, 168, 169
  see also Contributions; Newspapers and Periodicals
Manufacturing clause, 21, 23, 121–2 [16, 17, 107]
  books, 69–70
  illustrations, 96
  music, 129–30
  newspapers and periodicals, 134
  and UCC, 8, 101
Manuscripts
  protected at common law, 17, 66, 79–80, 184
  'publication' of, 150, 151–2
Maps, 14, 19, 21, 123, 151 [5f, 19]
  application form, 49, 76, 220
  in container or pocket, 41
  infringement of, 99
  relief maps, 49, 123
March of Time, 168
Marionette shows, 87
Mark Twain, 79, 168, 201
Masthead, equal to title page, 134, 137
Mechanical devices, directions for, 14

Mechanical reproduction of music, *see* Records and recording
Medical works, 92
Metropolitan Opera Association, 169
Miller, 98
Mimeographed copies, 36, 150, 180, 195
Mimicry, fair use, 91
Models, 7, 19, 21, 52, 54, 76 [5g, 12, 19]
Monologues, 48, 75, 114
Monuments, designs for, 54
Moral rights, 124–5
  in derivative material, 36
  infringement of, 157
  in International Copyright Union, 112, 113, 157
Motion pictures, 14, 19, 21, 77, 126–8 [5l and m, 12]
  application form, 50, 77, 225
  and assignments, 60, 117
  Buenos Aires, 106
  dances in, 73
  and fair use, 91
  and International Copyright Union, 113
  and moral rights, 124–5
  publication of, 151
  scripts, 72, 87
  titles, 165, 167
  UCC, 153
  unfair competition, 169–70
  unpublished, 174
Mottoes, not copyrightable, 15
Murals, 36, 54, 55, 61, 125
Musical plays and comedies, *see* Dramatico-musical works
Musical works, 12, 14, 17, 19, 20, 21, 129–31 [1, 5e, 9c, 19, 20]
  adaptations of, 36, 148
  application forms, 48–9, 76, 219
  in International Copyright Union, 113
  notice in, 137
  publication of, 150
  and radio, and television, 158–9
  renewal of, 161
  rights, 67
  UCC, 171
  unpublished, 174
'Mutt and Jeff,' 92, 169

N

Names, 15
  application errors, 50–51
  must be legal, 138–9
  in posthumous works, 139
  on renewals, 161
Napoleon, 4
National Geographic Magazine, 99

New editions, 20, 123, 132–3, 195–8 [7]
see also Reissued books
New versions, 20, 132 [7]
see also Versions, other
New works, 35, 36, 40–41
New Yorker, The, 91
News, 14, 15, 88, 135–6, 148
Newspapers and periodicals, 14–15, 19, 21, 22, 23, 134–6 [5b, 16, 20, 22, 23, 24, 107]
    application form, 48, 75, 214
    assignment of copyrights, 60, 65, 119–20, 135, 138
    deposit account for, 94
    foreign, 47
    in International Copyright Union, 113
    and manufacturing clause, 16, 122
    notice in, 16, 17, 137–8
    permissions, 155
    publication of, 150
    renewal of, 18, 162
    titles of, 165, 167, 168
Nichols, Anne, 98
'Nick Carter,' 168
Notice, 6, 7, 14, 15, 16, 17, 20, 21, 23, 137–40 [9c, 10, 19, 20, 21, 105, 106]
    in abridgments, 35
    in ad interim works, 37–9
    in advertisements, 40–41
    antedated, 90, 135
    in artist's name, 95; assignee's, 57; author's 64, 118
    in Buenos Aires Convention, 105
    in compilation, 82
    on containers, 40
    in contribution to periodical, 14, 40, 119–20, 135
    correction of, 19, 198–9
    date in, 62, 71, 132
    in digests, 35
    on a doubleton, 197
    in dramatic works, 88
    on dust jackets, 42
    errors in, 139–40
    on foreign books, 64, 101, 122, 151, 171; in foreign countries, 46, 63
    in Great Britain, 103
    in Havana Conference, 105
    on illustrations, 56, 95
    a legal name, 145–6
    by licensee, 118
    on maps, 123
    in motion pictures, 126
    on music, 129; and music dramas, 87
    necessary for copyright, 147
    on new editions (reissued books), 132, 196
    on newspapers and periodicals, 134–5
    omission of, 139, 199
    on photographs, 141
    postdated, 90, 152
    on posthumous works, 144, 201
    purpose of, 140
    radio and television, 159, 202–3
    of renewal, 162
    in Washington Conference, 106
    on works of art, 55
    see also UCC; C in a circle

O

Obscene works, 15, 64
Operas, résumés of stories of, 35
    see also Dramatico-musical works
Oral delivery, 19, 20, 48, 75, 97, 114, 174 [1, 5c, 12]
    see also Lectures, etc.
Originality, 13, 41, 54, 61, 83, 98
    and the author, 62
    in maps, 123
    in new versions, 130
    not in price lists, 41
'Other version,' *see* Versions
Outline of Copyright Law, 69, 93, 105
Outline of the Act of 1909, 19–24

P

Paintings, 7, 54, 76, 98
    see also Artistic works
Pamphlets, 16n., 40–42, 47, 74
Pan American Convention, 106
Pantomimes, 48, 73, 75, 87, 111
Paper dolls, 75
Parodies, 91
Patent Office, 7, 41, 75, 168
Patents, 7, 41, 54, 62
    books not subject to, 184
Patterns, 54
Pearson, Drew, 86
Pen names, 15, 65, 139, 199 [24]
    and unfair competition, 170
    see also Pseudonymous works
Penalties, 21, 22–3, 97, 100 [14, 18, 101–5]
    in early copyright laws, 6, 7
    for failure to deposit, 86
    for false affidavit, 44
    see also Damages
Performance, 7, 14–15, 19, 75, 87 [1d]
    amateur, 88
    in International Copyright Union, 110, 111–13
    of music, 129, 151, 158–9
    not publication, 88, 151
    rights, 97

Periodicals, *see* Newspapers and Periodicals

Permissible use, *see* Fair use

Permissions, 154–7
 for abridgments and adaptations, 35–6
 for anthologies, 82–3, 131, 180
 author's responsibility, 62
 under common law, 80
 for letters, 115
 for music, 130–31
 for photographs, 142
 for radio and television, 158–9
 if refused, 93
 from true owner, 99, 200
 see also Quotations

Philadelphia Suburban Life, 167

Philippine Islands, 106

Photo-engravings, 21, 77, 96, 141–2, 202 [16]

Photographs, 7, 12, 15, 19, 21, 77, 141–3 [5j, 12, 19]
 in advertising, 42, 188–9
 application form, 49, 141, 223
 of buildings, 53
 done for hire, 61
 infringement, 93, 98
 in periodicals, 77, 136
 under UCC, 171
 unpublished, 174

Pictorial illustrations, 7, 19, 21, 141–2 [5k, 19]

Picture books, 14, 74

Piratical editions, 3, 5, 6, 15, 23 [105, 106]
 importation of, 102
 and manufacturing clause, 38

Plagiarism, 13, 62, 98

Plans, methods, systems, 15
 architect's plans, 52–3, 54

Plastic works, 19, 21, 52, 54, 76 [5i, 12, 13, 19]

Plates, 121

Plays, *see* Dramatic works

Plots, 15, 88, 99

Poems, 14, 16n., 69, 133
 infringement of, 91, 127
 license to print, 118
 must be published to copyright, 17
 for oral delivery, 118
 in periodicals, 119–20
 quotation from, 155, 186, 199, 200
 see also Books; Contributions

'Poor Pauline,' 91

Pope, Alexander, 115

Postcards, 42, 50, 77, 142

Posters, 42

Posthumous works, 22, 103, 112, 144 [24]

notice in, 139, 146, 200–201
renewal of, 144, 161

Previews, 126

Price list, 41

Prima facie evidence, 17

Printers, 43, 97

Prints and labels, 5, 19, 20, 21, 40–42, 50, 77, 141–2, 150 [5k, 6, 19]
 application form, 224
 in early laws, 7, 12
 in magazines, 40
 notice, 40–41, 137
 renewal of, 160
 see also Advertisements

Privacy, right of, 42, 63, 65, 124–5, 142, 156, 188

Proceedings of societies, 75

Proclaimed countries, 107–9

Proof copies, 84

Property rights, 98, 169

Proprietor, 20, 21, 22, 145–6 [9, 19, 20, 24, 28]
 and the Act of Anne, 3
 of ad interim copyright, **37–8, 179**
 as copyright claimant, 16, 46
 holds copyright in trust, 119–20, 135, 145
 and renewals, 18, 146, 160–62
 and titles, 168

Prospectuses, 42

Prouty, Mrs. O., 124

Pseudonymous works, 103, 112–13, 125

Public delivery, for profit, 114
 not publication, 87–8, 114, 151
 right of, 97
 see also Dramatic works; Lectures; Music; Radio

Public domain, works in, 20, 147–9 [8]
 abridgments and adaptations of, 35–6, 62, 76
 art, 54
 foreign, 102
 illustrations of, 156
 maps, 123
 music, 54, 130
 new versions of, 88, 199, 201
 photo-engravings of, 55
 photographs of, 142
 titles in, 127, 166–7, 168
 UCC, 171

Public Information Office, 9

Publication, 14, 15, 20, 21, 22, 44, 66, 150–53 [10, 17, 24, 26]
 of architecture, 52
 of art and sculpture, 55, 76
 of books, 69, 174
 broadcasting not, 88, 158

of dramas, 88
defined, 150–51
'first,' 90, 101, 112, 150
in Great Britain, 103, 191
'limited,' 151–2
of motion pictures, 126–7
of music, 129
performance is not, 48–9, 88, 114
of periodicals, 134
of photographs, 141
simultaneous, 90, 110, 172, 191–3
telecasting is not, 87, 158
telegram not, 115
Publisher, 145–6
and assignments, 59, 60
culpable in infringements, 97
deposit accounts for, 94
and license, 118
of newspapers and periodicals, 135
of posthumous works, 113, 139, 144
may renew for author, 163, 204
Putnam, George, 6
Putnam, Nina Wilcox, 117

Q

Quarterlies, classification of, 14
Quotations, 62–3, 82, 154–7
for critical analysis, 154, 186
from foreign works, 102, 155–6, 192
in International Copyright Union, 113, 156
from letters, 115
of music, 130–31, 186
see also Fair Use; Permissions

R

Radio, 48, 87, 106, 158–9, 202–3
broadcasts, of copyright material, 97, 156
and fair use, 91
and license, 117
and moral rights, 124
and news, 136
rights, in International Copyright Union, 113
scripts, 48, 72, 75, 114
titles of, 168
and unfair competition, 169, 170
Radio News, 168
Ranch houses, infringed, 52–3
Read 'em and Weep, 154
Rebecca, 100
Reciprocal copyright relations, 20, 101–9, 171–3, 189–95 [9b and c]

Recordation of assignments, etc., 57–8, 60, 117, 135, 181–2
Records and recordings, 97, 105n., 106
Re-examination of Literary Copyright, 98
Register of Copyrights, 7, 10, 12, 17 [202–15]
Registration, 19, 20, 21, 22, 23 [5, 6, 11–13, 22–3, 209–10, 215]
before suit for infringement, 46, 86
in Canada, 104–5
fees for, 94
of published works, 51
see also Applications; Deposit
Reissued books, 14, 89, 132–3
see also New editions
Relief maps, 76, 123
Renderings, architectural, 52, 54
see also Architecture
Renewal, 22, 23, 89, 160–63, 203–5 [24, 25, 215]
application, 161, 226
by co-author, 65
in early law, 5, 6
fees for, 94
of illustrations, 95–6
overdue, 150
of posthumous works, 144
under UCC, 46, 86
by proprietor, 18, 146, 162–3
who may make, 18, 60, 68, 160
Reporting, not infringement, 135–6
Reports, published, 14
Reprints, 90, 117, 132–3, 195–8
in International Copyright Union, 113
Reproduction of work of art, 19, 21, 54–5, 76 [5h, 12, 13, 19]
see also Artistic works
'Reputation,' 97, 99, 169, 170
Residence, see Domicile
Review copies, and publication, 152
Reviews, 14, 42, 75, 134
Rights granted, 19, 66–7, 97–8 [1, 3, 4]
Romberg, Sigmund, 148

S

Sample copies, 151–2
Saturday Review of Literature, 91
Sayers, H. J., 93, 157
see also Spaeth, Sigmund
Scenario, see Scripts
Scenery, 87
Scholarly and scientific works, fair use in, 92, 154–5
may infringe, 99
Scripts, radio, 75, 126, 158

Sculpture, 54, 76
Search, 133, 147, 164
Secondary meaning, 41, 165, 167, 168
Seditious works, 15, 64
Selections, 15
    see also Anthologies
Serenade, 64
Serials, see Books; Contributions; Reissued books
Sermons, 14, 17, 48, 114, 136, 174
    see also Lectures
Short stories, see Books; Contributions
Slide rule, 74
Slides, 49
Slogans, mottoes, phrases, 15, 62
Smith, Betty, 91
Smithsonian Institution, 6
Soldier's letter, 116
Song, 98, 130
    see also Books; Lyrics; Music
South American copyright, 102, 105–6, 155–6
    see also Buenos Aires Convention
Southey, Robert, 64
Spaeth, Sigmund, 93, 154, 157
Speeches, see Lectures
Springboard use, 92
Staff writers, 61
Stage business, 87, 169
Stage sets, 54
Stationers' Hall, 4
Statues, 142
Statute of Anne, see Act of 8 Anne
Stella Dallas, 124
Strauss, Johann, 148
Stravinsky, Igor, 157
Street and Smith, 168
Struther, Jan, 91
Subject matter of copyright, 13–15
Subsidiary rights, 59, 64, 67, 117, 126–7, 182
Suburban Life, 167
'Subversive,' 64
Superman, 118
Swiss Confederation, 112
Symbol, copyright, see C in a circle
Synopsis, not abridgment, 92

T

'Ta-Ra-Ra-Boom Der E,' 154
    see also Spaeth, Sigmund
Tables, 14, 15
Tapestry, 49, 76
Technical works, see Drawings and plastic works
Telegrams, 115

Telephone book, 75, 98–9
Television, 158–9
    classification of televised works, 48, 50, 72, 73, 75, 78, 87, 114, 183
    in foreign countries, 106, 113
    licenses for use on, 117, 124, 127–8
    notice, 203
    telecasting not publication, 88, 112, 151, 158
    titles, 168
    unauthorized use on, 91, 97, 202
    unfair competition, 169, 170
Tenants in common, 65
Term of copyright, see Duration
Test Pilot, The, 167
Thayer, T., 92
Three Musketeers, The, 92
Title page, 21, 133, 198 [20]
    'evidence of authorship,' 113
    must precede text, 137–8
    notice on, 16–17, 134
Titles, 165–8, 205
    on application form, 69
    not copyrightable, 15, 165
    of dramas, 88, 166–7
    duplication of, 165
    fee for recording transfer of, 94
    of maps, 123
    of motion pictures, 127, 166–7
    of music, 129
    new, 35, 38, 133, 195–6
    of periodicals, 75, 134–5, 167–8
    of photographs, 141
    of radio and television, 158, 168
    on renewal applications, 161
    if search is wanted, 164
    and unfair competition, 165, 167, 168, 169, 170
    of unpublished works, 114, 125
    under Washington Convention, 106
Toys, 15
    designs for, 54
Trade marks, 41, 54
    do not prolong protection, 168, 201–2
    as titles, 135, 168
Trade names, in notice, 139, 145–6
Train, Arthur, 63
Transcription, 158
Translations, 19, 46, 55 [1]
    author of, 161
    of foreign books, 102–3, 194
    in International Copyright Union, 112–13
    licensing of rights, 117–18
    in UCC, 171–3
Travelogues, 50
Turn of the Screw, 163

Tutt and Mr. Tutt, 63
Type, must be set in the U.S., 121
Typewritten copies, 69, 150, 156

U

UCC, *see* Universal Copyright Convention
Unauthorized publication, *see* Infringement
Unfair competition, 41, 64, 92, 97, 169–70, 206
   and moral rights, 124
   and newspapers, 135, 136
   and radio and television, 159
   and titles, 165, 167–8
   and unprotected works, 148
United States Constitution, *see* Constitution, U.S.
Universal Copyright Convention (UCC), 20, 25–31, 101–9, 171–3, 189–95, 242–7 [9c]
   American edition of UCC books, 71
   and Berne Convention, 110
   and common law, 80
   duration under, 90, 160, 185
   and formalities, 45, 101, 121–2
   and moral rights, 124
   music, 130
   periodicals, 134
   photographs, 141–2
   posthumous works, 144
   'publication,' 153
   and registration, 75, 179, 212
   retroactivity, 149
   translations, 26, 172–3
   U.S. edition of UCC works, 75, 86
Unknown, 169
Unpublished works, 79–81, 174–5, 206
   art, 55–6
   in British countries, 90, 103, 190
   of deceased author, 144
   deposit of, 84–5
   dramas, 87–8

   duration of protection, 89–90
   infringement of, 97
   in International Copyright Union, 112
   letters, 115
   maps, 76, 123
   motion pictures, 126
   music, 129
   for oral delivery, 75, 114
   radio and television, 158
   under UCC, 171
   use, notice of, in music, 130 [1e, 101e]

V

Vend, 19, 97, 99 [1]
Versions, other, 19, 35–6, 66–7, 97 [1]
   of books in public domain, 133, 148
   and International Copyright Union, 113
   of music, 130
   for radio use, 156, 159

W

Wales, National Library, 86
Washington Convention, 106
Wat Tyler, 64
White, Pearl, 91
Whittaker's Reference Catalogue of Current Literature, 193
Widow, renewal rights of, 160–62
Wills, assignments by, 22, 57, 59, 67 [28]
Wood, William B., 69
Woodcuts, 76
Woollcott, Alexander, 100
Works done for hire, *see* Employer . . .
World series, 169

Y

'You Can't Stop Me from Lovin' You,' 91, 93, 187
'You Will Never Know How Much I Really Cared,' 146
Yukon Jake, 127